Doug Hurst retired in 1993 after 33 He has written numerous articles on military, contributor to *The Australian Dictionary of Biography*; contributed to the Time-Life series *Australians at War* and *The Dutch Down Under*; and has written three previous books involving RAAF history, including *The Fourth Ally—The Dutch Forces in Australia in WWII*, which was translated into Dutch in 2006. He lives in Canberra with his wife Doreen and a good deal of dependent birdlife from the hill behind their house.

The FORGOTTEN FEW

77 RAAF Squadron
in Korea

DOUG HURST

First published in 2008

Allen & Unwin
83 Alexander Street
Crows Nest NSW 2065
Australia
Phone: (61 2) 8425 0100
Fax: (61 2) 9906 2218
Email: info@allenandunwin.com
Web: www.allenandunwin.com

National Library of Australia
Cataloguing-in-Publication entry:

Hurst, Doug.

The forgotten few : 77 RAAF Squadron in Korea/author,
Doug Hurst.

9781741755008 (pbk.)

Includes index.

Australia. Royal Australian Air Force. Squadron, 77.
Korean War, 1950–1953 – Aerial operations, Australian.

959.704348

Maps drawn by Mapgraphics
Set in 12/13pt Bembo by Midland Typesetters, Australia
Printed and bound in Australia by Griffin Press

10 9 8 7 6 5 4 3 2 1

Contents

This book is dedicated to the men who became the Forgotten Few, with special thoughts for those who died in the Korean War and for Dick Cresswell, the greatest of them all.

Introduction

Those of us who joined RAAF fighter squadrons in the post-Korean War period have always had great respect for the remarkable group of men who are the spirit and essence of this book. As junior pilots finding our way in the fighter world, we came under the leadership of many Korean veterans. They were our flying instructors, flight commanders, commanding officers and officers commanding, our warrant officers and senior NCOs, and their combined influence was profound. Many have remained mentors and lifelong friends to this day. A number attained the highest levels in the Service.

From their small and invariably modest accounts of their part in it, I learned something about the Korean War. At first my knowledge was of the techniques of air combat, the hazards of weather and terrain, the importance of flying discipline and airmanship, and other aspects of day-to-day flying operations that helped a pilot stay alive in a place like Korea. Many lessons they learned in earnest were applied directly to our flying training, contributing to our own proficiency and survival. In later years as a member of the directing staff at RAAF Staff College I learned more about the Korean story, of the politics behind the war, the strategies that guided its operations and the tactics with which it was fought.

My understanding, however, was always patchy, with some key questions still unanswered about why things happened as they did. A number of good books have been written on Korea, and collectively they provided much of what I wished to know, but all had shortcomings for today's general reader. For example, George Odgers' otherwise excellent *Across the Parallel* told only part of the story, and like Robert O'Neill's invaluable official history, *Australia In the Korean War*, it was written before the collapse of the Soviet Union made available the knowledge of Russia's critical contribution to the air war.

Then, with the Soviet revelations, the full story was out there, spread though various books and in the memories of surviving veterans. All that was needed, it seemed, was the effort to pull it together in a single book telling what happened to No. 77 Squadron in Korea, and importantly, why. Easy to say, but a tough assignment to carry through.

Jim Flemming, the late Dick Cresswell and other veterans had long seen the need for such a book, aimed at the general reader. When Doug Hurst discussed it with them and decided to write this book, I happily agreed with his request to act as a researcher, and general assistant. With wonderful help from veterans here and in the UK, Doug has given us an incisive analysis of complex events. The book is, in my view, a significant addition to the seminal literature, and a sensitively crafted and fitting tribute to this unique band of brothers—a 'happy few' who have left a lasting legacy 'upon Saint Crispin's Day'.

Denis Stubbs
Group Captain (Ret'd)

Foreword

Even as North Korean President Kim Il-sung continued with his prolific rhetoric there was no real forewarning of war on the Korean peninsula in the midsummer of 1950. Surprise was complete as the northern armies crossed the 38th parallel and struck south; the situation became dire, triggering a near rout. Serendipity and solid leadership intervened: Russia had shunned the United Nations Security Council, enabling that body to react quicker than would have been otherwise possible, if at all. The United States took the lead and deployed forces to resist. Of these forces, it was air power that saved the day, especially in the critical first weeks.

Although the RAAF's 77 Squadron was on the brink of returning to Australia from Japan, it had been maintained at high operational efficiency. The squadron was well-led; the aircrew a nice mix of first-class World War II veterans and post-war graduates. The technicians and other support personnel were equally dedicated and skilled, and their Mustangs a proven and effective long-range, ground-attack aircraft. No surprise then that USAF Lieutenant General George Stratemeyer, commander of the Far East Air Forces, and General Douglas

MacArthur made personal bids for 77 Squadron's participation within days of the war starting. Lieutenant General Sir Horace Robertson, commander-in-chief, British Commonwealth Occupation Forces, strongly supported these representations to the Australian Government. Such was the squadron's reputation; 77 lived up to it.

Throughout the mobile phases of the war and the long static ground situation that followed, 77 Squadron operated with distinction, taking more casualties than the situation might indicate. It is noteworthy that throughout the squadron's participation was far from token in a hostile, well-stacked, anti-aircraft climate. Doug Hurst has written a top-notch story of their involvement. His history covers the full three years of the conflict; it is an important story, well-told and offering considerable insight and understanding to all readers.

Australia's spontaneous and vigorous participation not only yielded valuable combat experience; it also reinforced the lessons of World War II, provided a fresh view of the future and enhanced our diplomatic standing with the USA. We witnessed and experienced the importance of passive defence, the vital nature of reconnaissance, the new era of jets and helicopters in combat, and the application of air and maritime pressure to enable ground forces to operate effectively. There was a time when our force development sights blurred, but the Korean and subsequent wars sharpened our vision. Second best is to lose.

Air Marshal J. W. Newham AC
Chief of the Air Staff, 1985–87

Acknowledgements

Although I wrote most of the words, this book is a collaborative effort, with many people contributing material and memories; reviewing drafts and suggesting improvements of all kinds. Special thanks goes to Jim Flemming, Jake Newham and Jim Treadwell who also promoted the project and encouraged Korean veterans to contribute, and to Denis Stubbs for his invaluable help and advice on many things, especially fighter lore and some finer points of writing.

Via email, contributions and reviews came from as far afield as the UK, and thanks here goes to RAF pilots John Price, Don Smith and Sir Keith Williamson. Australian veterans included Bill Collings, Milt Cottee, Ross Glassop, the late George Hale, Dave Hitchins, the late Doug Hurst (the Elder), Lyall Klaffer, Keith Meggs, Bill Murphy, Sir Neville McNamara, Dinny O'Brien, Les Reading, Wally Rivers, Bill Simmonds, Cec Sly and the late Dick Wilson.

The late Dick Cresswell deserves special mention. Our many chats over the years helped spark the idea of this book and he strongly supported my early research with informal and formal interviews and books from his library. This turned out to be opportune; Dick is such a central figure in the story that I would not have attempted the book without his contribution.

And finally, thanks also to those listed in the bibliography who have previously written about Korea. Their work not only provided essential material for me, but also proved that while Korea may be the Forgotten War to most Australians, it is well-known to military historians. All were important, but two gave essential insight into those times: George Odgers' first-hand and factual *Across the Parallel* and Col King's *Luck is No Accident,* with its unequalled personal accounts of Meteor combat flying and insights into squadron life in Kimpo.

Author's Notes

In writing this book I set out to tell the story of what happened and why to 77 Squadron in Korea, not to write a detailed and complete history. As a result, those who served equally do not always get equal mention and much remains unsaid. These are unavoidable outcomes of telling the story the way I have, and I ask only that readers judge it accordingly.

When possible I have used given names instead of the initials normally used in the references. Most names were well-known, but despite considerable help from veterans others proved problematic; I suspect one or two may be wrong and apologise in advance if this is so. More difficult still was the determination of terminal ranks and awards for all who pursued post-war careers in the RAAF and the reader's indulgence is again sought with regard to omissions and mistakes in this area.

1

To War

The Korean War lasted three years, from 25 June 1950 until 27 July 1953. 17164 Australians served in the war and 340 died there. Of the Australian dead, 35 came from just one unit, No. 77 Squadron, Royal Australian Air Force. Six Royal Air Force pilots serving with 77 Squadron also died, bringing total squadron deaths to 41. Another seven pilots became prisoners of war and were treated barbarically.

Such levels of death and suffering in a single squadron were unusually high for the times, but they were not all in vain. No. 77 Squadron may well have tipped the balance in the early days of war, helping UN forces maintain a critical toehold on the peninsula's southern tip. From there the Allies fought back and eventually won. Had that toehold been lost, the war would have been lost with it. South Korea today would be under Communist rule, repressed and starving like its northern cousin.

But that didn't happen. And it didn't happen, in part at least, because of 77 Squadron. Theirs is a tale worthy of immortality, yet two generations later their efforts and sacrifice are largely unknown and unappreciated. To most Australians they are the forgotten few of a largely forgotten war.

In contrast, many of the survivors still have vivid memories of those times. Milt Cottee[i] is one. He flew on the first mission on the first day of 77 Squadron's Korean operations. It was 2 July 1950, and he flew one of three Mustangs sent to escort USAF C-47 Dakotas 'evacuating civilians out of Taejon, an airfield in the centre of South Korea'. North Korean YAK-9 fighters were active in the area and the Mustangs' role was to 'give fighter cover to the C-47s and the airfield.'[1]

The mission involved much that was new to Milt, who had only 100 hours on the Mustang and had not flown it at night. The task meant that, at short notice, he was faced with a night takeoff, visual navigation in unfamiliar territory, possible aerial combat and flying with drop tanks (which changed the aircraft's flight characteristics). Understandably, he was a bit anxious before takeoff and later wrote of 'a strange mix of fear, arising from some under-confidence with my ability to mix it in an air-to-air situation'.

There was no time to train—it was a 'come as you are war'. All they could do was plan thoroughly and this they did. Thanks to the planning, and a little luck, the night takeoff, climb-out and transit went well. They reached Korea from their base in southern Japan without incident, only to find to their frustration that they could not fix their position once there. Luckily, there were no enemy fighters and they loitered, making repeated attempts to rendezvous with the C-47s. When this failed they returned to base, their anticlimactic start to combat flying over.

Jim Flemming[ii] also flew that day and enjoyed better results, successfully escorting giant B-29 bombers on missions against North Korean airfields. He well remembers the disappointment of initially aborting with an unserviceable aircraft, and the nervous excitement of later flying in what many expected

i   Later a test pilot, retired as a Group Captain AFC, and now lives in Canberra.
ii Continued flying fighters. Is now a retired Air Vice Marshal AO, US DFC and Air Medal and lives in Canberra.

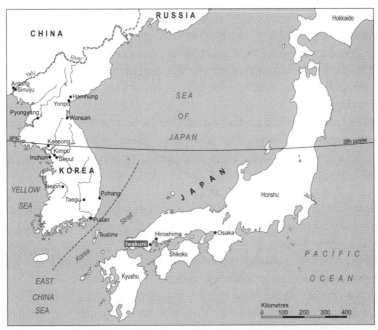

War began with Korea divided along the 38th Parallel, the Communist North backed by China and Russia, South Korea supported by the US and its allies and 77 Squadron based in Iwakuni, Japan.

to be a brief affair once the Americans got their act together. Memories of the giant bombers spread out below him in loose formation over Korea's jagged coastline and its rugged, brown terrain—so unlike the neat and green Japanese countryside he was used to—have also stayed with him for life.

In all, sixteen No. 77 Squadron pilots flew that day on three separate missions. All flew Mustang fighters from Iwakuni, in southern Japan. Based there as part of the British Commonwealth Occupation Force (BCOF), until now they had operated only within Japan and its surrounding waters. Although Korea is a mere 200 kilometres or so from Iwakuni, they had not previously been there, and knew little or nothing about 'the land of the morning calm'.

3

Only a week before there was no thought of war in Korea—or anywhere else for that matter. The squadron was packed up, ready to leave Japan for good and return to Australia. Then North Korea invaded the South, and they were suddenly at war in a country they knew little about, fighting an enemy about which they knew even less.

No one in the squadron could have anticipated the war from what they knew, but the same cannot be said for those in charge of Australian defence and government. After all, trouble had been brewing ever since the atomic bombs had ended the Pacific War suddenly and unexpectedly in August 1945, freeing Korea from Japanese colonial rule, and catching the Allies with no detailed plan for its future. By general agreement the Soviets (who were still an ally) occupied the north and the Americans the south until Korea was unified—but how this would actually happen was not decided.

One story goes that when the war ended suddenly, two US colonels were tasked with dividing Korea into temporary occupation zones in which the US and Soviets could accept the Japanese surrender. They chose the 38th parallel, the Soviets agreed, and the arrangement became entrenched both politically and geographically.[2]

Unification proved elusive as the emerging Cold War drove a wedge between the Communist North and the non-Communist South. Despite this, in 1948 the newly formed United Nations scheduled elections for a single government. The North Koreans and the Soviets refused to cooperate and held their own elections.

Princeton-educated Syngman Rhee was elected in South Korea as their first president.[iii] Kim Il-sung, a Korean resistance fighter against the Japanese in the 1930s, and later a Soviet Army officer, became the leader of the north.[iv] From the start, neither

---

iii Syngman Rhee, while in exile, was President of the Provisional Korean Republic from 1919-1941.

iv Father of Kim Jong-il, the current North Korean leader.

leader showed any signs of giving in to the other, and both indicated that the situation might have to be resolved by war.

War so soon after the massive destruction of World War II had no appeal to the US or the Soviets. Wishing to avoid hostilities, both acted to restrain the respective leaders. Stalin refused to give Kim the Soviet backing he needed to invade the south, and the US kept the South too weak to invade the North by limiting their arms build-up to purely defensive forces.

Indeed, despite the obvious potential for trouble, the Soviets withdrew their troops from Korea in 1948 and the US withdrew all but a small advisory group the next year. It seemed that US interest in Korea had waned. This view was reinforced in late 1949 when General Douglas MacArthur—in Japan as commander of US occupation forces in the Pacific—told a British journalist that 'our defence line runs through a chain of islands fringing the coast of Asia' and went on to describe an area that did not include Korea.[3]

Other regional Allied forces too were being reduced. Most British occupation forces in Japan had been redeployed to Malaya to counter Communist terrorists there. Australian occupation forces too were much reduced; by 1949 the original three RAAF Mustang squadrons were down to one, No. 77 Squadron, and it was going home mid-year.

In the north, Kim Il-sung watched these force reductions very keenly. Despite a population of only nine million to the South's twenty million, he had built a strong army with the aim of uniting Korea by force. He continually badgered Stalin to support an invasion but was always rebuffed. Eventually, however, everything came together for Kim in the second half of 1949.

The Communists now ran China and the Russians had exploded an atomic bomb. These facts, along with the shrunken US and Allied presence in Korea and Japan, led Stalin to believe that US President Harry Truman would not act, as he 'would not want to start a third world war over such a small territory'.[4] With this thought in mind, he gave Kim the OK.

As 1950 progressed, Kim began preparing for a mid-year invasion, beginning one Sunday when much of the opposition was stood down or sleeping in. The signs of Kim's build-up were there to see. In March 1950, the US Central Intelligence Agency (CIA) predicted a North Korean attack in June. A little later, senior intelligence officers on MacArthur's staff in Tokyo reported that 'a massive build-up of communist shock troops was underway'.[5]

This was high-quality intelligence. It is difficult to understand why the South Koreans did not know more of the North's intentions and strengths, or why regional Allied forces were not more on the alert. It certainly seems that Korea was now a very low priority for distant countries like the US and Australia.

This may be unfair to some senior officials, but there is no doubt that pre-war Korea had a low profile in Australia, even within the military. Dick Cresswell was then CO of 21 Squadron, a Citizen Air Force squadron flying Mustangs at Laverton, near Melbourne. A Pacific War veteran, he was 77 Squadron's first operational CO and would soon be its CO again (although he did not know this at the time).

Familiar with the Korean situation—having recently done a tour at the RAAF Staff College—he was not surprised by the invasion and remembers thinking it would be a 'dirty war'. This informed reaction was rare, however, and the war was 'a total surprise to most' he knew in the RAAF. Furthermore, it initially sparked little interest in the press or the wider public.[6]

To the average Australian or American, such ignorance mattered little if at all. For the South Koreans it was a very different story indeed. For them, ignorance meant that they were neither properly forewarned nor adequately forearmed. As it was, the North had a strong offensive force of some 200 000 troops, with over 1000 artillery pieces, some 150 tough, battle-proven T-34 Russian tanks, 132 tactical aircraft (mostly Il-10 ground-attack aircraft and YAK-9 fighters) and 22 twin-engine transport aircraft.[7]

The South had a force of about 100 000, but it was almost entirely defensive. Poorly equipped even for that role, it had no effective combat aircraft, no heavy artillery, ineffective anti-tank weapons (in desperation, South Korean soldiers sacrificed their lives in vain attempts to stop the tanks) and little to counter Il-10 and YAK-9 tactical air power. In all, the war was a considerable mismatch, as Stalin had anticipated.

Fortunately for South Korea, Stalin misread President Truman. Deeply disappointed with the failure of the League of Nations before World War II, Harry Truman was determined that the United Nations would not follow the League's example. Instead, he was determined it would take decisive action when needed. He saw Korea as the UN's first big test, and when told of the invasion proposed an emergency session of the UN Security Council.

The Council convened at 2.20 p.m. on 25 June 1950 (New York time). The Soviets refused to take part, and without them the Council quickly decided that North Korean actions had violated UN charter principles. It then adopted a resolution declaring the invasion 'a breach of peace and calling for immediate withdrawal of North Korean forces to the 38th parallel.'[8]

North Korea ignored the UN decision, and on 27 June Truman committed US air and naval forces to assist South Korea and appointed General Douglas MacArthur (in Japan) to take over all regional US forces. He also ordered the US Seventh Fleet into the Formosa Strait (the strait that separates Taiwan and mainland China) to deter the mainland Communists from attacking the Nationalists in Taiwan.

Later that day the UN Security Council passed a resolution urging member states to assist South Korea. The UN was being decisive, just as Truman had hoped. Good news indeed, but not good enough to stop North Korea from capturing the South Korean capital, Seoul, the next day, 28 June 1950.

The South Koreans were losing badly. MacArthur had to act quickly to optimise existing forces and build for the future.

What he had looked a bit thin on paper, and was even thinner in reality. Existing US forces had been hit hard from five years of peacetime budget cuts that had reduced numbers and readiness. When fighting began:

> US Army units stationed in Japan (4 divisions) were at only 50% of combat readiness,
>
> the Fleet Marine Force was down to only 24 000 men,
>
> the Air Force F-80 jets were based in Japan and could remain over any Korean target for only 15 minutes at most, and
>
> the Seventh Fleet had only one large *Essex*-class carrier, two cruisers, 12 destroyers and a few minesweepers and auxiliary craft in the area.[9]

The only good news was the Allied naval forces. With Commonwealth ships included, they were vastly superior to the North Koreans, who had only 'four dozen small and insignificant craft'.[10] These strong Allied naval forces controlled the seas around Korea throughout the war, protecting vital supply lines into Allied areas (especially through ports like Pusan in the south) and providing air support from their carriers.

Thus, carrier-based aircraft played an important role, especially in the early stages of the war, but much more air power was needed. With USAF F-80 jets limited by range, endurance and airfield availability[v] to only 15 minutes or so over Korean targets, longer range aircraft like 77 Squadron's Mustangs were needed to provide the air power MacArthur needed to first contain the enemy and then to hit back.

As it was, he only just got 77 Squadron. As mentioned, the squadron was packed up ready to go home when the North

---

v The jets needed long runways for takeoff and landing, and had only four suitable strips in Japan and none in South Korea when war broke out.

invaded. In another week or two it would have been well on its way back to Australia. Flying had ceased, the aircraft were packed in plastic cocoons and the Australians in Iwakuni were enjoying a round of farewell activities. The best of these was a 'Ship Wreck' party at the Sergeant's Mess on 24 June 1950—the eve of the invasion by North Korea.

Some RAAF pilots were then sergeant equivalents and most of the experienced maintenance and support staff were sergeants or above. A Sergeant's Mess party, with the officers invited, allowed all the pilots, and the senior maintenance and support men, to all celebrate together. Money was no object. The mess, with a healthy bank balance, was about to close and there were more than enough funds for something memorable. The chosen theme was a 'Ship Wreck'.

Invitations went out on sea charts stating the need to be dressed 'as you would be if you were ship wrecked'. The response was wholehearted. Some wore bathing trunks or old shorts with a tie about the waist, and one original thinker came in a night shirt with a bottle of 'snake-bite cure' under his arm.

A model sailing ship was built outside the mess though which guests entered before walking the plank once they had drunk the statutory number of lethal cocktails needed to qualify for entry. At the main door they were met by two 'pirates', normally known as Blue Thornton and Jim Flemming. The latter had a canister of Scotch and a water pistol which he used to squirt Scotch into the mouths of all who wished to enter.

As they swallowed the Scotch, all but the vague began to realise that this was no ordinary party. Further confirmation came when they entered the mess building. There they found a world of palm trees, treasure chests and rubber dinghies for seats—there were no chairs. Discipline was strict. An iron jail near the bar housed anyone found guilty of not drinking enough 'snake-bite cure' until they were judged sufficiently inoculated to again enter respectable society. Those deemed guilty of not being properly dressed for a shipwreck were given a 'fair trial' and dipped in the fishpond—a not always unwelcome punishment as the weather was hot and sticky at the time.[11]

The commanding officer, Wing Commander Lou Spence, and his wife Vernon, attended dressed in tennis clothes—for deck tennis they said—and were adjudged properly dressed and allowed to drink and eat the supper served, Japanese style, on long low tables. The food included local prawns and oysters and Western food, all eaten with chopsticks. Abundant local fish were also available, thanks to a sortie the previous day when 'a Mustang dropped a couple of live 500 pound bombs in the sea off Iwakuni to provide fish for a party'.[12]

In all, it was a great party and a wonderful way to say farewell to what had been a unique experience both culturally—with life among the polite and helpful Japanese—and professionally—with a unique mix of veteran and tyro pilots. This mix was a feature of the squadron, for the veterans included some impressive men, four of whom led the squadron.

Lou Spence, the CO, had earned a DFC[vi] flying Kittyhawks in the Middle East. A fine pilot, he won a second DFC in the Pacific where he flew Kittyhawks again and commanded a Spitfire squadron in Darwin. Approachable and honest, with a friendly manner, he was liked and admired by all, down to the junior airmen. The operations officer, Graham Strout, was also a World War II veteran, having flown with Nos 12 and 86 Squadrons. He too was an excellent pilot and popular leader.

The 'A' Flight commander, Stuart 'Brick' Bradford, was a quiet man, but an effective and popular leader nevertheless. He also had fought in the Pacific and was most capable in the air. John 'Bay' Adams, the 'B' Flight commander, was, in one pilot's words, 'an institution'.[vii] Bay had flown Typhoons in Europe in World War II with the great French air ace Pierre Closterman

---

vi   Distinguished Flying Cross—awarded for bravery in the air.
vii   Bay Adams became an Air Vice Marshal and was the Air Officer Commanding Operational Command, in charge of all RAAF operational units, prior to retirement.

who, in his book *The Big Show*, described Adams as 'that remark-able Australian who feared neither God nor the Devil'. He was a deadly shot and had recently won the US Far East Air Force Weapons Competition—a shoot-off between the region's Allied fighter pilots.

These four, and the other experienced men, had welded 77 Squadron into a well-trained and competent peacetime unit. Originally in Japan to provide air defence, their main roles now were more general. They 'showed the flag' with fly-pasts on appropriate occasions, flew local area surveillance patrols, and 'kept watch on the movements of vessels in the Inland Sea and Tsushima Straits to check the smuggling of aliens into the country, especially Koreans who made for Hiroshima, the main settlement area in that part of Japan'.[13]

Importantly, some key combat skills were also maintained. Fighter skills were honed, and gunnery, using a little uninhabited island off Iwakuni in the Inland Sea as a target, was regularly practised. This meant that although 77 Squadron now had no combat role, it was still proficient in aerial fighting, strafing and general reconnaissance. Although war would initially find them lacking in other areas, these basic combat skills would prove invaluable. But this was yet to come, and members of the 'Ship Wreck' party no doubt reflected that these hard-won skills would gradually fade when they were dispersed into a range of new jobs back home.

The party showed all the benefits of abundant funds and good planning as the Japanese band played on into the night and all but the older and wiser partied on. Lou Spence, in accordance with usual practice for a CO, left reasonably early so as not to inhibit proceedings too much, and the Operations Officer (Ops O) and flight commanders, experienced warriors all, decided eventually that discretion was the better part of valour and followed their leader's example.

The band had stopped playing well after midnight but the 'stayers' were still there in number when dawn broke. At 8 a.m.

some ate breakfast while others just sat around the mess, keeping the moment alive. The band came back and began playing. About mid-morning the telephone rang and was answered by one of the young pilots, Ray Trebilco.[viii] The caller was an American who told Trebilco that North Korea had invaded the South and 77 Squadron was on standby. Thinking the American was joking—their American friends all knew the squadron was pulling out—Trebilco replied, 'You can't pull that one on me', and hung up.

Some 30 minutes later, at about 11 a.m., a more senior American called back. This time Trebilco believed the caller and put him on hold while he spoke to Graham Strout, who had just come into the mess.[14] It turned out that the American had been trying to contact them for some hours with an important message—the North Korean Army had indeed crossed the 38th parallel around dawn and was attacking the South Korean Army.

The US 5th Air Force had been alerted and placed on standby. The American concluded by saying he thought they might be going to do something about the invasion. This was certainly an important message. 77 Squadron was under the operational control of the 5th Air Force while in Japan—and if the 5th Air Force was on standby, so was 77 Squadron.

Graham Strout jumped in a jeep and drove to the CO's house. He was just in time. Lou Spence and his wife were in the hall, with bags packed, about to leave on a holiday with their two children before returning to Australia. On hearing the news, Spence told his wife that the holiday was delayed by at least a day until things clarified, but they kept their bags packed in the hope it would all blow over. It didn't, and the Spence family never got their holiday together.

Meanwhile, there was a real possibility that 77 Squadron would go to war, and preparations began. Strout rang the two

---

viii   Retired as an Air Vice Marshal, DFC.

flight commanders, Brick Bradford and Bay Adams, and asked them to go back to the mess where he assembled all the pilots in the billiard room. He then told them the news, ordered them not to tell anyone and to stop drinking alcohol.

In reply to the questions that came thick and fast Strout then told his men that the aircraft were to be armed, and drop tanks fitted to extend their range should they have to fly over Korea at short notice. He then directed that all pilots be at the hangar by 1.30 that afternoon to help prepare the aircraft.

By the time they assembled, all had a dozen unanswered questions in mind and speculation was rife. Would they actually be involved, or would it be a border skirmish that fizzled out? If it was a major war, would the Russians be involved? Could it all get out of hand and trigger off World War III? Could the North Koreans attack Iwakuni and how would 77 Squadron fare against the YAK-9?

No one knew the answers to such questions. All they knew was two things. Firstly, they must prepare as soon as possible to defend themselves and their base if need be, or to enter the war if told to. Next, if they did go to war, Korea was not far away, well under an hour's flying across the Tsushima Straits in a Mustang, and they would quickly be in the thick of things.

In the early afternoon of a hot and humid summer day they set to work immediately, stripped to the waist in most cases. Although many sweated profusely in the humid heat, their spirits were high, and it's a fair bet that the old RAAF joke 'if I knew I'd be this thirsty now, I'd have had more to drink at the party' did the rounds.

The aircraft were readied and the pilots began a thorough version of the checks they normally carried out before each flight. Samples of fuel were tested for water, glycol (the engine coolant) and oil levels were checked and the engines run. Next, the airframes were inspected for damage and flight controls checked for 'full and free' movement consistent with control column and rudder pedal movement.

Most of the armourers had already left for Australia, so the pilots helped the remaining few belt the Mustangs' 50-calibre ammunition and load the ammunition bins. Milt Cottee worked that day and remembers that once the ammunition was loaded

gun barrels were given a pull through and all particular parts of the Browning guns inspected and oiled. Some aircraft needed to have their guns and gun-sights harmonised. With the aircraft in the flying attitude we would fit special mirrors to look down the gun barrels allowing them to be aligned on a spot 300 yards distant. The gun sights were then aligned . . . All rounds were then expected to fire through the gun-sight aim point plus or minus a foot or two.[15]

This meant that the guns were most accurate at 300 yards (about 270 metres), and would shoot high at closer ranges and low at longer ranges. The Mustang's gyro gunsight took this into account and also allowed for deflection shots[ix]—provided the pilot set the enemy aircraft's wingspan and turned the ranging knob on the throttle to fit the enemy's image within a graticule. As a result, gunsight operating procedures became one more thing to think about when contemplating flights into enemy territory.

They also had to constantly think about fuel, especially on long flights. Fitting drop tanks gave them more fuel, but this increased weight, reduced speed and affected handling and manoeuvrability. Thus, when they could, pilots dropped the tanks before aerial combat to lighten and clean up the aircraft.

Flying with drop tanks placed extra demands on everyone, especially those like Milt Cottee who were still learning about the Mustang, but there was no option. To operate effectively over Korea the extra fuel was essential and maintenance staff worked feverishly to fit all aircraft with drop tanks. Others

---

ix   Shots against targets crossing at an angle in front of the attacker.

worked equally hard to fix unserviceable aircraft and make as many available as was humanly possible.

When this work was underway, Spence, Strout and the two flight commanders held a council of war to produce an interim plan until things clarified. They decided to place eight aircraft on immediate standby to cope with an attack on Iwakuni, or for some other task as directed, and placed eight pilots on standby to fly them if need be.

The response from the pilots provided an interesting measure of squadron morale. It would be natural for the eight chosen to be apprehensive at the thought of the possible dangers ahead, and for those not selected to be obviously relieved, but this was not the case at all. The chosen eight were clearly most happy to be selected, and most of the rest 'bitched and moaned' about being left out and possibly missing something that would be over before they knew it.

Had they known what lay ahead, the bitching and moaning may well have been more subdued, or totally absent. But they didn't know, and all sat around the crew room until nightfall, hoping for some definite word and speculating about the future. Talk naturally turned to combat, with the young Mustang pilots asking the veterans how best to cope with a YAK-9 or, should the Russians be involved, a jet.

They also discussed their possible tasking, and it soon became obvious their mission planning would sometimes be much more thorough and demanding than in peacetime. It was one thing to fly in the familiar surrounds of Iwakuni and southern Japan, but another thing altogether to fly to the far reaches of the Korean peninsula to find and hit a target in country they had never seen before.

To do so they would need detailed pre-takeoff briefings on the target and how the flight and attack would be conducted. Navigation planning would select the shortest possible route that gave them good visual fixes along the way and avoided known enemy anti-air installations. On receipt of the meteorological forecast, the headings and expected times for each leg, fuel required and total flight time would be worked out. Safety heights would be calculated for different areas and alternate and emergency airfields selected. It was all basic stuff they had been trained to do, but seldom did, and needed urgent revision.

Thoughts also turned to how best to equip each pilot for war. The supply 'pipeline' from Australia had already been turned off for things like flying clothing, and many pilots were wearing locally made white flying suits. Others wore suits they had traded from Allies, especially the Americans who would happily trade a pair of Australian leather fur-lined flying boots for a flying suit and gloves.

Slouch hats were even more valuable, and with astute bargaining could produce a .45 Colt pistol, flying suit, flying boots and gloves. The eternal favourite with Americans, a case of Australian beer, also proved its worth on many occasions and some, perhaps more adventurous than usual, helped solve Australian supply problems for a bottle of Corio Whisky.

This local production and trade kept the pilots in flying clothing during the last weeks of peace and during the first months of war. Dressed in what they could beg, borrow or trade, 77 Squadron pilots were anything but sartorially uniform in these times. The supply pipeline eventually got running again, but even then it did not include things like the cold-weather gear needed for outside work in Korea's winter.

That problem was some months off as it was now summer, and often very hot and sticky with it. Mustang safety equipment included a dinghy pack, a parachute which formed the pilot's (not very comfortable) seat and a yellow survival vest universally and unfailingly called a 'Mae West' after the busty film star. With its bubble canopy the Mustang cockpit got very hot in summer especially at low level and when operating over land in Japan few pilots wore their Mae Wests.

This would change with regular flights to and from Korea, making the Mae West essential equipment. As soon as they could, pilots added a survival pack including some US dollars, ten gold sovereigns and a silk square on which was printed an Australian flag and Korean writing stating that they were members of the UN forces. A pistol, a .38 Smith & Wesson revolver, was also provided. Deemed much inferior to the US .45 Colt automatic, it was usually replaced by a Colt as soon as a trade could be arranged. This was seldom difficult as the Americans seemed to have an endless supply of .45 Colts and an insatiable appetite for Australian slouch hats and beer.

All of which would make dressing for war a far more bulky and uncomfortable business than dressing for a local area flight in peacetime, but so be it. As it was, news of the war was slow in coming. The first reliable account came from the US Services newspaper *Stars and Stripes*, which confirmed that the North had invaded the South, and added that 'President Syngman Rhee in Seoul had telephoned to Tokyo an appeal for American aid'.[16]

This confirmed in print that there really was a war on, but did nothing to clarify if or how 77 Squadron would be involved. Under existing arrangements, they were controlled by the US 5th Air Force for specific tasks within Japan only. This had effectively made them part of the 5th Air Force as they had operated only in Japan.

Operations in Korea would require new arrangements. Approval would have to be given by the commander-in-chief, British Commonwealth Occupation Force, Lieutenant General Sir Horace 'Red Robbie' Robertson. He in turn would need approval from the Australian Government to commit forces to an unexpected war. This probably meant that the squadron could not be sent to war immediately—but it did not, obviously, rule out North Korea attacking them and the need to fight back if this happened.

Their fate was clearly in the hands of others and all they could do was get ready to fight, if need be, and await developments. As it was, the developments that sent them to war took only a few days, driven by the urgency of the situation, the quick assessment of the situation by the US regional commander, General Douglas MacArthur, and his decisive action that followed.

MacArthur was then a household name in much of the world and America's best known general in the Asia–Pacific area. Highly decorated in World War I, he had become the youngest ever chief of the US Army, and in World War II headed the Allied forces in the South West Pacific Area, successfully using an 'island hopping' strategy to push north from Australia though island bases to the Philippines and on towards Japan. He had taken the Japanese surrender on the deck of the battleship *Missouri* and then, as head of US Occupation Forces in the Pacific, had ruled Japan wisely and well, setting it on the path to become a modern democracy and winning the affection of the large majority of the Japanese, many of whom referred to him as 'Field Marshal Macassar'.

Despite all that, he was a controversial figure. Many critics claimed, with good reason, that he had bungled the defence of the Philippines when the Japanese invaded and taken far too long to understand the adverse affect Papua New Guinea's extreme terrain and weather had on land and air operations, and that his fame owed much to brilliant self-promotion, especially through control of press releases.

The critics had a point, but at the start of the Korean War the best of MacArthur came to the fore. Knowing the situation was bad and deteriorating, he decided there was no alternative but to go to Korea and see for himself. This he did on 29 June 1950, flying with his senior generals in his DC-4, named *Bataan*, despite foul weather and attempts to dissuade him by Lieutenant General George Stratemeyer, commander of the Far East Air Forces (which included the 5th Air Force).

Ever mindful of the role of the press, he also invited four Tokyo news agency chiefs along, warning them that there was no fighter escort to protect them against the North Korean Air Force due to a lack of long-range Allied fighters. Sensing a big story, all four accepted the invitation despite the danger, giving

MacArthur a key tool to get the forces he needed and to polish his image.

During the three-hour flight from Tokyo, MacArthur briefed the journalists on the dire situation and talked with his generals. A radio newsflash heard during flight announced that the British Government was promising the UN 'all-out naval help' from the British Far Eastern Fleet, which included two aircraft carriers and was then in Japanese waters.[17] This would at least double Allied naval strength, and perhaps more importantly, significantly and quickly increase Allied air power.

The extra air power was especially welcome. MacArthur and his generals had already agreed the need to maximise air power to compensate for their lack of ground forces. As MacArthur was not yet supreme commander, UN Forces, Korea—he was formally made so on 7 July 1950—a message was sent to the British Fleet proposing combined US–UK carrier air operations. Thoughts then turned to gaining air superiority so that Allied aircraft assisting ground forces would be safe from the North Korean Air Force, which operated from bases north of the 38th parallel.

MacArthur was not then authorised to send forces north of the 38th parallel. This effectively gave the North Korean Air Force a sanctuary from which they could attack south of the parallel at will. With the initiative and safe bases, they enjoyed a huge advantage over their larger but very constrained US-led opponents.

MacArthur decided to attack North Korea's airfields as soon as possible. Time pressed and he pondered ways to avoid the prolonged process of convincing Washington's decision-makers of the urgent need to bomb north of the parallel. In the end, he decided to act and seek legal sanction after the event. The necessary messages were sent and bombing missions against North Korean airfields began the next day. As MacArthur expected—having presented his government with a *fait accompli*—all the missions were approved later the same day.

The need for more ground-attack aircraft was also raised. General Stratemeyer told MacArthur that he needed long-range ground-attack aircraft like 77 Squadron's Mustangs—at that time the only fully operational Mustang unit in the Far East—ready for immediate service. US Mustangs had all been replaced by jets, which were much faster than propeller-driven aircraft like the Mustang.

Their speed advantage made the jets superior to the Mustang for air combat and intercept roles, but they were gas guzzlers and could not, by a big margin, go as far, or fly for as long, as the Mustang. And to make matters worse, most of the American Mustangs had been sent back to the US to be flown by the Air National Guard. One hundred and forty-five were quickly chosen for service in Korea, but before that happened they would have to be shipped to Japan and Korea and their pilots made combat ready on arrival—all of which could take many weeks.[x]

Stratemeyer told MacArthur that 77 Squadron was the best fighter squadron in Japan, Bay Adams was the best shot in the Far East Air Forces and the squadron, from their base in Iwakuni, well placed to work in southern Korea. In the circumstances, No. 77 was indeed a prize. It would have to learn the business of war fighting, but it was strongly placed to do so, with 25 well-trained pilots and 26 front-line aircraft in excellent condition[18]—thanks to the fine work of Australian fitters and the skilled and loyal Japanese who worked with them. So meticulous was this care that the aircraft were all polished with Fuller's Earth,[xi] which gave them a smooth, gleaming finish and, pilots believed, an extra 4 or 5 knots top speed. At least twelve more aircraft were held in reserve and were immediately available.

The Mustang was the best propeller-driven fighter of World War II, easily outclassing most rivals with its top speed of over 700 kilometres per hour and range (with auxiliary fuel) of more

---

x   The first two of six US Mustang squadrons began operations on 30 July 1950.

xi   A non-plastic clay used to remove oils and grease.

than 2500 kilometres.[xii] Its armament was varied and effective, including six .50-calibre machine guns and a combination of standard bombs, high-explosive rockets, fragmentation bombs, napalm tanks and armour-piercing, high-velocity rockets.

There were three guns in each wing and Les Reading[xiii]— who was there when war broke out and stayed on to fly Meteors—later wrote that: 'Each inner gun carried 400 rounds of ammunition, while the middle and outers carried 270 rounds. This allowed about 25 seconds of firing with the middle and outers, and the remaining time in the inners was often held for self-defence.'[19] In other words, the guns could fire more than 1000 rounds in 25 seconds and still have 800 rounds as a back-up. Something, one imagines, that was much better to give than to receive.

Additional pilots and aircraft would almost certainly be available should Australia commit 77 Squadron to the fray. MacArthur then acted with his famous disdain for protocol— probably to ensure this valuable prize did not slip though his fingers—and sent an 'in the clear' (i.e. unclassified) message to General Robertson requesting 77 Squadron for use against North Korean forces operating south of the parallel, and ensuring the journalists travelling with him knew about it. Surprised at receiving such an important message unclassified, General Robertson re-classified it 'Secret' and sent it to his superiors, the Australian Chiefs of Staff in Melbourne.

He then told Lou Spence of the request and Spence passed the news on to the squadron pilots and senior men. Believing that the request would be granted, they double-checked everything, pored over maps, sought out the latest intelligence (especially on the YAK-9), flew as much as they could to hone their combat skills, and otherwise prepared for war.

---

xii   Kilometres per hour. 700 kph is about 430 mph or 380 knots (nautical miles per hour).
xiii Retired as a Group Captain DFC.

Having landed at Suwon, south of Seoul, MacArthur toured the combat zone with his staff. In George Odgers' words:

> He was appalled by what he witnessed. Mangled corpses lay where desperate refugees had plunged from bridges across the Han which were prematurely dynamited. Most of the South Korean troops and their equipment were thus trapped on the north bank of the Han. After the seizure of Seoul, South Korean Army strength had fallen from 93 000 to 22 000.'[20]

Things were even worse than expected. MacArthur quickly told Washington that US ground forces were needed, without delay, if South Korea was not to be lost to the Communist invaders. President Truman, after much deliberation, approved the use of the US ground forces under MacArthur's command. What until then was being called an incident, was now a war to which 21 UN member states eventually contributed.[21]

But much of that was still to come. On return to Tokyo, Roy Macartney, one of the four journalists travelling with MacArthur, reported MacArthur's request for the Australian squadron to the British and Australian press. This made the request public knowledge and turned the spotlight on the Australian Government, which had welcomed the cost savings associated with the withdrawal of forces from Japan. Now, it suddenly found itself under pressure to fund further defence efforts far from home in North East Asia.

The pressure came in three main areas. Firstly, Australia was discussing a potential 'Pacific Pact' with the US and the commitment of combat forces, especially given the strong US response, would show they were a good ally. Next, having strongly backed the creation of the UN, Australia was now obliged to support it in one way or another. In effect, the UN was on trial. If it failed to stop North Korean aggression, this could embolden other aggressors, leading who knows where and possibly on to World War III. Swift reaction, on the other hand, would send a strong message to the world that such aggression would not be tolerated, hopefully preventing far bigger and worse conflicts.

And last, but not least, there were strong and legitimate concerns about the growing spread of Communism—then widely promoting itself as an international force, and as a unified bloc of countries (now including China) bent on world domination. With Communist parties also active in much of the non-Communist world, and the splits that eventually shattered Communist solidarity yet to emerge, these grandiose plans were hard to dismiss and were sending shivers up many a democratic spine.

With all this in mind, on 30 June 1950 the Australian Cabinet decided to send forces to Malaya to help counter Communist terrorists there and committed 77 Squadron, and other elements of the occupation forces, to the Korean War.

MacArthur had his Australian squadron of Mustangs. That same day, President Truman also authorised flights north of the 38th parallel and a naval blockade of the entire Korean coast. As well, the US 24th Division in Japan was transferred to Korea, tasked with blocking the road from Seoul to the southern port city of Pusan—soon to be the entry point for so much of the vital equipment the Allies needed to wage war.

In the weeks ahead, the successful defence of the 'Pusan Perimeter' would allow the Allies to turn the tide of war and see 77 Squadron play a part in that victory out of all proportion to its size.

2
Iwakuni Ops

For the first three months of war, 77 Squadron operated from Iwakuni, flying to Korea and returning each day. The three flights on their first day at war—2 July 1950—were fighter escort tasks. The emphasis soon changed to ground attack and interdiction,[i] but these first flights were good predictors of what was to come.

It was soon obvious that the priorities, and some of the rules, had changed. Flexibility and mission achievement now ruled supreme, beginning with the very first mission sent to escort some Dakotas flying out wounded from Taejon. In that mission a flight of four, with Graham Strout leading, simply became a flight of three[ii] and pressed on when Brick Bradford turned back with radio trouble.

The Taejon mission also established the fact that from now on they would often fly when they would not have done so in peacetime. In this case, night flying standards were a concern.

---

i   Opposing the movement to combat areas of troops and supplies by road, rail, animal or human means.
ii   Graham Strout, Milt Cottee and Tom Murphy.

New arrivals like Milt Cottee were not the only ones lacking night-flying experience on Mustangs; most squadron pilots were in the same boat. And cloud cover above the airfield further complicated things, requiring a climb out through cloud after the night takeoff. In peacetime they simply would not have done this without current night-flying practice. Now, with no time for such practice, they just prepared as best they could and went.

Happily, the Mustangs departed safely, and when the cloud layer stretching to Korea made visual navigation impossible they pressed on regardless. The cloud cleared as forecast, giving them their first look at Korea, bright and clear in the early morning light. What they saw, to put it bluntly, was not encouraging. In George Odgers' words:

> it looked grim and dirty. There was a monotonous sameness in the colouring. Normally it was reddy brown with sparsely wooded hills and cultivated valleys. The torrential rains filled streams and rivulets with muddy water, and turned the red surface to a dirty chocolate colour ... the whole country looked like a dirty piece of parchment on which had been scrabbled a thousand little water courses and meandering streams ... a chaotic patchwork.[1]

One stream looked much like another—especially with maps that soon proved unreliable—and they were unable to fix their position on the Naktong River as planned, or be sure that they were at Taejon. There was an airfield below, on time as expected, but no Dakotas. Either their navigation was out, or the Dakotas were in the wrong place. Unable to fix their position from land features or contact Taejon by radio, they could not solve their problem and returned home.

The flight back to Iwakuni was a happy contrast. The early cloud had cleared, giving them a good view of the Korean coast as they crossed it and a clear run back to Japan. Navigation was no longer a problem as they flew with good visibility into familiar territory. Iwakuni tower was equipped to provide bearings of radio transmissions from aircraft. This helped pilots locate the airfield in cloudy weather, but with clear skies it was not needed. They did a visual approach, landed and climbed out of their aircraft with mixed feelings—disappointment at missing the rendezvous, but elation at having gone into enemy territory and returned unscathed.

But however they felt, the fact was that 77 Squadron's first mission had failed. A combination of persistent cloud, the confused and alien landscape, poor maps and the resultant navigational uncertainty had thwarted them. Also, lack of experience flying the Mustang at night, with drop tanks, had added to the risk and difficulty of the task. There was much to ponder after just one flight.

There was, however, an up-side. This was only day one of their war, and work could begin immediately to deal with the problems. Unfortunately, problems do not all have solutions— especially quick and easy ones. Sometimes, all you can do is work around them as best you can and try to fix them as you go. In 77 Squadron's case, some problems (like navigation in bad weather) were intractable and plagued them throughout their time in Korea.

Despite that, most missions were flown successfully, beginning with the other two that first day. Lou Spence led the second mission of seven (the eighth, Jim Flemming, dropped out with an unserviceable aircraft)[iii] to escort 17 USAF B-26 Invaders on a bombing raid against an undisclosed target. They rendezvoused near Pusan, on the peninsula's southern tip, and headed north towards Seoul.

No enemy fighters were seen, but two USAF F-80 jets mistook the Mustangs for the enemy and opened fire before realising they were friendly. Luckily, the attackers' marksmanship

---

iii   The others were Bay Adams, Ken McLeod, Bill Horsman, Brian Nicholls, Wally Rivers, and Geoffrey Thornton.

was as bad as their aircraft recognition and they missed.[iv] As the B-26s and Mustangs neared Seoul, anti-aircraft guns opened up. A good deal of flak began bursting around them. For some, it was the first flak they had seen and their excited comments on the radio reflected this. Luckily, no one was hit.

As they approached Seoul it became obvious the target was the railway bridges. These bridges crossed the Han River to the city's south and facilitated the movement of troops and supplies in and out of Seoul, now in enemy hands. The B-26s split into two groups, one to bomb the bridges and the other to then attack with rockets. The first group began with an exhibition of precision bombing, straddling a bridge and knocking out a complete section. The bombing done, the other B-26s went in for their rocket attacks.

Apparently satisfied with their work, the B-26s headed south. The Australians escorted them as far as the southern coast before heading for home, impressed by the precision bombing and most happy to have survived their first 'flak' attack unharmed. They landed just before noon and, their adrenalin levels still high, excitedly joined the three pilots from the first mission to compare notes.

Brick Bradford led the third mission of six, including previous reluctant withdrawal Jim Flemming.[v] Their task was to escort USAF B-29 bombers flown up from their base in Guam, in the Mariana Islands. They rendezvoused with the B-29s at Kangnung, near the 38th parallel and headed for the target, Yonpo airfield, just south of Hamhung. Well inside North Korea, it was selected following MacArthur's decision to attack the enemy's airfields to help neutralise their air force.

---

iv   Other F-80 attacks on Australian Mustangs took place in the first weeks of war, but luckily all were detected early and evaded. When USAF Mustangs entered the war during August 1950 and North Korean YAK-9s were no longer a threat, the attacks ceased.

v   The other four were: Gordon Harvey, Carlyle 'Nobby' Noble, Max Garroway and Dick Turner.

MacArthur had requested and been granted 77 Squadron for use 'operating south of the parallel'.[2] Now, only three days later, they were flying well north of the parallel on an offensive mission. To those involved, the mission made sense and they were happy to go along. It must also have made sense to those above them as the restriction was ignored thereafter.

The B-29s did considerable damage to Yonpo airfield and impressed those like Jim Flemming who had not seen the giant bombers at work. He later recalled that 'it was the first time I had seen pattern bombing. They dropped all their bombs within the perimeter of the airfield—quite fantastic—despite quite heavy flak against them.'[3]

The mission also demonstrated the value of the Mustang where range and endurance were needed. They had flown four and three-quarter hours by the time they landed back at Iwakuni, just after six in the evening. No contemporary jet fighter could fly for anywhere near that long, and none could have escorted the B-29s as the Mustangs had done. The flight also showed the 77 Squadron pilots how vulnerable airfields were to bombing attacks—a thought they shared when they joined in the evening's discussions.

As the various experiences were aired, it became clear that although they were well trained for their peacetime work, this was different. In peacetime most sorties were an hour to an hour and a half at most—and flown during daylight hours, in reasonably clear weather, over familiar country with good maps, and seldom with drop tanks and a full weapons load. Now much of that had changed, usually for the worse.

They now had to be able to fly long sorties of four to six hours at night and in bad weather, over unfamiliar country that was poorly mapped—and usually with drop tanks and weapons to slow them down and restrict their manoeuvrability. And while they were doing it, people on the ground were shooting at them, trying to kill them. In all, their job had suddenly become considerably more difficult and much more dangerous.

There was little they could do about it except put up with it. Five hours sitting on a parachute in a confined cockpit made them stiff and sore, but it had to be done. So too the bad weather. When widespread cloud completely hid their targets or made navigation impossible, they didn't fly. But whenever possible they flew, knowing that the outnumbered Allied ground troops would suffer even more than usual if they didn't.

Many peacetime rules were ignored, especially those relating to weather conditions. Things were done as a matter of routine that would seldom if ever be done in peacetime. On high-priority missions, pilots at times descended through cloud using an estimated position, rather than a positive fix—a potentially dangerous procedure only used in peacetime to locate an airfield when all other options were exhausted.

Their post-flight debriefs also indicated that the North Korean Air Force—with no bombers and now being quickly neutralised—was little threat to their base in Iwakuni. This was not just comforting, but good news operationally. Iwakuni was not just an airfield. It was a fully equipped base with all the facilities and amenities needed to sustain indefinitely the Mustangs and the people who flew and supported them.

It was also home to 77 Squadron's communication flight of two C-47 Dakotas and two Austers, run by Flight Lieutenant Dave Hitchins (who also flew Mustangs on occasions and later flew some combat missions with the squadron).[vi] Within days of the war beginning, they were joined by a USAF B-26 Invader squadron of the Third Bombardment Group, one of many Allied squadrons hastily brought into the area.

The urgent need for the B-26s to be based near the action was obvious to all, but the way it happened was bizarre to say the least. Dave Hitchins later wrote:

---

vi   Had a long RAAF career flying transports, was OC RAAF Darwin when Cyclone Tracey hit and played a key role in the air evacuations, and retired as an Air Commodore AM AFC.

I do not know what orders the Americans had, and I'm sure that our CO, Wg Cdr Spence did not know either. There was an immediate move to take over the base. Offices and hangars were commandeered. MPs went into the local village where we had lived for three years and tacked *Off Limits* signs on shops and other buildings. They were soon followed by a jeep load of our airmen who pulled the signs down. I did not see it, but I believe there were several punch-ups.

A group of our men went into the swimming pool and were told by a guard that it was off limits. They threw him in the pool and then had to pull him out because he couldn't swim. Lou Spence was arrested trying to return to his home at night. They had imposed a curfew without reference to anyone … Five days passed before the Australian Government committed 77 Squadron to operations in Korea, and I think there was some notion that we were sitting back while the Americans did all the dirty work. Not all the fault was with the Americans. A senior RAAF officer objected to a pretty American nurse attending our Officer's Club because she was black.'[4]

After this extraordinary start, things were soon sorted out and relations between 77 Squadron and the USAF were not just good, but excellent for the rest of the war.

Later, when the squadron moved to Korea, it operated from USAF bases, enjoying strong support from the Americans and cordial relations. Shared bases and facilities became the norm and Iwakuni, with its RAAF Mustangs and USAF B-26s, set the pattern for 77 Squadron for the rest of the war.

Iwakuni is some 30 kilometres further down the coastline from Hiroshima, on a river delta at the southern end of the island of Honshu. It was built initially as a training airfield for the Imperial Japanese Navy. During World War II Kamikaze pilots trained there, in sight of Miya Jima, the sacred island of eternal life they would visit before leaving on their one-way missions. Taken over post-war by the occupation forces, Iwakuni was modernised by the RAAF's Airfield Construction Squadron and now contained good-quality hangars, workshops, domestic areas and married quarters.

All work needed to keep the Mustangs flying for years could be done there. Front-line maintenance did the routine things needed for day-to-day operations—things like checking tyres, oil and coolant levels, serviceability checks, component replacements and such. Deeper level maintenance repaired damage caused by accident, combat, corrosion or fatigue and overhauled moving parts like engines, gear boxes and brakes. This effectively restored worn or damaged aircraft close to 'as new', so greatly prolonging their useful life.

In practice, deeper level maintenance was scheduled and linked with front-line maintenance. Later in the war, when the squadron moved to other airfields, front-line maintenance men and supplies went with them. Deeper level maintenance, however, always stayed at Iwakuni, with the Mustangs, and later on Meteors, ferried back and forth.

Japanese were employed extensively on the base, working as personal servants, mess staff, cleaners and—to the surprise of many newcomers—as skilled aircraft maintenance staff who played a vital role once the war in Korea began. To young arrivals from Australia, it was something of a culture shock. Milt Cottee was one such newcomer in late 1949 and wrote:

> Iwakuni and Japan were not as I expected four years after the end of war. As a member of the British Commonwealth Occupation Forces (BCOF), I felt sure I would have to be aggressive and be prepared to defend myself. But whilst we were issued with rifles there was no ammunition provided and in fact we were not permitted to take weapons off the base.[5]

Indeed,

the Japanese … accepted their defeat completely and without outward signs of animosity. Their Emperor had decreed their standard of behaviour and that was that. It was a great help to have Ray Trebilco around as he had already served a tour in Japan post-war as an interpreter …

On the flight line:

the beautiful looking Mustangs with their highly polished fuselages were parked in a precise line on the tarmac. Each aircraft had a Japanese worker assigned whose job was to affect the high polish to the fuselage.

Once airborne, he found himself

flying over beautiful looking island countryside around the Inland Sea. Iwakuni had one main concrete runway of about 6000 feet [1800 metres] … An oil refinery off the northern end of the runway was coming back into commission, having been knocked down during the war. A large number of Western style houses filled an area known as the cabbage patch.

A good number of dependants were still there when the war broke out. Most were soon sent home to safety, but during the first weeks of war many of the men flying off each day to war still had their families with them. It was decided that pilots' wives would not go down to the flight line to see their husbands off. In reality, this did little to reduce the stress for either partner. The married quarters were close enough to the strip for the wives to see the aircraft climb away and approach to land when they returned—and they counted them out and counted them back in.

In this regard, wartime operations from Iwakuni were almost surreal. The base was peaceful, with a peacetime environment, yet in under an hour's flying the pilots entered an alien world of inhospitable country and enemy forces, only to re-enter the peacetime world again on return. Although this gave them a sanctuary to retreat to each night, the strain on families as well as the pilots was considerable. For that reason, and for their safety should the base be attacked, Lou Spence arranged to have families repatriated to Australia as soon as possible.

On their second day of operations, 3 July 1950, they did the first of the many ground-attack missions that thereafter dominated their tasking. Although the North Korean Air Force was being neutralised, their army, with superior troop numbers, artillery and T-34 tanks, was still sweeping all before it. With UN ground forces still assembling, or yet to arrive, all possible air power was directed at the North Korean Army, its supply lines, and key facilities like communications and headquarters buildings.

The main targets were enemy troops, tanks, fuel and ammunition dumps, rail and road bridges, trains, trucks and other road transport, and key buildings. Only occasionally did 77 Squadron fly in direct support of Allied troops in the field. More usually, targets were selected from the list above by their tasking authority, the 5th Air Force, on the basis of the most recent intelligence.[6]

This was logical as it theoretically made best use of available air power—provided, of course, the intelligence and the tasking both got it right. In the fast moving ground war of the times this didn't always happen. And for 77 Squadron, it didn't happen on their very first ground-attack mission.

Lou Spence led the 3 July attack mission of eight aircraft against 'targets of opportunity' in an area near Suwon, about 35 kilometres south of Seoul.[vii] The original area, tasked the previous night, was changed that morning to one further south.

---

vii   The others were Bay Adams, Bill Horsman, Gordon Harvey, Blue Thornton, Ray Trebilco, Bill Harrop and Ken Royal.

Lou had doubts that the North Koreans had got that far south and rang the tasking agency on the fighter base at Itazuke querying the new area. The USAF major he spoke to also had doubts, but after checking confirmed that the mission should proceed as ordered. This suggested that the North Koreans had actually moved that far south—a real possibility given their successes to date—and essentially ended the matter at the time.

They took off about 2 p.m. and after an hour reached their assigned area, clearly identified by a distinctive river estuary and railroad junction. A train and some road transport—important targets that would slow a rapidly advancing enemy if destroyed—were clearly visible. Bay Adams was preparing to attack the train when he spotted a South Korean flag and delayed his attack to double-check that they were in the right area. They were, and reasoning that it was probably a South Korean train captured by the North Koreans, they attacked with guns and rockets to fire the first shots by Australian forces in the Korean War.

It was the sort of thing they had trained for on the range near Iwakuni and they set about their task with confidence and skill. The train was thrown clean off the rails, a number of trucks and a staff car were damaged or destroyed and nearby buildings attacked. Having done considerable damage, after some 20 minutes the attack was broken off and they returned to base, more than happy with their day's work.

Things had indeed gone well. They had done considerable damage—which would no doubt slow the enemy's advance—and had all returned home safely. The well-earned celebratory beers that followed in the mess were being drunk in high spirits when the Intelligence Officer came in with a grave look on his face. The news could not be worse. Lou Spence's concerns about target verification had been valid, as were Bay Adams' worries about the flag on the train. The enemy had not yet come that far south. They had attacked American and South Korean forces.

This was terrible news. The celebratory mood died instantly and some felt so sick in the stomach that they retched. To add to their woes, reports that Australian aircraft had attacked Allied forces were soon widely reported in American newspapers, including *The New York Times*. Consistent with its preference to deal only in good news, MacArthur's headquarters denied the reports.

This silliness didn't help the Australians cope as they knew the reports were true. Some solace was eventually gained, however, when Major General Earle Partridge, the commander of the 5th Air Force, told Lou Spence the squadron was not to blame, and his boss, General Stratemeyer, later absolved the Australians during a Tokyo briefing.

Such things happen in wars, especially fast-moving and confused wars like this one in which 'the fog of war' is common-place. Sometimes, things change so quickly that those in charge simply can't keep up. But in this case, there was more to it than that. The targeting had been done at the Itazuke airbase in Japan by staff with no way of keeping up with all the latest changes. Not only were there too few staff, but the communications and intelligence systems were such that information was often incomplete and dated when it reached them.

And they could do nothing about the time lag, usually some hours, between tasking an aircraft and its actual arrival in the target area. By the time the aircraft arrived, mobile targets, like trucks and trains, could have moved or the situation could have changed markedly in some other way. To improve the system a number of changes were made. A better system of establishing 'bomb-lines' was introduced and South Korean vehicles were marked with distinguishing white stars on their tops and sides.

And perhaps more importantly, the use of airborne controllers,[viii] operating close to the action, was much improved. In many cases the targets allocated by the controllers were

---

viii Later called Forward Air Controllers, or FACs, as they are still termed today.

obvious, like a tank or truck, and were simply referred to as such. When operating with ground forces, special fluorescent panels were laid out (when possible) to direct the attack—with directions such as 'attack 200 yards, zero two zero degrees from the panel'. In the absence of panels, distinctive ground features were used. All operations were 'real time', greatly reducing the chance of another 'Suwon incident', and much improving the effectiveness of air attacks in general.[7]

A Joint Operations Centre (JOC) was quickly established in South Korea to coordinate all Allied air strikes and allocate attack aircraft to airborne controllers. This was a major improvement, allowing real-time operations and much reducing scope for error. Unfortunately, it also further complicated squadron navigation problems.

Three map scales were needed for their work, with three levels of detail. The first was a big area map needed to get to Korea and back. The next was used to navigate about Korea, with more detail and so covering less area. The third level, used to locate specific targets, was more detailed again and so covered quite a small area. Until now pilots had a good idea where their targets would be and could select the required maps before leaving and arrange them in the expected order of use. Now, with much less knowledge of target location, they had to carry all the maps and quickly find the right ones when allocated targets.

Les Reading recalls that there were 32 maps involved, all carried in a special bag made by the squadron safety equipment people. To simplify things, some flight leaders split up the problem among flight members, and maps were then readied accordingly. This helped, but with unexpected changes pilots still had to sort through a bag of maps to find the right one with one hand while flying with the other. And having found the right map, they then had to find where they were on it and the target, which was not always easy.

Although a big improvement, the JOC system did not entirely eliminate the chance of 'friendly fire' incidents, as the squadron found out just three days after Suwon. That morning, Lou Spence led two sections of Mustangs to escort some of the Iwakuni B-26s to bomb near Seoul. They returned unscathed to learn of four Mustangs[ix] about to launch on an urgent attack mission in Korea. Tasking would be supplied by the JOC and an airborne controller when within radio range. No drop tanks were fitted as internal fuel was considered enough for the mission.

They got off just after 5.30 p.m. on 6 July, and when Graham Strout turned back with mechanical troubles, Ken McLeod took the lead. Once over the peninsula they checked in with the JOC and were allocated a 'Mosquito' airborne control aircraft, who Milt Cottee later wrote, was 'wanting aircraft to strike a bridge to hold up a T-34 tank column advancing south along the main Seoul/Taejong highway at Pyongtaek. We didn't think we would be very effective against a bridge but we were the only aircraft he could get.'[8]

A fuel check showed they were close to 'bingo'—the fuel state when they had only just enough fuel to return to base. They told the controller they could only spend a short time in his area and headed towards the position he had given them. With about 25 kilometres to go, the now agitated controller suddenly called that he was being attacked. They immediately went to full power to close as quickly as possible.

Milt Cottee arrived first and saw 'the Mosquito aircraft and then another type flying down a valley'. He decided to attack the aircraft following the Mosquito and was about to do so when he saw South Korean markings on it and broke off. Les Reading then closed for a better look and Milt, thinking he was preparing to attack, sent out a hasty radio call. Les had, in fact, just identified the aircraft as friendly and wouldn't have fired. Nevertheless, Milt had prepared to attack and Les had got close enough to do so. Each had made his decision in only a few seconds. Had either mis-identified the South Korean aircraft in the few seconds

---

ix   Graham Strout, Milt Cottee, Les Reading and Ken McLeod.

available, another 'friendly fire' tragedy could have occurred.

Good aircraft recognition proved its worth, but by coming to the rescue they had passed 'bingo'. With too little fuel to reach Iwakuni, Ken McLeod decided to head for Pusan (on the southern tip of the peninsula). He told the controller, who suggested they land instead at his base, Taejon, which was closer, had suitable fuel and was long enough to take Mustangs. They agreed to do so and, as this gave them a small fuel surplus, turned to the bridge they had come to attack.

Their rockets hit the sturdy concrete bridge but did not destroy it, so they strafed troops in the area and headed for Taejon, arriving just on dusk. The airfield was crowded with Mosquito aircraft all trying to land and park before dark. It was a bit tricky but they all got down safely, becoming the first Australian pilots to land in Korea during the war. They also became the first 77 Squadron members to sleep overnight there—albeit in body bags on the floor of a Korean house taken over by the US Army, lulled to sleep by a substantial tot of Bourbon and prune juice[x] provided by the Americans.

At Taejon they requested Iwakuni be notified of their safe arrival, but the overloaded communications system was accepting only the most important operational messages and their request was refused. When no message was sent, Iwakuni assumed they were missing in action. Not knowing what had happened, Iwakuni staff had to act on what they knew.

As Les Reading was single, his next of kin in Australia were notified he was missing. Milt Cottee's and Ken McLeod's wives, who were still at Iwakuni, were told personally that their aircraft had not returned. One can imagine the collective feeling of relief when the three overdue pilots, having refuelled at Taejon, landed safe and sound at Iwakuni early the next morning.

---

x   Hard to believe, but true, and the source thereafter of jokes about its 'regular' qualities.

Unfortunately, this good news was soon followed by bad. Later that day Graham Strout was killed; the first Australian to die in Korea. He was leading a flight of four[xi] and put in the first attack against railway targets on the east coast at Samchok as part of an offensive to slow rapidly advancing enemy troops in the area. Tom Murphy, who was just commencing a dive, saw a bright flash and believed Graham had hit a target that exploded. The other two saw nothing, and assuming Graham had radio trouble, continued the strike and returned to base. It was only when they contacted Iwakuni tower that they learned their Operations Officer had not returned.

Apart from the flash, there was nothing to confirm he was dead until wreckage seen by a reconnaissance flight the next day was assessed as almost certainly from his aircraft. Although they were not absolutely certain, there was little doubt. Lou Spence then had to do the saddest thing a CO can do, and told Graham Strout's wife that her husband was most probably dead.

The reaction to Graham Strout's death, Jim Flemming recalled recently, was one of

> Complete shock. Complete shock on all parts, until people like Lou Spence and Bay Adams got us all together and told us what war was all about, and this was inevitable, and looked us in the eye and said: 'and a lot of you others won't be here either at the end. We've got to realise it's a real war.' And then it came home to us straight away that the whole thing had changed. We'd gone practically overnight from our peacetime thinking to a wartime footing. It changed the whole demeanour of the squadron from then on in.[9]

It also drove home the fact that ground attack was a dangerous business, requiring considerable skill. Les Reading, who did more of it than most, recalls that

---

xi   The others were Tom Murphy, Max Garroway and Geoff Stephens.

for accurate results all conditions had to be spot on: roll-in height, airspeed and revs, angle of dive, balanced flight, correct aiming allowance including a wind factor, release height, and release speed ... [10]

In most cases, a dive angle of about 60 degrees was used for bombs and 35 to 40 degrees for rockets and guns. Judgement of the pull-out from the dive was critical, especially in hilly and poorly mapped terrain. High-speed and evasive manoeuvring approaching and leaving the target were normally used if ground fire was expected—and it usually was.

High 'G' loads resulted, placing considerable stress on the pilots, who sometimes neared blackout when recovering from their dives.[xii] A good standard of physical fitness was required, and even then most found it tiring. Overall, the training effort was high and risk ever present. This price was paid because ground attack was such an effective way to quickly hit targets within a large area of enemy territory. The enemy knew this, and often produced vigorous opposition.

Important fixed targets were usually defended with anti-aircraft guns. Some fired patterns designed to explode as the aircraft flew into them, and some (the most dangerous) were radar controlled and could track an aircraft across the sky and adjust their firing to intercept it. Range varied gun to gun, but some fired shells which could be pre-set to explode at heights of up to 7000 metres, creating the flak pilots often saw exploding around them.

To defend mobile targets, pistols, rifles and machine guns, or anything else that could shoot at attacking aircraft were used. Aircraft could be hit at up to 3000 feet [900 metres] and where possible they flew at 3000 feet above ground level (AGL) or higher. But as most attack runs were done at low level, there

---

xii G loads refers to Gravity equivalent increases or decreases an aircraft and crew experience during maneuvers. Most fit pilots can withstand up to 6 G before blood draining from the head causes 'blackout'.

was no escaping the danger. For pilots, there was no way around it. The majority of attack runs attracted ground fire and chance often determined the attacker's fate. It didn't matter how skilled or experienced a pilot was, it only took one hit, in the right place, to bring an aircraft down.

Experienced men knew this and planned for possible losses. There was also a need to systematically replace pilots and ground crews over time with fresh men from Australia, and extra pilots and ground crew were soon on their way. The RAAF then had half a dozen Mustang squadrons in Australia, and twelve experienced pilots were chosen from within them, along with 28 ground staff. In most cases, they got only a day or two's notice.

Fred Barnes was one.[xiii] A World War II veteran, he had done a previous tour with 77 Squadron in Iwakuni, flown Mustangs since his return to Australia and was about to do a flying instructor's course at East Sale, in Victoria. He arrived there on 3 July 1950, only to be told he was headed for Richmond, west of Sydney, by 5 July. Ian 'Pip' Olerenshaw, whose wife was pregnant, was given even less notice—only a day to get from Newcastle, where he was living, to Richmond. Another World War II veteran, Robert Hunt was orderly sergeant on the base in Canberra when told, and was able to spend a few hours with his wife before leaving for Richmond only because another NCO stood in for him.

These three stories were no doubt repeated in various forms throughout the RAAF's Mustang squadrons, not just for the pilots, but for the hastily-chosen ground staff as well. The sudden and drastic change to their immediate future was no doubt met with dismay by some and mixed feelings by most; but not everyone was unhappy. Lyall Klaffer[xiv] had been

---

xiii Later an Air Vice Marshal DFC, AOC Support Command and Deputy Chief of the RAAF.

xiv Later flew F-4 Phantoms with the USAF in Vietnam, commanded a RAAF F4E squadron and No. 82 Bomber Wing at Amberley, and became an Air Commodore AFC before retirement in Adelaide.

enjoying a posting flying Mustangs with No. 3 Squadron and had gone on posting to the flying instructor's course at East Sale with 'a heavy heart'. What happened next, and his reactions and observations, are best told in his own words:

> I checked into the Sergeant's Mess ... and adjoined to the bar ... where the other NCO pilots, who were also posted to the course, had gathered. The main topic of conversation of course, was the war in Korea ... About 4.00 pm, the Orderly Officer, Flight Lieutenant Don Hillier (later killed in a Meteor in Korea) walked into the Mess, and called for attention. When the noise subsided, he announced that several pilots, who were to undergo the Flying Instructor's Course, had been re-posted to No 77 Squadron and were to leave for Japan the next day. He read out the names, and yours truly featured on the list. I was delighted of course, and immediately set about re-packing my gear—some to be sent home to Adelaide and some to accompany me to Japan.
>
> Next day we boarded a Dakota aircraft and departed East Sale for Richmond ... where we ran into some other pilots bound for 77 Squadron.[xv] A few days later, after the usual clearances, inoculations etc, we proceeded to Sydney Airport, where we boarded a chartered Qantas Constellation aircraft bound for Japan, via Manila in the Philippines ... We arrived in Iwakuni on 8 July, and after the aircraft landed I ... was greeted by Milt Cottee and Ray Trebilco ... with the news that Squadron Leader Graham Strout ... had been killed in operations in Korea the previous day. This news had a very sobering effect indeed on the group.
>
> We soon split into groups and departed for our various messes ... There were about 100 Japanese civilians working on the base ... We even had Japanese room girls who made

---

xv   The other nine pilots not yet mentioned were Eric Douglas, Andrew Hankinson, Bill Michelson, Don Brackenreg, Ross Coburn, Stan Williamson, Dick Wittman and John Murray.

our beds and cleaned the living quarters. Some of the fellows formed quite an attachment to these girls, but not me. Mine was about four feet tall and the same distance around the middle.

That evening at 5.00 pm, we were introduced to life in Iwakuni. I was having a beer in the mess when I heard a Mustang flying very low over the base. The Mustang, flown by Wally Rivers,[xvi] was spraying the base with a kerosene-based mixture to reduce the number of mosquitoes. When I looked in my glass, I had spots of kerosene on top of my beer. I didn't go in the beer garden the next night.[11]

Like all the newcomers, Lyall soon found there was more to worry about than keeping his beer free of kerosene during the late afternoon anti-mosquito run. First up, there were some lectures on intelligence and operating procedures, especially those for the JOC and air controllers, and for various weapons. They then did some local area training flights to get familiar with key landmarks and fired some rounds at the range. After that, they were ready to go. From now on, their training would be mostly OJT (on the job).

The new arrivals brought squadron pilot numbers to 36, giving it 50 per cent overmanning to cater for further losses and future postings out. Normally this would be a good thing, but in July Korea's notoriously hot and humid summer produced cloud and storms that limited flying opportunities. Consequently, despite having been rushed to Korea, on arrival some newcomers experienced a 'fairly slow' flying rate until the weather improved and, according to Lyall Klaffer, 'some pilots, including Milt Cottee, were sent back to Australia after they had flown 50 combat missions'.[12]

Tour lengths in Korea varied during the war, but 100 missions or six months soon became the most common. Milt

---

xvi Flew 319 combat missions and was awarded a DFC.

Cottee went back after 50 to do a flying instructor's course. Jim Flemming, Max Garroway, Brian Nicholls and Bob (Stormy) Fairweather also left after 50 missions to provide operational input to the Mustang Operational Conversion Unit (OCU) then being formed at Williamtown, near Newcastle.[xvii] Lyall Klaffer flew a fairly typical '105 operational missions and accumulated 300 operational flying hours'. Others, like Les Reading, Ken Murray and Wally Rivers, volunteered for extra tours.

The summer weather was not just frustrating the new arrivals, but, more importantly, it was helping the enemy. The North Koreans knew that UN ground forces would take time to deploy, and were trying to quickly take over the entire peninsula before UN forces were strong enough to stop them. The summer cloud and storms were a godsend to them, greatly restricting the all-out effort UN air forces were mounting against them.

This was especially important as air power was still the UN's main weapon. Fortunately, some flying was possible and by the second week in July UN air forces were averaging 300 missions a day. While this was well below their clear-weather potential it was a vital contribution; every sortie that slowed the enemy, even by a small amount, won extra time for the UN ground commanders to muster their forces.[13]

Time was indeed of the essence; the speed of the North Korean advance and the time available for the UN to deploy its forces were two sides of the same coin.

No one understood this better than Lieutenant General Walton Walker, the commander of the US 8th Army in Yokahama, Japan. He had begun progressively deploying his forces to South Korea in early July and watched anxiously as UN ground forces were inexorably pushed south, hoping that they would

---

xvii Until the OCU became active, replacement pilots were selected from operational Mustang squadrons or trained on type at No. 3 Squadron in Canberra.

resist long enough for his forces to fully deploy. This looked like a forlorn hope as, on 8 July, the Communists closed on Chonan, some 100 kilometres south of Seoul.

But Allied luck then turned. Some good flying weather arrived and stiff air resistance checked the Communist advance in a number of places. On 9 July, Gordon Harvey[xviii] and Jim Flemming contributed by knocking out the first T-34 tank destroyed in the war. It happened on the road between Osan and Chonan during a 'target of opportunity' mission, with Gordon leading, when they surprised two tanks and attacked one each. Having previously used up their rockets, all they had was 50-calibre bullets and they attacked with these.

Gordon's bullets simply bounced off the tough Russian tank, but Jim had better luck. The tank crew had forgotten to close its rear radiator doors, and on his second pass his rounds went into the engine cavity and the tank exploded. On return, Jim was interviewed by US Army and Air Force officials keen to find out the weaknesses of the tough T-34, until then virtually unstoppable.

Thanks to the better flying weather Gordon and Jim were but two of hundreds who flew that day, checking the enemy, but not stopping him entirely. In response to the continuing enemy advance, by 12 July regional US ground forces had withdrawn to the more easily defended Kum River near Taejon—now the provisional South Korean capital and regional US headquarters. There they would fight, with help from the air, to either stop the enemy, or delay him and buy time.

Slowing the enemy advance with air power wasn't a win in the usual sense, but in this case anything that hurt the enemy and bought time was a win, and air power had done this since day one of the war. The strategic decision to maximise air power was being vindicated daily. Its results had no more enthusiastic supporter than General Walker who, on 13 July said: 'Had it not been for the Far East Air Forces [which included 77 Squadron]

---

xviii Retired as a Group Captain DFC.

there would not be an American in Korea today.'[14]

This was true, but the North Koreans were still moving south, albeit at great cost. On 13–14 July, they crossed the Kum River and, after heavy fighting on 20 July, took Taejon. From there they continued south 40 kilometres to Yongdong, which they took on 24 July. Desperate for a quick victory, they fought on regardless of very high losses,[xix] many inflicted from the air.

By the end of July, in George Odgers' words:

> They pushed on down until the United Nations forces were compressed in the Pusan defence box behind the mighty Naktong River. Had the enemy possessed air power matching the United Nations, it would have been all over by the end of July.'[15]

But they didn't have such air power; and because the UN forces did, the US had time to move in reinforcements before everything was lost. And, of particular importance to our part of the story, General Walker had enough time to deploy the US 8th Army from Japan to South Korea. By the end of July, believing he had enough forces to halt the Communists—and knowing that UN naval forces could guarantee his supply lines into Pusan—he made his famous statement: 'There will be no retreat. We must fight to the death to hold what we have.'

The Pusan Perimeter, based mainly on the Naktong River, was now a reality in fact if not yet in name. The fighting to hold the perimeter would not just be along it, but along all the approaches to it from the north and west. Anything that would weaken the enemy and reduce his ability to breach the perimeter and push further south would be targeted. When Taejon fell, the government moved to Taegu, south of the Naktong. General Walker established his headquarters there, in an old school

---

xix   Reported in some sources to be as high as 58 000 casualties in June–July.

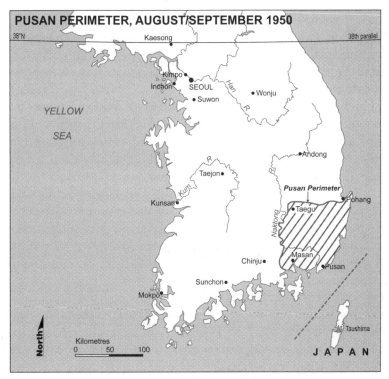

PUSAN PERIMETER, AUGUST/SEPTEMBER 1950

38°N
38th parallel
Kaesong
Kimpo
Inchon
SEOUL
Han R.
Wonju
Suwon
YELLOW
SEA
Andong
Taejon
Pusan Perimeter
Kunsan
Pohang
Naktong
Taegu
Kum
Chinju
Masan
Sunchon
Pusan
Mokpo
Tsushima
North
Kilometres
0   50   100
J A P A N

Korea, showing important locations and the main airfields 77 Squadron operated from during the war.

house, and began planning to defend this now vital perimeter that would eventually turn the tide of war.

Meanwhile, at Iwakuni the new pilots had been progressively introduced to operations. The more experienced went first. Having already done a tour at Iwakuni, Fred Barnes did only a single area familiarisation flight on 10 July, and flew his first combat sortie the next day, after just three days in country. The following day, 12 July, Ross Coburn joined a 'four' led by Tom Murphy[xx] to Chochiwon (about 50 kilometres north of Taejon) where an air controller directed them to six camouflaged tanks.

---

xx   The other two were 'Stormy' Fairweather and Tom Stoney.

They attacked with armour-piercing rockets and guns, destroying five tanks and a nearby fuel dump. They then followed the road south and found more tanks, which they attacked, destroying one and damaging others. Ricocheting incendiary bullets hit a nearby fuel dump, setting it on fire. By all criteria, Ross Coburn's first combat sortie had been successful. Later that day another new arrival, John Murray, also tasted success when he flew on a strike led by Blue Thornton that knocked out another two tanks and a fuel dump, bringing the squadron tally that day to eight tanks and two fuel dumps confirmed destroyed.

The ability to damage and destroy tanks from the air was a boon to the Allies, whose ground troops until then lacked the firepower to counter the tough Russian T-34 tanks that were playing a critical role in the Communist push south. From the Allied perspective, the more tanks destroyed, the slower the Communist advance—and with this in mind, tanks were a prime target from day one of the war.

Thus, the missions of 11–12 July were typical for those times, and with clearer weather there is no doubt 77 Squadron and its colleagues in the Fifth Air Force would have done even more damage. But, the weather being what it was, they were unable to fly the next day, 13 July, and most attempts the day after were forced to abort. Eventually, it cleared enough late in the day for Ken McLeod to lead a flight of four[xxi] to the Kum River area where the Communists were making the crossings that preceded their attack on Taejon.

The mission began like all before it, only to end in a way that would change how the squadron operated from then on. Their first attack, with rockets on a bridge, scored direct hits but did little damage. The controller then directed them to enemy troops trying to cross the river in boats and caught in the open. Sitting ducks, many of the troops were killed by strafing runs. Two boats mid-stream were sunk, staining the river red and

---

xxi The others were Gordon Harvey, Bill Horsman and Nobbie Noble.

turning the stomachs of their attackers—a reaction many would experience again when forced to attack defenceless enemy troops or other human targets.

The mission completed, they then landed at Taegu where they refuelled and flew back to Iwakuni—the first 77 Squadron aircraft to use the airfield that would soon become their second home (albeit a somewhat less salubrious one then Iwakuni). This development was inevitable; flying from Iwakuni involved two hours or more in transit for each mission. Recovery to Taegu to refuel for the return leg allowed more time on task. Missions flown entirely from Taegu, with their much reduced transit times, produced even bigger gains.

There were some problems with Taegu, however. To begin with, it was not an established base like Iwakuni, with permanent maintenance facilities and buildings, a 1800-metre concrete strip and secure fuel supplies. Instead, it was mostly a temporary affair. The buildings were hastily erected and the runway, taxyways and hardstands (used for parking, refuelling and rearming) were made of PSP (pierced steel plating), laid down in patterns of interlocking plates. The PSP had sunk into soil made soft by summer rains and sat under a thin layer of mud. White markers were placed on the mud to outline the strip, taxyways and hardstands.

Fuel was stored in giant bladders flown in from Pusan each day by C-119 transports, along with almost everything else, including food and weapons. This daily airlift was critical for the first weeks of operations because Taegu was under constant threat. Secure in an old walled city to the north during the day, the Communists sometimes took over parts of the airfield at night and had to be driven off in the morning. Along with valuable items like weapons, spares, communications equipment and the like, the aircraft were flown out each night to more secure airfields. When flying in again the next morning, before landing pilots often strafed the airfield perimeter to clear it of lurking North Koreans.

Consequently, for much of July, aircraft using Taegu flew in and out each day. It was only as security improved into August did they dare to stay overnight, and it was September before they could be based there with reasonable security. The effort required to operate Taegu under such conditions was immense, and a tribute to the US logistics people who moved everything in and out each day, and always ensured there was enough fuel and adequate weapons supplies to meet daily tasks.

This was all achieved, Milt Cottee tells us, despite 'the ever present sound of not so distant gunfire to the north'. He also added that: 'Without complete air superiority we would have been very vulnerable.'[16] This is certainly so for the RAAF C-47 transport which flew in from Japan each day, often at considerable risk from ground fire, with supplies and men to help support 77 Squadron operations.

This support was at times critical, but as Jim Flemming points out, without the fuel and weapons provided by the USAF each and every day, 77 Squadron operations from Taegu would not have been possible. This fact simply emphasises the key role of supply in war, and does not in any way diminish the value of the RAAF C–47 Dakota support in Korea.

Beginning with two aircraft—a transport and General Robertson's VIP aircraft which he quickly gave up for general transport duties—the Dakota flight eventually grew to four aircraft, and then to eight to become a squadron. Throughout the war it supported all Australian forces in Korea with regular transport flights and special flights like medivacs. Here, at Taegu, it often flew in harm's way and would do so elsewhere as the war progressed.

The impressive logistics effort allowed Taegu—despite the base's rudimentary state—to become the hub of the UN air effort along most of the Pusan Perimeter and adjacent areas to its north. Until early August, most of the action was directed at North Korean forces yet to reach the perimeter, but steadily closing. Milt Cottee flew out of Taegu in July and found the ground handling effort quite impressive in the circumstances. He later wrote of

> my first landing on the PSP strip at Taegu to join the queue of aircraft being refuelled and rearmed. We stayed with our aircraft and moved a few times in a queue to be eventually armed with refilled guns and 5 inch American rockets.
>
> These rockets were very different to our British style rockets ... They only had 5 inch warheads, so were much smaller than our 60 pound heads. Some of these 5 inch rockets had special armour piercing heads employing a shaped charge, used to penetrate thick armour.

Their different designs gave the rockets very different flight characteristics and 77 Squadron pilots had to learn the launch criteria of the US rockets as they went, there being no time for dedicated training flights.

Later that day Milt

> went on another mission with the special tank busting rockets looking for enemy heavy armour—T-34 tanks. We soon found some in an orchard. We blew the turret off one with a rocket and it burned. Finding some trucks, we hacked into them using guns ... Then back to Taegu for fuel, followed by a flight back to Iwankuni in late afternoon. A long day's work with 7½ hours flying.'[17]

The system Milt experienced, in which armed aircraft queued ready for immediate takeoff, was called 'Cab Rank'. Developed in World War II, it sometimes also included airborne aircraft in holding patterns to cut reaction times even further. Cab Rank operations usually sent out four aircraft at a time to nearby targets, but sometimes only two aircraft were launched. Whoever was at the head of the queue went. At Taegu in those times it could be four RAAF, mixed numbers of RAAF and USAF, all USAF, or a mix including US Navy aircraft as well.

Flight times were often short, as little as 25 minutes, and on one occasion Jim Flemming flew six Cab Rank missions in a day.

By August, the North Koreans were closing on the Pusan Perimeter and so were moving closer and closer to Taegu. Aircraft operating from Taegu often reached their targets after only a few minutes' flying. This was a hectic time for all concerned in 77 Squadron and required stamina and skill from pilots. Ray Trebilco later wrote that

> We would then land at ... Taegu ... rearm and refuel, take off for a further mission, sometimes even contacting an airborne controller during the climb and rolling in on a target very close to the airfield, landing back at Taegu for re-arming and refuelling again (perhaps even twice more), complete a final mission and, finally, return to Iwakuni.
>
> All this was done on dead reckoning, a combination of time and distance, airspeed and course and a cockpit full of military topographical maps of differing scales: 1:1 000 000, 1:1 500 000 and 1:50 000. We had no navigation aids other than mental calculations and map reading abilities ... When being passed from controller to controller, as might be required by the developing ground situation, flight to a new reference meant a new struggle with target maps and a renewed battle with terrain and weather.'[18]

These problems were ever present, but the hectic pace of many Taegu operations compressed time scales and exacerbated them.

Taegu operations also highlighted something few would have anticipated—problems associated with RAAF pilot ranks following the sudden change from peacetime operations in Iwakuni to war in Korea. The RAAF then used a system for non-commissioned aircrew, in which many pilots held one of five rank levels: pilot 4, 3, 2, 1 and master (the highest and roughly equivalent to a warrant officer). Everyone was a pilot 3 or above after six months and all lived in the Sergeant's Mess.

Pilot 3s otherwise were treated as corporals and placed on corporal duty rosters, like guard commander, at times with little recognition of the pressures operational flying imposed on them. This didn't matter too much during peacetime; if a pilot was too tired to fly he simply didn't. Now, in most cases, he had to fly. And when flying, if he were the most experienced man, he might then lead a flight that included officer pilots—despite being the lowest paid and lowest ranked man in the flight.

Lou Spence did what he could to sort out the mess. He took the pilot 3s off the corporal rosters and approved the wearing of officer ranks by all 77 Squadron pilots when flying over Korea—in the hope of better treatment should they become POWs.[xxii] On arrival at Taegu, they mixed easily with USAF pilots, who were all commissioned, and quickly contrasted their odd world with the much more straightforward world of the USAF.

The RAAF reverted to traditional NCO ranks soon after and eventually commissioned all pilots. But in the meantime, 77 Squadron pilot 3s had to live in a world where they had the disciplinary powers of a corporal at Iwakuni and were treated as officers on USAF bases. This may sound trivial to anyone who has not been in the military, but it wasn't. Flying an armed warplane in combat is demanding enough without the added pressure of not being able to order people to do mission-critical things, and going flying tired-out from spending a night on guard.

At first, only a handful of 77 Squadron missions used Taegu, but as the enemy moved further south they used it more and more. By the end of July, operations from Taegu were a major part of squadron life. But in mid-July, many of the enemy were still further north, and air strikes were planned with the aim of keeping them there as long as possible, or hurting them enough to prevent them coming at all.

---

xxii This made no difference—POWs were treated equally badly irrespective of rank.

In these times Lyall Klaffer finally joined the fray, on 16 July, flying with Bay Adams in a flight of four. Understandably a bit nervous, Lyall gained confidence from Bay's apparent lack of nerves and brief to: 'Go in low and hit them hard.' This sage advice may have sounded trite and perhaps gung-ho to some, but it was actually a succinct distillation of years of hard-earned experience. A fast, low-flying aircraft on the attack is hard to counter and so more likely to succeed and survive. Bay Adams knew this from experience, and encapsulated it in his simple one-liner.

The mission was to Konju, some 100 kilometres west of the Pusan Perimeter, to attack ground forces with bombs and guns. A week later Lyall flew even further, as one of four[xxiii] attacking enemy ground forces and tanks at Hamhung, well north of the 38th parallel, where he attacked a tank and set it alight. The squadron was now ranging far and wide about the peninsula. On the same day, Milt Cottee and Nobby Noble put in a napalm attack on troops sheltering in a town just south of Taejon, and the next day the squadron attacked tanks and troops near Yongdong.

They continued this pattern of operations throughout July, hitting key enemy targets throughout Korea, and attacking the advancing Communists as they pushed south. To do so they were still flying mostly from Iwakuni, but using Taegu more and more as the enemy moved south. Significantly, on 31 July, they flew five missions against an estimated 800 enemy troops in the hills near Hadong and Chinju, within only 50 kilometres of the Pusan Perimeter. It now looked as if the enemy would reach the perimeter and the fate of South Korea would soon be decided one way or another somewhere along the Naktong River.

This proved to be true and the tempo lifted in August as the battle for the Pusan Perimeter built to a climax. Targets were many and varied and ground fire a fact of life near most of them. Stan Williamson almost became the squadron's second

---

xxiii The others were Bay Adams, Tom McCrohan and Bill Harrop.

casualty on 10 August when he was hit by small-arms fire. He headed for Pohang, on the east coast of Korea and arrived safely. Unable to lower his flaps, he was overshooting when the engine failed and he crash-landed. Luckily, he emerged unharmed and hitched a ride back to Iwakuni on a US transport plane, a further reminder—if anyone needed it—that this was a dangerous way to earn a living.

During the pivotal month of August the Allied air effort concentrated mainly on hitting the enemy throughout the approaches to the perimeter, and eventually at the Naktong River that defined most of it. To do so, in August 77 Squadron flew 1745 hours on 812 sorties to destroy 35 tanks (and probably destroy or damage 31 others), 182 trucks, 30 other vehicles, 4 locomotives and 14 box cars, and 13 ammunition and fuel dumps[19]—an outstanding performance by any standards.

This fine effort did not go unnoticed. The distinctive squadron callsign, 'Drop-kick', meant everyone knew when the Australians were on a task. This no doubt helped the squadron gain recognition, but it was the quality and quantity of work done in just seven weeks of war that brought them to the notice of 'Genial George' Stratemeyer, head of US Far East Air Forces. On 22 August he called at Iwakuni.

Lou Spence had just returned from a mission and was still in his sweaty flight suit when they met. True to his nickname, Stratemeyer greeted Lou cordially and publicly presented him with a citation for 'outstanding leadership in the preparation of his unit for combat', and added that Lou Spence's 'deep devotion to duty and personal courage reflect great credit on himself and the RAAF'. The general then presented Lou with an American Legion of Merit. These awards were warmly welcomed by everyone present and spontaneous applause broke out at what was widely seen as a compliment to the squadron as well as its popular CO.[20]

The recognition lifted squadron morale, but had no other effect on the war, which was nearing maximum ferocity. Kim

Il-sung, knowing there was only limited time to take the peninsula, had demanded victory by 15 August from his North Korean forces. In response, his military leaders drove their troops mercilessly throughout August, applying heavy pressure to the Pusan Perimeter despite constant heavy losses. Their plan was clear to all—an all-out offensive to cross the Naktong and push the UN forces into the sea.

Of these times, George Odgers wrote that: 'they crossed the Naktong at seventeen points, in barges, boats and underwater bridges.'[21] The crossings all took place between 5 August and 1 September, the decisive point of the battle for the Pusan Perimeter. Jim Flemming flew against troops crossing the river and still remembers vividly that 'the North Korean troops were trying to cross a ford and the air controller was calling everything possible onto the troops'.[22]

Most aircraft used against the river crossings operated from Taegu, with 77 Squadron's Mustangs making up about 30 per cent of them.[23] To make that contribution, 77 Squadron worked long and hard. On most days, four flights of four Mustangs left Iwakuni before dawn, flew all day out of Taegu, and often landed back in Iwakuni after dark.

It was exhausting stuff. Pilots were out of bed at 4.30 each morning and spent much of their day, hot and sweaty, in a Mustang cockpit—either on the ground waiting, or flying at low level. It was no picnic for the ground crews either. They frequently worked all night repairing battle damage and readying the aircraft for flight next day. Some travelled back and forth to Taegu where they worked long hours in the mud and heat. With time, a semi-permanent maintenance detachment stayed there for days at a time, living in tents.

The main river crossings were close to Taegu, and by using the Cab Rank system, the Allies were continually attacking from the air, with devastating effect. Indeed, there were, Jim Flemming remembers so many dead it was amazing they were still coming. With each successive attack, we could see the pile of bodies mounting, and eventually the river ran with blood. It was a shattering experience. We were not used to shooting at people, especially on such a large scale.[24]

Of all their work, 'shooting at people' was the hardest thing to do, not just at the Naktong, but everywhere. Tanks, trains and even trucks were one thing. But when the target was something like troops in the open, or an ox-cart and the people with it, this somehow personalised things and made the task much more distasteful. Almost everyone had second thoughts about such work—even though ox-carts were a popular way to transport weapons and, along with troops, were legitimate targets.

Even worse were attacks against individuals wearing the flowing white robes and distinctive black hats of some Koreans.[xxiv] The flowing robes were ideal for concealing ammunition and explosives and were often used that way. But to many, their wearers looked especially innocent and vulnerable and some pilots could not bring themselves to attack them, even though they often blew up when hit.

Ironically, the very success of the Allied air effort produced more human targets for them to attack. Norman Bartlett[25] explains that

> when naval and air bombardment drove the North Koreans off the good coastal roads they took to the sheltered inland tracks. In this sort of country, tanks, aircraft and heavy transport were at a disadvantage. The Communists used horse carts, handcarts, pack animals and human carriers. They impressed refugees of both sexes to carry supplies. A woman could carry ten grenades, a boy could handle a belt of cartridges, one hundred men were equal to a motor truck.

---

xxiv Most Koreans adopted white dress, a sign of mourning, when the Japanese took over their country in 1905, and many still wore it during the war.

In these circumstances, refusing to fire for moral or personal reasons at people deemed legitimate targets was not allowed. It was seen by the system as cowardice, or LMF (Lack of Moral Fibre) and reason to be taken off operations and sent home, effectively in disgrace. While the 'system' saw things that way, few pilots did, and Jim Flemming cannot recall any pilot condemning another for 'LMF'. Rather, they all accepted that some could always shoot whatever the target, and some couldn't, and made no further judgements. It was simply a fact of war.

The Naktong River experience was especially horrible, but along with other Allied successes in August it stopped the enemy enough to secure the Pusan Perimeter—and with it the UN presence in Korea. During the first week in September, the enemy was still applying strong pressure, but it was waning. On 12 September, General Walker stated that 'the worst was over'. The UN had kept a toehold on the peninsula, a toehold from which they could, and would, fight back, and without which the war almost certainly would have been lost.

MacArthur and Stratemeyer's early decision to maximise air power was vindicated. In the critical first two months of war, air power 'had accounted for 81 percent of all enemy tanks destroyed, … 75 percent of all trucks, 72 percent of artillery and 47 percent of the personnel killed.'[26] In short, airpower had made the difference. And where it counted most, at the Pusan Perimeter, 77 Squadron had provided 30 per cent of the air power from Taegu when the fighting was at its fiercest.

UN forces now had a secure hold on southern Korea, but the war was far from over and fighting was still widespread. Taegu was no longer seriously threatened, but North Korean troops were still active just to its north. Above the parallel, US bombers were still pounding North Korean targets, reducing the enemy's ability to wage war. On 3 September four B-29s were sent to bomb Pyongyang, the North Korean capital, escorted by four 77 Squadron Mustangs led by Ken McLeod.[xxv]

It was a long flight and the Mustangs were fitted with drop tanks. The B–29s bombed from 20 000 feet (6000 metres) and, when no longer required as escorts, the Mustangs headed for Taegu. En route, they were contacted by an airborne controller to attack a target some 30 kilometres north of Taegu. Ken McLeod had engine trouble and headed straight for Taegu, while the other three attacked some enemy troop positions. Lyall Klaffer later wrote that they:

> encountered quite a bit of ground fire. When Bill Harrop called up, and stated that he had only 20 gallons of fuel remaining, we called off the attack and headed towards Taegu. Then Bill reported that he had been hit and that his engine was losing power and he would have to force land. He landed safely, wheels up, on the banks of the River Nakong near an orchard. I watched him get out of the cockpit unharmed. He waved to me as I flew down over him. Michelson told me to cover Bill, while he headed to Taegu, only five miles away, to organise a rescue. Bill ran into an orchard and hid in a hut there. I circled the area … until four US Mustangs arrived on the scene … Down to 20 gallons of fuel … I left the area and landed at Taegu.[27]

A rescue helicopter sent from Pusan did not arrive until much later, by which time Bill Harrop's luck had given out. The area was now teeming with enemy soldiers and the helicopter could not land to rescue him. His fate remained unknown, but the squadron feared for the worst, knowing the habits of the enemy. Months later, when the area was back in UN hands, Bill Harrop's body was found in a shallow grave near the orchard. He had been shot several times.[28]

The knowledge that Bill Harrop was probably dead had a sobering affect on everyone. Or maybe he was a prisoner.

---

xxv The others were Lyall Klaffer, Bill Michelson and Bill Harrop.

No one knew for sure, and that in itself did nothing for the mood. Life went on, of course, and the very next day the squadron lost another aircraft—piloted by Ross Coburn—on the return leg to Iwakuni, following a rocket strike at Kigye, just inland from Pohang.

A generally tough aircraft, the Mustang's weak point was its glycol cooling system which, if hit, could lose glycol, causing the engine to overheat and even fail. Whether Ross Coburn's cooling system was punctured by ground fire during the attack on Kigye, or if it suffered other problems, is not known. What is known is that while crossing the Tsushima Straits with Jack Murray and Gordon Harvey his engine started to overheat, glycol fumes entered the cockpit and glycol could be seen streaming from the radiator shutter.

They had reached Japan when the engine finally gave out and the violently vibrating Mustang began to lose height. Although in cloud and over mountains, there was no option but to bail out. Ross jettisoned the canopy, undid his seat harness and stood up into the hurricane-force airflow. Levering himself with the windscreen frame and the armour plate at the rear of the cockpit, he dived towards the starboard roundel, pulling himself into a ball. When clear of the aircraft he pulled the parachute ripcord and the 'chute opened.

A little later, Jack Murray saw the parachute nearing the ground and Ross wave to him after landing. Unlike Bill Harrop, his luck was good. He was in Japan, not Korea, and was quickly surrounded by helpful Japanese. Two hours later he was picked up by a jeep sent from Iwakuni. According to one chronicler: 'They gave him a couple of beers to drink and he was right as rain.' Such is fate.

Fate can also be cruel, and was cruel indeed just five days later on 9 September. Bad weather made it impossible to reach Taegu that day, but conditions were good enough for operations from Iwakuni to Korea and return. Early that morning Lou

Spence led a flight of four,[xxvi] three armed with napalm, on a strike directed by a controller onto the town of Angan-ni. On the way, Ross Coburn had diverted to Pusan with engine problems, leaving three for the attack.

Lou Spence put in the first attack and was killed doing it. The aircraft was seen to hit the ground and explode—probably hit by ground fire, but no one knows for sure.[xxvii] The other two, seeing there was no possibility that Lou had survived, continued the attack and recovered to Iwakuni with the news.

This was terrible news, not just for his family, but for the entire squadron to whom he was not just an inspiring leader but a friendly and helpful boss and a much admired figure. He had been selected for staff training in England in preparation for higher rank and there is no doubt he would have achieved it. In this regard, Jim Flemming is strongly of the view that he had the qualities 'to make CAS (Chief of the Air Staff, the head of the RAAF)' and many others who knew Lou Spence say similar things. However it is seen, he was a great loss.

The two senior men were now gone. Both had been respected and admired, one almost to the point of adulation. The affect on squadron morale was shattering. Their leaders killed, the squadron desperately needed a strong and competent leader to take them through these bad times and restore their morale and fighting spirit. Fortunately for 77 Squadron, and for the RAAF, the ideal man for the job was available, and Dick Cresswell was posted in as CO almost immediately.

---

xxvi The others were Dick Turner, Ross Coburn and Andrew Hankinson.

xxvii Some accounts say he probably misjudged his pull out, but those who flew with him doubt this as he was an expert in such attacks and had taught many of them.

3

Mustangs in Korea

There was much about Dick Cresswell that made him the best man in the RAAF to replace Lou Spence. To begin with, he had done the job twice before and done it very well—despite being only 21 years old when first appointed CO of 77 Squadron in April 1942.

The squadron was then being formed near Perth, Western Australia. Its Kittyhawk fighters were still in crates and his brief was to oversee their assembly, ready the squadron, and take it to war in Darwin. The local RAAF base was overcrowded, so he took over a golf course, joined two fairways for a runway and used the clubhouse and local houses as accommodation. The resultant airfield became known as Guildford.

RAAF Darwin too was overcrowded and could not meet their needs. In response, Dick secured funds and sent a carefully selected team to Adelaide to buy everything needed and trucks to carry it to Darwin. In mid-June the trucks drove north, laden with everything from tents to teapots and including a ton of beer, and the aircraft flew, navigating via the 'iron compass' (the transcontinental railway) and the dusty Adelaide to Darwin road.

On arrival, the base commander passed a message from the RAAF chief, Air Marshal George Jones, asking 'What took you so long?' With customary directness, the recently appointed Squadron Leader Cresswell replied: 'With due respect, Sir, tell the chief to look at a map.' Jones did not reply and never spoke to Dick again.

Jones's churlish behaviour did not alter the fact that this was a remarkable feat for a 21-year-old, achieved by some excellent organisation, good communication, and a willingness to trust competent men to get on with the job. He had also led from the front, setting the example on the ground and in the air.

In Darwin he became the first Australian to shoot down an enemy aircraft in Australian airspace at night when he attacked three Betty bombers, hit all three and followed one down for a definite kill. When asked by a journalist what he felt like after shooting down the aircraft, Dick replied: 'Breakfast.' It had been a long night. Later in the war he was himself shot down, at Milne Bay, during his second tour as 77 Squadron's commander, and served in and around New Guinea at places like Noemfoor, Biak and Moratai.

He finished the war as a wing commander and stayed in the post-war RAAF with the lower rank of squadron leader and a reputation among his peers as an outstanding operational commander. Buster Brown, who flew with him in Milne Bay and later took over 77 Squadron, admired his leadership and believed that Dick was:

> The greatest organiser, on the ground ... and in the air of what we were going to do tactically. He ran a squadron the way it should be run—you keep everyone informed ... then everyone is allocated their task, they are trained to handle that task, and the whole thing is brought together. In the air ... their training is so good, on a word of command they will do anything ... everyone knows what to do.' [1]

In September 1950, as CO of 21 Squadron in Melbourne Dick was current on Mustangs. Along with his war record, this made him the logical choice and he was again appointed CO of 77 Squadron on 12 September, just three days after Lou Spence's death. He left Sydney via Qantas on the 15th and was flying operationally from Iwakuni on the 20th.

He quickly saw that the squadron was 'well equipped, well organised, operationally trained, and could do a good job—and thanks to Lou Spence ... it was led perfectly in all the jobs it did'.[2] In that regard, the two flight commanders, Bay Adams and Brick Bradford, were running things very well. But running things well didn't replace their lost CO. His death was keenly felt and his strong leadership and positive example were sadly missed.

Dick Cresswell's job was to provide that leadership and example, to re-focus the squadron, to get them concentrating on the task at hand and the job ahead. To do so he decided to gain some practical flying experience, demonstrate competence and win the respect he needed to engender the focus he wanted.

His first sortie was a strike mission as No. 2 to Bay Adams, who had been leading the squadron since Lou Spence was killed. He flew three more sorties that day and a total of eleven in the first week, learning about the war and leading from the front, showing the squadron that their new CO was neither a figurehead nor a desk wallah.

The ploy worked well, as many veterans can attest. What Milt Cottee later called 'dismal times', were replaced by good spirits and confidence among the pilots once their new CO had taken charge. Of these times, Lyall Klaffer wrote that 'Dick was a great pilot and an energetic and enthusiastic officer' who 'very quickly earned the respect of every pilot in the squadron'.[3] Jim Flemming has similar memories, recalling that the early casualties had 'seriously lowered morale, but Dick Cresswell led from the front and soon had the squadron on its feet again'.[4]

And it was just as well he did. As he was boarding his Qantas flight from Sydney, the first US Marines were already beginning

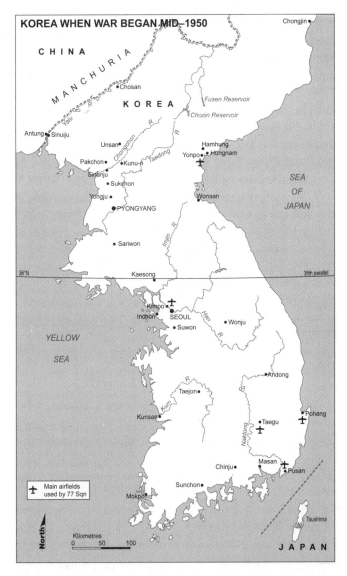

Following rapid North Korean advances, UN forces made a stand at the Pusan Perimeter. By maximizing air power, they held the perimeter, saved South Korea and turned the tide of war.

an audacious landing at Inchon, near Seoul, to take the enemy from the rear and cut his supply lines. It was typical MacArthur. He had publicly discussed the fact that in the history of war 'nine out of ten times an army has been destroyed because its supply lines have been cut',[5] fuelling speculation that an amphibious landing was being planned.

The big question was 'where?' and this was kept a carefully guarded secret. As it happened, no one of consequence among the enemy seems to have picked Inchon, notorious for treacherous approaches and tides that vary the water depth by 10 metres. Clearly not expecting an invasion there, the North Koreans had a force of only 2000 to protect Inchon.

This small force proved no match for the 70 000-strong 10th Corps that landed. Audacity, surprise and good planning were all evident, but the degree of risk was high to many eyes—including some high up in the Pentagon who opposed the plan—and critics claim MacArthur was lucky to pull it off. Again, his critics have a point, but the fact is he did pull it off and Inchon quickly turned the war.

The first Marines of the 10th Corps landed on Wolmi Island, just off Inchon, at 6.30 on the morning of 15 September 1950, heavily supported by air power and naval gunfire. The supporting armada was huge—261 vessels from eight UN nations—and showed again the complete maritime superiority the Allies enjoyed. The Allied forces, George Odgers tells us:

> quickly crushed the feeble Inchon defences, seized the major nearby airport of Kimpo[i] and then, after a bloody struggle, liberated Seoul, the capital. The Inchon landing had slammed shut the door on the North Korean divisions, which, far away in the south-east, were still hammering, to no avail, at the Pusan Perimeter defences.

---

i   Which would, in less than a year, become 77 Squadron's home base until the end of the war.

The North Koreans had become palpably weaker. Desperately short of food, ammunition and transport, they melted away into the mountains. Only 25 000 eventually reached North Korean territory beyond the 38th parallel. By 27 September, General Walker's 8th Army, moving north, joined forces with the 10th Corps on the following day. At Government House in Seoul, General MacArthur restored the symbolically important city to President Syngman Rhee and his government.[6]

With South Korea back in South Korean hands, the question arose, what next? For many UN countries, the aim had been to nip the aggression in the bud, stop it spreading, wind up the fighting as soon as possible and use negotiation from here on. There were also fears that if matters were pushed too far, the Russians and/or Chinese might join in.

MacArthur, on top of his game and feeling hawkish, disagreed with the 'doves' and demanded a North Korean surrender. When there was no response the US Chiefs of Staff gave him permission to move troops north of the 38th parallel. On 7 October, the UN General Assembly also authorised troops north of the parallel, and the establishment of a UN Commission for the Unification of Korea.

Meanwhile, China was not behaving quite as passively as MacArthur had expected. They began a 'hate America' campaign and on 30 September stated that 'the Chinese people absolutely will not tolerate seeing their neighbours savagely invaded by the imperialists'. Typical Communist rhetoric of the times, it completely ignored the fact that North Korea was the aggressor and left open the question of just what the Chinese were prepared to do, and what would cause them to do it.

The very next day, they answered the question. The Chinese Foreign Minister, Chou En Lai, told the Indian Ambassador that if American troops entered North Korea, China would enter the war. MacArthur decided it was bluff, and President Truman, probably influenced by MacArthur's brilliant success so far and confident judgements, agreed. As a result, MacArthur pushed on into North Korea. As October progressed, the catchcry became 'North to the Yalu', the river that forms the border between North Korea and the Chinese state of Manchuria.

Meanwhile, to support Inchon General Stratemeyer had maximised the air effort, hitting the enemy on the battlefield, at his bases and especially along his supply lines. By 14 September—the eve of Inchon—most movement of military supplies and equipment within enemy territory had ceased. On the 16th, General Walker went on the offensive and by 19 September the 8th Army had crossed the Naktong River and forced the enemy into a disordered retreat.

Operating from both Iwakuni and Taegu, 77 Squadron was in the thick of things, flying far and wide, wherever worthwhile targets could be found. Some flew with US Marine and Navy pilots in support of the Inchon landings and others supported Allied troops crossing the Naktong. On the 19th a flight of four[ii] supported a secondary amphibious landing at Pohang—which, though they did not know it, would soon be their first base on the peninsula. Soon after that, a flight of seven found a tank on the road from Waegwan to Kumch'on (northwest of Taegu), destroyed it and killed the crew.

Others went much further from home. On 24 September, Lyall Klaffer was one of four that attacked the airfield at Pyongyang, where he destroyed a YAK fighter on the ground. Until then, his targets had been 'tanks, railway engines, railway tunnels, trucks and boats' and he found it very satisfying 'to finally destroy an enemy aircraft, albeit on the ground'.[7] A number of squadron aircraft were hit by ground fire, but none was forced down.

Following an attack on an electrical sub-station, intelligence told them that such targets were off limits so the electrical grid

---

ii   Fred Barnes, Ken Royal, Bill Michelson, and Don Brackenreg.

could be used by the Allies as they took back territory. The substantial grid was the one technically advanced aspect of an otherwise backward country and well worth protecting. Built by the Japanese during their 40-year occupation of Korea, it used the mountainous terrain with its many rivers to produce hydro-electric power and distribute it throughout much of the country.

As a result, even remote villages with mud and thatch houses often had electric lights, although few had piped water or sewage systems, and garbage and human waste was collected and carried in 'honey carts' to fertilise rice paddies. Sanitation was an unknown concept, and in summer the pilots could often tell they were flying over a village by the smell wafting up from below.

On 22 September, the commander of the 5th Air Force, General Partridge, awarded US Air Medals to Bay Adams, Brick Bradford, Nobby Noble and Charles Taplin, a Dakota pilot. In an accompanying speech he said: 'I have watched you in the air, I have seen you dive-bombing and I have seen you on the ground at Taegu and everywhere I go you are doing wonderful work ... we are doing exceptionally well and it looks as though we have the North Koreans on the run.'[8]

The North Koreans were indeed on the run. So much so, in fact, that the rapidly shifting lines made ground attack difficult to organise and on 1 October close-support missions were temporarily shelved, replaced by armed reconnaissance over the 38th parallel. 77 Squadron now found itself on many sorties like the flight to Pyongyang on the 24th, flying further and further north to seek out the enemy.

Anticipating this possibility, early in the war General Robertson had recommended that 77 Squadron be moved to Korea when the circumstances allowed. On 10 August 1950, the Australian Chiefs of Staff approved his recommendation and from then on it was only a matter of time until a suitable airfield became available. On 11 October, 77 Squadron moved to Pohang, in Korea's southeast, near the extreme end of the Pusan Perimeter.

On the eve of their move, the 10th Corps made another amphibious landing—this time unopposed—into Wonsan, midway up the east coast of North Korea. There it linked up with South Korean forces that had pushed up the east coast. No attempt was made to link up with the 8th Army in Seoul, as this would take time and MacArthur's plan was to keep the enemy on the run and bring the war to a quick conclusion. For 77 Squadron, this translated into plenty to do once they got to Pohang.

The nicest thing that can be said about Pohang is that it greatly increased everyone's appreciation of Iwakuni. The airstrip was an old Japanese concrete one about 1350 metres long, with a significant dip just before the Mustang lift-off point that made for some deep breaths and bouncy takeoffs. The enemy had recently occupied the base and only withdrawn following Inchon. Until they left, it was the regional location of choice for Allied aircraft to drop unexpended ordnance after missions. As a result, there were no serviceable buildings and the nearby town was in ruins.

Scattered pockets of the enemy were still about and Les Reading's 'notable memories include the zing of bullets ricocheting nearby and adding urgency to business at the open-air thunderboxes'.[9] He also remembers walking on the nearby beach and finding human body parts left over from recent fighting washed up with the tide. In peacetime Pohang could have been quite a nice place to be, but right now it was pretty dreadful.

They were the third Mustang squadron there, one of three in the USAF 35th Fighter Group, of which they were now part. Its commander, Lieutenant Colonel Jack Dale, had served in Australia and New Guinea during the Pacific War, as had a number of other USAF pilots. They liked Australians, knew how they operated and made the squadron welcome.

Operationally, being part of the 35th Fighter Group worked very well—77 Squadron had been working with the USAF for months now, spoke the same language and were well regarded. And, perhaps even more importantly, domestically it proved to be a godsend—for without American help they could not have survived.

In simple terms, the Australian supply system let them down badly, both in Australia and in Japan. Dinny O'Brien's experience was typical.[iii] An airframe fitter, he had previously done a tour in Iwakuni and was one of the 28 ground staff rushed to Korea just after the war began. Like everyone else he had 'no time to settle domestic matters' and took a train to Richmond as soon as possible. Following inoculations, they went to the clothing store for an issue of extra clothing: 'two pairs of pyjamas, a dressing gown, a pair of slippers, and two sets of woollen long-john type underwear'.

Nice to have, but apart from the long-johns, no use for outside work in the Korean winter. But in Dinny's case, that didn't matter because they wouldn't give him any. As he later explained: 'They told me there was only one issue, you only got this issue once, and as I had been to Japan some four years previous I'd used my issue and they didn't have authority to give me a second one. So half our crew went away without the additional clothing.'

Dinny arrived in Pohang in early November and found the conditions there 'absolutely appalling. We were living under canvas, there were no tracks or paving and we were sloshing around in thick mud. The temperatures were so low, we had never experienced anything like it. However, the Americans came to the fore when they realised we were inadequately clothed.'[10]

The type of clothing they received is only seen on the

---

iii   Dinny was later commissioned, spent 20 years as an Engineering Officer, and retired as a Squadron Leader with an MBE to live near Newcastle.

snowfields in Australia, so it is understandable that the normal provisioning system did not stock it. What is unforgivable is that no one in Australia bothered to find out what Korean winters were like and arrange clothing supplies from the Americans. In Australia, the 38th parallel is near Melbourne, where the RAAF headquarters was then based. Perhaps those in charge assumed that the climate in Korea, at and about the 38th parallel, was like Melbourne's. If they did, they did so in ignorance of the 'Siberian Wind' that sweeps across that part of the world, unchecked from the Arctic and almost as cold, producing temperatures of 20 below zero and worse for weeks on end.

Knowing Korea was once called Chosen, the squadron soon labelled Pohang 'Frozen Chosen'. The cold caused serious problems for maintenance staff. For some tasks, Dinny remembers: 'You'd have to take off your gloves, and, without thinking, take the appropriate tool, and realise it was stuck to you hand, it was frozen. You'd then race to the flight line tent where they had a brazier burning all the time … and hold your hand over it until the tool fell off, and then get your glove back on and go to work.'[11]

Even worse was an unprotected hand stuck to a frozen aircraft. If no hot water was available, sometimes the hand had to be urinated on to free it.

When not at work they lived in old Indian Army camouflage tents and used a lot of old World War II equipment, mostly provided by BCOF stores in Japan. Unsuited to the task, the tents kept out little cold and everyone suffered accordingly. This fact, along with the lack of adequate clothing, was an immediate headache for the new CO who would have rather concentrated on operational matters.

For him, everything came to a head when:

I lost two pilots in a tent fire one night. We were using old fashioned wiring … and it caught fire … and they couldn't get out of their sleeping bags. I screamed blue murder.

General Robertson[iv] was on my side, so was Air Vice Marshal Scherger,[v] who said: 'Look, whatever you want, I'll back you'. And I suppose he was the only senior member of the air force that really backed 77 Squadron … He knew what was going on and had a fair idea that we were in trouble in all sorts of ways—equipment worries and so on. In the end, I got all American gear; I signed for everything and the Yanks … were quite happy to give it to us, and they did.'[12]

Australian army troops also needed winter clothes. To transport them the RAAF C-47 Dakotas from Iwakuni made a rush trip to Pusan to pick up winter clothes and then fly on to Pyongyang despite freezing conditions and a 100 kilometres per hour head wind. From there the clothes were trucked north to the men of the Royal Australian Regiment, still fighting in their summer uniforms. It seems the RAAF was not alone with its supply inadequacies.

Other supplies were also obtained by direct action from the squadron, often with little help from the Australian supply pipeline. To make matters even worse, the camouflage paint on the burning tent was found to have fuelled the fire. Had they been using fire-resistant American tents, the two men almost certainly would not have died. Overall, life in Pohang was one long challenge to everyone's morale, even the most positive of men.

That said, in such times there are always positive people who don't take adversity lying down. Dick Cresswell knew this, and with his support they built hot showers, arranged movies and reading material, opened a wet and dry canteen and connected electrical power were they could. And on the first Tuesday in November, they ran the traditional Melbourne Cup

---

iv   Dick always spoke highly of the support, personal and operational, he received from General Robertson.
v   Later Air Chief Marshal, Chief of the Air Staff, Chairman of the Joint Chiefs of Staff, Chairman of the Australian Airlines Commission and Australia's first 'four-star airman'.

sweep. Nothing could be done about the mud and cold, but these self-help measures got people working together, made life more comfortable, and helped lift morale.

A week after 77 Squadron shifted to Pohang, all RAAF units in Korea and Japan were placed in a new 91 (Composite) Wing. As well as 77 Squadron, the new wing included 30 Communications Flight with two C-47 Dakotas and two Austers, 491 Maintenance Squadron and 391 Base Squadron. The Dakota flight later received two more aircraft and became independent, and was renamed 36 Squadron when its fleet numbers were increased to eight in 1953.[vi]

Except for the Mustangs and front-line ground staff, everything was based in Iwakuni, including the 91 Wing commander, Group Captain Arthur Charlton, who was now Dick Cresswell's immediate boss. These new arrangements had no immediate impact on those at Pohang, who gained only from being nearer the action. Operations began soon after their arrival, supporting troops near Kaesong (the old capital, near the parallel) and escorting bombing missions against enemy targets to the north.

Along with the other two squadrons at Pohang, they were placed on 'maximum effort' and were soon doing everything—close support, strikes, bomber escort, reconnaissance, the lot. The main Allied objective now was to take the North Korean capital of Pyongyang. Some of the air effort was directed accordingly and some simply aimed to hit the enemy wherever he was found.

So far they had done little close support for ground forces, but now found themselves providing a good deal of direct support for troops on the ground. On 15 October, Fred Barnes led a four to support Australian troops advancing on the village of Namchonjom. On arrival, they could see the troops about 3 kilometres from the village and were asked by the controller

---

vi   36 Squadron remained a transport squadron thereafter, was re-equipped with C-130 Hercules aircraft and based at Richmond until its recent re-equipment with C-17 Globemasters and transfer to Amberley.

to subdue enemy fire coming from the village. They napalmed gun positions near the village to good effect, but ran into a problem when Fred Barnes had a 'hang up' of the napalm tank under his left wing.

The napalm tank could come loose at any time and he climbed to clear the area, forced to fly over the Australian troops as he did so. As he neared them, the tank came off and tumbled end over end towards the troops, landing with a great burst of flame in a paddy field about 200 metres from the soldiers. Very scary and a close call, but luckily no one was hurt. After a quick apology to the controller, they strafed enemy positions in the village and flew back to Pohang.[13]

The noose was now tightening around Pyongyang. On 19 October, Republic of Korea (ROK) soldiers entered the city and the next day it was clear of enemy forces. MacArthur was justifiably buoyed by this success and next day assured the UN that the fighting 'was very definitely coming to an end shortly'.[14] Being 'home for Christmas' was a realistic hope for UN troops.

But there was still much to do to bring that about. A large paradrop was planned north of Pyongyang, in the Sukchon–Sunchoo area. The area was 'softened up' from the air before the drop. 77 Squadron played a major role, with eighteen aircraft, led by Dick Cresswell, attacking enemy targets with rockets and strafing runs before recovering to Kimpo, where they stayed overnight.

The squadron had attacked Kimpo a number of times and when they landed on the rough runway, Milt Cottee realised some of the roughness was from filled-in bomb craters he had made recently with two 500-pound bombs. They had also recently strafed and bombed the terminal building and now had time to inspect their handiwork as they spent the night in the burned and beaten-up buildings.

Milt also flew to protect the transport aircraft carrying the paratroopers of the US 187th Airborne Regiment and to protect the troops after the drop. It was a big affair, about which he later wrote:

> We were up at first light and there, scattered over every available parking space, were C119 Packets and C47 Gooney Birds loading up with para-troops and equipment … We watched from our cockpits as streams of these aircraft took off and formed up into huge formations … After they had taken off, it was our turn and our twelve Mustangs took off to catch up with the transports. We took up top cover positions above the huge formation. Soon they were disgorging thousands of parachutes on the selected drop zones.
>
> Air controllers were already in position to direct our close support. We were soon at work suppressing sporadic ground fire from enemy troops. Often we found ourselves dodging around parachutes and giving encouraging waves to those descending. The enemy ground fire was short lived and we took every opportunity to pick off machine gun positions … I was elated to have been able to provide direct covering fire for the descending troopers, some of whose lives may have been preserved as a result. Complete surprise seemed to have been achieved and this force did much to cut off large sections of the enemy.[15]

Similar Allied success was being enjoyed almost everywhere. As October progressed, Allied forces continued to push north. On 26 October, ROK soldiers marched into Choson, on the Yalu River and within sight of Manchuria, to fulfil an earlier goal to 'wash their swords in the Yalu'. The North's President Kim had relocated to Kanggye, further up the Yalu, where he was expected to make a stand, but most saw this as a vainglorious act rather than something that could turn the war. He had gambled by starting the war without adequate air and naval forces, lost the gamble and now was losing everywhere. Allied victory and a quick end to the war seemed certain.

Unfortunately, this was not to be and the Koreans suffered accordingly, along with the UN forces. So far, tens of thousands of Korean soldiers had died on both sides in what for them was civil war, dividing families and friends. Much of the civilian population had been killed, wounded, displaced and enslaved as the Communists drove south, only to be caught up again in the fighting as the Allies swept back north. During the next few months, many of these unfortunates would be embroiled again when the Chinese Communists joined the fray to support the paranoid ideologies of their leader, Mao Tse-tung.

The full extent of Mao's influence on the war has only become known since the collapse of the Soviet Union and greater freedom in China to access records and interview veterans. Since then, researchers have learned that millions of Koreans (and hundreds of thousands of Chinese) suffered and died to further Mao's political ends. He feared invasion and grasped the chance to fight the potential invaders in North Korea instead of in China. He then deliberately prolonged the war, believing it to be the ideal opportunity to exhaust America and lower its international standing.

Massive Chinese losses meant nothing to him. His field commander, Lin Piao,[vii] suffered heavy losses which he attributed 'to the failure of the Chinese central Government to furnish air and tank support as promised'[16] but his angry reports detailing his inability to win in such circumstances changed nothing. The Chinese Army continued to suffer terrible losses, and Mao told Stalin that he was 'ready to persist in a long-term war, to spend several years consuming several hundred thousand American lives, so they will back down'.[17]

To do so, he sought Stalin's aid for military equipment, training and arms factories. Stalin agreed the aims and the aid, happy to make America suffer at the cost of North Korean and

---

vii   Also spelt Biao. Later assassinated when the airliner in which he was fleeing to Russia was shot down by Chinese fighters.

Chinese lives, but baulked at the arms factories just yet. For Mao the longer the war lasted, the more chance he had of getting Russian factories and a Chinese arms industry.[18]

Had this been known to MacArthur and the UN partners in Korea, many decisions would have been different. Kim Il-sung too would have had second thoughts, as Mao was about to take over his war and prolong the suffering of his people by two years or more. But it wasn't known to any of these people, and there is no way they could have known at the time. Based on what they knew, both sides planned their war.

On the UN side, what was known was far from reality. Although the Chinese were quietly entering North Korea in large numbers, they managed to hide the fact from UN intelligence. Indeed, they were so successful in their subterfuge that, although they had 300 000 troops in North Korea in mid-November, 8th Army intelligence only knew of 9000.[19] Other estimates were higher, but not hugely so.

Thus, in early November, planning for 77 Squadron aimed only to keep it operational until North Korean forces—with whatever help they got from the few thousand Chinese then known to be in-country—capitulated. Hopefully, this would be in just a few weeks, or months at best, but planning had to be for however long it took. With this in mind, in early November the first rotation of pilots took place when five 50-mission men were sent home. Fifty missions was set as a tour early in the war, but most volunteered for a second tour and did 100 missions, or thereabouts. A tour of six months soon became standard, during which 100 or more missions were usually flown.

Two 50-mission men, Milt Cottee and Jim Flemming, have already been mentioned. Milt went home via Iwakuni, where he did a number of maintenance test flights and ferried a replacement aircraft to Korea before leaving. Jim[viii] went to 3 Squadron in

---

viii And also Max Garroway, Brian Nicolls and Bob 'Stormy' Fairweather.

Canberra, then training pilots to fly Mustangs in Korea. This was critical work as the pool of experienced Mustang pilots in Australia was shrinking fast, and by December 1950 it was obvious the squadron would not be 'home for Christmas'—not that year, anyway.

There were then only 42 fully trained Mustang pilots in Australia and 22 others doing refresher training. The inevitable result was that as the war progressed, average pilot experience levels at 77 Squadron dropped. The original 25 at Iwakuni when the war started and the twelve experienced men who joined them soon after were increasingly replaced by men straight off flying training and Mustang conversion. With time, the casualty rate reflected this drop in experience level.

As mission totals grew, leave in Japan was introduced as a break from combat flying. The first batch of seven went in early November, temporarily reducing pilot numbers to 27. Group Captain Charlton,[ix] in Iwakuni, criticised this temporary reduction, pointing out that the tempo of operations was high and no end to the war had been declared. Dick Cresswell, who had authorised it, believed the leave was essential for men who had been in combat for months, and that by criticising the decision Charlton was questioning his operational judgement—something Dick resented, later stating he believed Charlton was not 'operationally minded'.[20]

Although Charlton had raised a valid concern, Dick came to feel that RAAF staff in safe and comfortable Iwakuni did not fully understand the stress of combat flying from some hell-hole like Pohang. He held this view throughout his time as 77 Squadron CO in Korea. At times he bypassed 91 Wing and went direct to General Robertson, who invariably supported him—which suggests he too thought 91 Wing was sometimes out of touch.

An operational CO does not need problems like these, but to Dick they went with the job. As the man on the spot, he happily

---

ix   Arthur Dallas Charlton—retired as an Air Commodore CBE.

made quick decisions when required, and then lived with the consequences. When a young pilot arrived and announced he had just married, Dick sent him home, reasoning that Korea was too dangerous for a young newlywed. The posting authorities, with emerging problems providing pilots for Korean duty, were not amused. Dick, however, saw such things as his 'call' and stuck to his guns.

He upset the 'posters' further when he requested 'some more colour-blind pilots',[21] having found that his handful of partially colour-blind pilots could see camouflaged targets more easily than the rest. The problem was, such people did not officially exist. All RAAF aircrew were given rigorous tests to weed out the colour blind before training and every year thereafter. The fact that some had slipped though the tests could not be admitted, and his request was ignored without comment.

When the 35th Fighter Group was transferred to Yonpo airfield, near Hamhung, he immediately proposed the squadron go with them, as he was most happy with the existing operational arrangements and the continuing domestic help they received.

An advance party was sent on 10 November. Six days later, ten C-119 Packets and four C-47 Dakotas flew most of the Fighter Group to Yonpo airfield.

Normally referred to as Hamhung, their new home was well over the parallel near the east coast. It was nearer the action, but currently even colder than Pohang, thanks to a pool of cold air that had moved in from Siberia just two days before they arrived.

Lyall Klaffer had been on leave in Japan and was

flown back to Korea by Dave Hitchins in a Dakota ... to Hamhung ... We had bombed the airfield on several occasions, and I doubt there was a building on the airfield with intact windows. There was about 18 inches of snow covering the airfield, and it was bitterly cold. We boarded up the window frames in our hut, but it did not keep the howling winds at bay.

Some of the problems of operating in such weather are illustrated by Lyall's further comments:

The next morning I briefed for a mission, and we went down to the tarmac area to get our parachutes, which were stored in a tent by the side of the runway. Each parachute had a flat rubber water bottle on top of the seat cushion as part of our survival kit. We went to our aircraft and I handed my parachute to one of the ground staff, who put it in the cockpit while I did my pre-flight check.

We then waited while an air traffic control jeep was driven down the snow covered runway to show us where the runway was located. At last I strapped in, started the engine and taxied out to the end of the runway. I thought the seat was a little hard, but put it down to the fact that I had not flown for a couple of weeks. When we got airborne, I checked the water bottle and found I was sitting on a slab of ice …

Ice could be not just uncomfortable, but very dangerous, as he later found out. One day, when returning from a mission,

the aircraft felt sluggish and I thought I may have sustained some battle damage, so I used extra power on final approach. It was a sound decision, because the aircraft quite literally dropped out of my hands as I flared for landing. I taxied to dispersal … and climbed out of the cockpit onto the wing. The foot on the wing slid away from under me, and I crashed down onto the ground twisting my back at an awkward angle.[22]

When able to stand he found some 3 centimetres of ice on the upper surface of the wing. The ice had increased aircraft weight and interfered with the smooth flow of air over the Mustang's 'laminar flow' wing, to which it owed much of its performance. This had reduced lift, increased drag, raised the stall speed and caused the heavy landing. A later X-ray revealed three crushed discs in Lyall's back, which, along with the rough landing, were directly attributable to the freezing weather and the resultant ice on the wing. With sub-zero temperatures and snowfalls every day they were in Hamhung, such cold weather problems became part of life.

Maintenance was no less of a trial than in Pohang. An advance party began each day well before dawn, armed with brooms to sweep the snow off the aircraft so the fitters could do their work, checking fuel, tyres, etc. and helping the armourers load bombs, rockets and rounds. Extra checks were done to detect things like frozen brakes—in one case an aircraft's frozen brakes stayed locked under full power and the wheels had to be removed to clear the ice from the brake discs.

Fuel was supplied from American tankers—all 77 Squadron contributed was its aircraft, pilots, ground crew and some tools and spares. The fact that the Americans were also flying Mustangs was a big help, allowing Australians and Americans to swap parts and help one another in many ways.

Experience and initiative were in high demand and in this regard Dinny O'Brien pays special tribute to the senior technical man, Darby Freeman, who was

> father confessor to the troops and highly respected by the officers and aircrew because Darby ran the whole show … He was a great man … a flight sergeant, he took his crown and put it on the front of his cap. The Americans thought he was a major, he knew that, but he won some things for us.[23]

Although without windows, their accommodation was now buildings instead of tents, and every spare pair of hands was put to work on cleaning and repairs, and fitting electricity and heating stoves. Wood from the rocket boxes was especially prized, being ideal for shoring up windows and other simple carpentry jobs. Within a week things were much better and a snowfall on the

23rd was a nuisance more than a trial. Domestically, things were definitely on the up for the shivering Australians.

Operationally, a very different story was emerging as the Chinese presence gradually made itself felt. Poorly armed—but with decades of experience fighting the better armed Nationalists—they knew how to take the initiative on day one against their better equipped foes. With no announcements and no fanfare, they entered the war surreptitiously, crossing the Yalu from Manchuria under the cover of smoke from forest fires and moving at night and on foot.

With no formal declaration of war, the first indication of Chinese involvement came from sudden and unexpected strengthening of resistance from North Korean forces in late October. Then, on 25 October, an ROK battalion near the Yalu was wiped out in an ambush by Chinese forces, removing any doubt that the Chinese had arrived.

And, of particular importance to our story, on 1 November six Russian-built, Chinese MiG-15 jet fighters made a brief pass at some US Mustangs over North Korea. Large numbers of MiG-15 jets were also seen at Antung, just across the Yalu in China, and on 8 November the first jet air battle in history took place between US F-80s and MiG-15s in the Sinuiju area, just inside the North Korean border. The Americans scored one kill to none and won the fight.

The Chinese were clearly now in the war, but their strength was still not known—thanks to their surreptitious entry. The bulk of their forces was thought to still be in China, and would need to cross the Yalu to enter the war. To prevent this MacArthur ordered the bridges on the river be bombed. But he was too late. The winter was one of the coldest on record and began early. The Yalu River froze and the Chinese walked across it at will.

Oddly, MacArthur's GHQ publicly denied the presence of Chinese forces until well into November. Had they asked 77 Squadron and their colleagues at the 35th Fighter Group, they would have ceased this farce. After all, on 5 November, while still at Pohang, 77 Squadron had engaged Chinese forces near Pakchon, 100 kilometres or so from the Chinese border, and attacked Chinese troops frequently thereafter.

Pakchon was not just their first brush with the Chinese, but also another chance to provide close support to Australian troops who, in this case, were besieged by enemy troops in nearby hills. Bad weather the previous day prevented flying, but despite strong crosswinds a section of four, led by Pip Olorenshaw,[x] was able to fly to the Pakchon area and support the diggers. Dick Cresswell too got airborne to lead a four to the same area, attacking a tank and some enemy trucks in the face of some determined anti-aircraft fire. This type of sortie became their main work for the next few days.

Persistent Chinese attacks forced General Walker's 8th Army to withdraw south into the narrower part of the peninsula. The Chinese then withdrew, but General Partridge saw this as a temporary move and threw the 5th Air Force against additional troops and supplies being brought in from Manchuria.

Still at Pohang, 77 Squadron flew almost to the Yalu to search roads coming in from Manchuria. In just two days they attacked some big Chinese army convoys, destroying twenty or more vehicles and damaging many others. On one occasion, Dick Cresswell and three others[xi] found a convoy of tanks and trucks just 13 kilometres from the border town of Sakchu. There were 60 camouflaged vehicles in all, in a mountain pass about 3 kilometres long, many still burning from a previous air attack. The Mustangs attacked, destroying four more and damaging others before running out of ammunition and calling on the air controller to send more aircraft.

This he did and soon after, Fred Barnes, Kevin Foster and Dick Wittman arrived and destroyed twelve more vehicles, all

---

x   The others were Dick Wittman, Bill Michelson and Tom Stoney.
xi   Tom Stoney, Cec Sly and Lyall Klaffer.

disguised as haystacks but too numerous to be so in that area. It was good hunting, but the almost 90-minute transit each way made for long sorties. This fact, along with General Partridge's wish to get them nearer UN forces in the northeast, was a major factor in the move to Hamhung.

The appearance of the Chinese MiG-15s meant that the Allies no longer had air superiority everywhere and the squadron was now under threat of air attack. Seeing the need to review fighter operations, Dick Cresswell called all the pilots together, gave them the latest intelligence and discussed what they would do if attacked by MiG-15s.

The briefing was timely as they continued to operate in MiG territory near the border, and some days later damaged or destroyed 43 trucks near Sakchu. Again, the trucks were disguised as haystacks, but were in this case too large and square to fool anyone. Having refuelled at Pyongyang, they later found seventeen more 'haystacks', set eleven on fire and damaged the others. In all, it was a busy few days.[24]

The weather continued to be very cold, and at times cloudy and windy, making flying difficult and sometimes impossible. As it was, bad weather delayed 77 Squadron's first flight from Hamhung until the 19th when Ross Coburn led a four to attack targets in support of ground forces near Chonju, over near the west coast. This type of tasking became their main work, but when larger attacks were needed, the 35th at times pooled resources and flew with aircraft from all three squadrons.

This happened on one memorable occasion on 22 November when the 35th attacked a Communist Party headquarters near the Russian border, just south of Vladivostok. Lieutenant Colonel Jack Dale led twelve aircraft—four from each squadron—with Dick Cresswell leading the Australians. The target was in the mountains some 300 kilometres from Hamhung and consisted of a collection of buildings, dominated by a multi-storey building with a circular driveway and a huge red star set in the lawn.

The weather was far from ideal and as it closed in they flew in line astern and descended to 1000 feet (300 metres) above ground level (AGL) and entered the valley leading to the target. They were in between mountains, with visibility at times down to 2 kilometres or less, and occasionally had to descend to 300 feet (less than 100 metres) AGL, reducing their margin for error to close to zero.

Jack Dale called that he had the target in sight just as Lyall Klaffer looked down and saw a large, multi-storey building with a big red star on the front lawn. Realising they were attacking the wrong target, he immediately told his leader who responded by telling him to take over and lead them to the correct target. This required a backtrack from twelve aircraft flying at only 500 feet (150 metres) AGL, with varying visibility, in mountainous country—a recipe for disaster in normal times, but something for which months of flying in all sorts of conditions had prepared them. They turned about with some trepidation but without incident, followed Lyall in, delivered six rockets each into the headquarters building and strafed the other buildings.[25]

There was little ground fire, possibly because the Communists thought they were safe from air attack in among the mountains in such weather. And they would have been safe just months earlier when the 35th's pilots entered the war, armed only with their peacetime training and some memories from a previous war. But now they were hardened veterans, practised at flying in marginal weather, finding their targets and attacking with ruthless efficiency.

Necessity is, the saying goes, the mother of invention. In this case, it was also the creator of skills and judgement few of them would otherwise have possessed. And it was just as well they had become thus, for they were about to be tested to the limits in one of the worst events of the war—the fighting near the Chosin Reservoir.

The entire incident owed much to the clever way the Chinese had moved hundreds of thousands of troops into North Korea with only a few thousand being detected by UN intelligence. Not knowing what they were up against, throughout most of November UN forces continued to press to the Yalu and occupy more of North Korea. They reached the river city of Hyesan on 20 November, then paused before pushing on. Although they did not then know it, this was as far as they would go before being rapidly driven back.

The Chinese moved at night whenever they could and used camouflage during the day. On one flight near the Chosin Reservoir, before the main fighting began, Dick Cresswell and his flight saw a 'white movement' in a snow-covered depression 2 kilometres or so wide. It turned out to be thousands of Chinese in white uniforms moving slowly towards American troops in the area. Out of ammunition, all they could do was tell the local air controller—who contacted USAF and Navy aircraft to attack the Chinese—and report the sighting on return, to be told by intelligence that 12 000 to 15 000 Chinese troops were expected in the area.

This suggests that regional intelligence agencies knew there were large numbers of Chinese in the area—although there is nothing to suggest they suspected anything like the actual number of 300 000 plus. MacArthur's headquarters clearly knew little of actual Chinese troop numbers. On 24 November, he visited the 8th Army in Korea, and repeated the 'home for Christmas' prediction—based on the intention to continue the push north to the Yalu wherever possible and force an end to the fighting.

His main forces were in three groups: the 8th Army in the west, ROK forces in the middle and the 10th Corps in the east. On 24 November, the 8th Army began moving along roads to the north without opposition. Then, the next day, reality hit. On 25–26 November, the Chinese launched a massive attack against the ROK forces in the middle, overwhelming them and taking the town of Tokchon. Elements of the 8th Army were sent to help, as were some nearby Turkish forces, but to no avail.

The Chinese were simply too numerous and were driving all before them.

To help ease the pressure, UN forces—the largest of which was the 22000-strong 1st Marine Division from the 10th Corps—were sent to push in behind the Chinese at the Chosin Reservoir. The Chinese suddenly appeared in great numbers from the hills where they had pre-positioned and surrounded the Marines and other UN forces. The seriously outnumbered UN forces then had no option but to try to fight their way out[xii] towards Hamhung and the nearby port of Hungnam.

Similar scenes were repeated throughout the region as the Chinese forces, without air forces or heavy artillery, used sheer numbers to win, and keep winning. It soon became obvious that the UN forces, thought so recently to be on the brink of victory, now faced defeat. All possible air power was thrown at the Communists (who also included some 30000 North Koreans).

During 25–26 November, 77 Squadron flew a maximum effort to support the 8th Army and stricken ROK forces. Fred Barnes led a four [xiii] on the morning of the 25th for close support. They found enemy troops firing from ridges and blocking advancing UN troops, napalmed them and rocketed and strafed the ridges. Dick Cresswell and another four did similar work for ROK troops later in the day and another four[xiv] caught some 200 enemy soldiers on a road and strafed and rocketed them as they tried to take cover in a creek.

At Hamhung, 77 Squadron was only some 100 kilometres from the 1st Marine Division surrounded near the Chosin Reservoir and quickly became part of their battle. Before takeoff the pilots would look across the flat coastal plain that housed

xii Only some Marines managed to fight their way out. They suffered some 7000 casualties—about half in battle and half to cold—making the Chosin Reservoir the worst loss of life in US Marines history.
xiii And Tom Stoney, Don Brackenreg and Ken Royal.
xiv Murray, Turner, Foster and Ellis.

Humhung to the high snow-covered mountains where the battle was raging. With each look at the mountains they were reminded that the conditions up there were far worse than in freezing Hamhung. If the UN forces stayed there too long they would freeze to death, even if they out-fought the Communists. Everything possible had to be done to help get them out.

At first light on the 27th, Ross Coburn led a four to support the beleaguered Marines, checked in with the controller and was directed to enemy forces blocking the Marines, which they attacked with rockets and 50-calibre bullets. They were soon followed by Dick Cresswell and another four, and then Fred Barnes and Tom Stoney, diverted while returning from a reconnaissance mission.

More flights followed that day, led by Murray and Olorenshaw, and yet another by Dick Cresswell, who on return to Hamhung had learned of the desperate plight the Marines were in. The tempo increased even more and they flew 22 sorties on the 28th and 24 on the 29th—a Herculean effort in the circumstances.

One mission on the 29th was transiting over the mountains at 11 000 feet (3300 metres) for a strike near the Yalu when they spotted 200 to 300 Chinese cavalry riding along a ridge, beautifully clothed in winter uniforms. The riders waved to them—obviously believing them to be friendly—only to find out they were wrong when the flight attacked and destroyed them. Having spent all their ammunition, they cancelled their primary target and returned to Hamhung.

Flying ceased at night for everyone except Dick Cresswell and the three who flew with him one night to Chosin. There, the controller directed them to Chinese troops camped with blazing fires and making so much noise the air controller could hear them while airborne and relay the noise to the Australians over the radio. The cloud base was low, the night dark and they clearly did not expect an air attack. No doubt they were surprised, and not a bit inconvenienced, when four Mustangs came out of nowhere to strafe and rocket them in conditions they had been told no one could fly in.

The air effort did considerable damage to the Chinese, but with huge numbers on their side they just keep coming. The tempo was intense for the squadron, both in the air and on the ground. Knowing men work better in such circumstances when they understand what is happening, Dick Cresswell—along with the intelligence officer, doctor and flight commanders—held nightly briefings for everyone who could attend to tell them the current situation and the plans for the next day.

Some briefings were as late as midnight, but all were well attended. With time, the audience included increasing numbers of American pilots and ground crews who had no access to such candid and timely intelligence. Oddly, American policy forbade such briefings and Dick went against orders to hold them. The American policy, the reason for which is unclear, was later changed to encourage the kind of briefings Dick and his team had done.

Despite the intensive air effort, and some spirited defence on the ground, by the 29th fighting was within 6–7 kilometres of Hamhung and closing and the base periphery was attracting fire. That night, Colonel Frederick Gray, who commanded the wing controlling the 35th, decided to prepare to withdraw the squadrons. The base was protected by 500 troops—far too few given the Chinese strength—and everyone was issued with arms varying from pistols to heavier weapons like Bren and Owen guns. These were carried at all times and some hasty target practice arranged.

Dick briefed the squadron, telling them that the Chinese had driven a wedge down the centre of the peninsula, the 8th Army was in orderly retreat in the west and a perimeter around Hamhung and the nearby port of Hungnam was to be held for as long as possible—hopefully with help from Marines and other forces retreating from the Chosin Reservoir.

Aircraft were arriving from overrun airfields, crowding Hamhung and making operations difficult. Also, Hamhung was needed as a transport air head, to fly supplies in and wounded out. Faced with this situation, it was decided to withdraw the 35th's squadrons and relocate them to Pusan, and preparations began immediately to do so.

Some hard decisions were called for. The weather and crowded airfield restricted the number of transport aircraft available, and with the Chinese closing quickly it looked like not everyone could be flown out. When the Americans told Dick he would have to leave some people behind he called for volunteers and a list of 19 was drawn up.

Things looked desperate, but routine work like test flights still had to be done if they were to defend themselves and fly out the aircraft. Les Reading had a very close shave on one of the test flights and later wrote:

Our Hamhung base was surrounded as we prepared for evacuation, and we were attacking the enemy virtually in the circuit area. My most abiding memory of Hamhung is of testing a Mustang a couple of days prior to evacuation.

At about 3000 feet [900 metres] the fire warning light came on, all power was lost, and smoke issued from the cowls. A single round in the cooling system was the culprit. Normally a fire warning light that won't go out is alone a mandatory reason to bail-out, but with all those angry fellas down below who were being strafed, rocketed and napalmed, the likelihood of reaching the ground alive seemed pretty slim. So I stayed with my friend the Mustang, hoping the pair of us would not be blown to smithereens.

It was my habit, when things got a bit hairy, to take a detached look at myself to see how things were coming along in the mind … Here was a case of take it easy … hope we make the airfield OK (we didn't, quite), don't stretch the glide, under control, but a tad worried. Shaking of legs on rudders

approaching touchdown told the true story. A tad worried?
Scared youknowwhatless, more like!'[26]

It was close, but Les was uninjured and flew again as soon
as he was needed. Fortunately, the Chinese moved slower than
expected and no one had to stay behind. Air attacks, UN ground
forces and the extreme cold had all inflicted heavy losses on the
Chinese, and with their supply lines from Manchuria stretched
to breaking point they checked their advance. The Chinese
successes had, in fact, hidden from the Allies the terrible suffering
their troops had experienced, and would go on experiencing.

Pleas to Mao to be content with the recapture of North
Korea fell on deaf ears, as this would not achieve his aim of
tying up American forces for years and causing them great
losses. But whatever Mao wanted, even fanatical Chinese troops
could not do the impossible and were eventually forced to pause,
regroup and re-provision. The extra time this took allowed all
squadron personnel to get out of Hamhung by 3 December,
and prolonged the use of the airfield and the nearby port for
another three weeks.

Most of the air transport was American, but two Dakotas
from 30 Communications Flight in Iwakuni did all that could
be asked of them. Noel Elliot, a World War II bomber pilot
now flying Dakotas, found Hamhung rather chaotic at first, but
soon found order in the chaos as '77 squadron was pretty well
organised. There was no panic … It all worked in an orderly
manner. They got all they could back.'[27]

Noel had started flying early that morning and flown all
that day and throughout the following night. He returned, tired
out, to Iwakuni, had a shower and a drink and woke up some
hours later sitting upright in a mess armchair. With Hamhung,
it seems the gods had decided that nothing would be easy for
anyone who went there.

An American spare part got the last Mustang out. Its radiator
was badly damaged and two fitters were held back to repair it,

along with a Dakota to fly them out and a Mustang pilot, Lyall Klaffer. Knowing they had no spare, the fitters on the job, Ted Wilson and Dinny O'Brien, got a replacement radiator from the Americans and fitted it in record time, at the cost of 'a lot of skin, a lot of frostbite on thumbs and fingertips … When we closed it up we knew it was serviceable, apart from little things, like lock wiring, the straps that go around it and a few screws on the cowling. We made a note of the tail number—when we got to Pusan we'd fix it up.'[28]

Despite the cut corners, it was well done and Lyall flew the Mustang out to Pusan, followed by the Dakota with the last 77 Squadron personnel on board. They had been in Hamhung for just over two weeks of frantic and freezing activity, and shed no tears on leaving. Thanks to some spirited Allied effort, and the slowdown in the Chinese advance, the airfield stayed in UN hands for a few more vital weeks. In that time many thousands of UN troops straggled wearily in, to be flown to safety down south or moved on to the nearby port of Hungnam to be evacuated by ship.

On withdrawing from Hamhung, some of the Mustangs flew strike sorties in the Chosin Reservoir area before going on to Pusan. On arrival they were readied for combat as soon as possible and flew sorties the next day. The Chosin Reservoir fight was not yet over and the Chinese were still advancing across a wide front. To some minds, this meant that the Chinese were in such strength they would be unstoppable, and 'a gloomy MacArthur warned that the UN forces would be driven into the sea unless immediate and strong action was taken against China'.[29]

How much this reflected his true thoughts, and how much it was aimed at getting him the reinforcements he needed is not known, but there is no doubt MacArthur was very worried at the rapid turn of events. Inchon and the early triumphs were now history, along with symbolic gestures like washing swords in the Yalu. The grand plan to unify Korea had collapsed, the

Communists were ascendant, and many UN troops had suffered so badly they were losing the will to fight. In all, things looked grim and it was hard to be optimistic.

But that was not how Dick Cresswell and the veterans in the squadron saw things from their new vantage point in Pusan. Bad as things were, they reasoned that the Chinese had lost some of their early advantage. The element of surprise was gone—the Allies now knew roughly how many they were and where they were—and they were moving further away from their supply sources. Furthermore, the UN naval blockade meant that they would have to resupply over land, making them targets for air attack.

The Chinese were also operating in the neck of the peninsula, which would place them closer to carrier-based aircraft and those like 77 Squadron flying from secure southern bases. All of which meant that, provided they were hit hard enough and often enough, the Chinese would find the going increasingly tough. This turned out to be the case, but not yet.

Pusan was very crowded with both combat aircraft and transport planes, all needing somewhere to park and be serviced. Having been stripped as the Allies went north, it was also now very basic. PSP was widely used and when an aircraft landed, muddy water would spray up through the holes onto the undercarriage, brakes and wheel wells, and into the radiator intake, increasing the ongoing maintenance task. When the rain stopped, the mud eventually turned to dust that got into everything—including the engines, which had to be constantly monitored. But on the plus side, the airfield was secure and there was little snow.

And in the circumstances, despite all its problems, it was the best place available to develop into a more permanent base. As soon as they could, the Australians arranged wooden frames to throw their tents over, wooden floorboards and, perhaps best of all, the hot showers Hamhung had lacked. Soon after, mail that had not caught up with them at Pohang and Hamhung arrived and a regular mail service was established, greatly aided by the daily Dakota courier service to and from Japan and regular flights to and from Australia.

With time, the squadron was housed in permanent huts with concrete floors and quite good petrol heaters (which were safer than they sound, with the petrol stored outside the hut and smoke and fumes piped out through a chimney). Not exactly five star—in fact, probably not even one star—but the best yet since leaving Iwakuni.

As usual, a little self-help worked wonders. The pilots occupied a 30 x 7 metre hut. It accommodated twenty stretcher-type beds and had little room to spare, but they still managed to put up a partition at one end for a bar. The bar quickly became a popular spot to entertain pilots and friends from other squadrons. Through it, they got to know their comrades-in-arms from the 35th Fighter Group even better, and some long-term friendships and a good deal of mutual respect resulted. And, it should be added, because they invariably 'talked shop' their work together improved, and the power of a few convivial beers to oil the wheels of progress was proven yet again.

Not that there was much time for relaxing during their early days in Pusan. They were now further from the Chosin Reservoir, but their work there was far from done. Many Marines and other UN forces were still either trapped there or fighting their way to the coast through the rugged and frozen country, with its numerous ambush sites along the way.

The main Marines push to the coast and safety began on 6 December. Chinese radio had already boasted that the Marines would be destroyed and they threw everything they could at the Americans. The Marines fought on, burying their dead as they went and finally reaching Hamhung after crossing a bridge dropped from the air and assembled under enemy fire. It was a terrible but heroic three weeks, during which Hamhung and the vital nearby port of Hungnam were kept in Allied hands by gunfire from UN ships, the air effort and troops on the ground.

By 24 December, all who could reach Hamhung (Hungnam) had done so and been evacuated. In all, 105 000 men from the 10th Corps and other UN units, 350 000 tons of supplies and 91 000 Korean civilians were taken from Hungnam in more than 190 ships, mostly to Pusan. As the North Koreans had retaken Pyongyang on 4 December and the 8th Army had withdrawn to below the 38th parallel, this marked the end of the UN campaign into North Korea.

But until then, to support the Marines and Hamhung security, the squadron flew every day the weather allowed, beginning the morning after they arrived at Pusan. This meant that, despite shifting bases three times in six weeks, they had managed to fly every day the elements permitted—a proud achievement in the cold, slush and primitive conditions they had to cope with.

Targets were now of all kinds: static targets like bridges, tunnels, troop concentrations and fuel and ammunition dumps; interdiction targets like road convoys, trains and other transport systems; and direct support for troops in the field. There were plenty of worthwhile targets, many identified by aircraft from the US 67th Tactical Reconnaissance Wing. Their information was fed into the intelligence system, which, Dick Cresswell believed, 'by December 1950 was very good indeed'. Targets could now be prioritised, markedly increasing the effectiveness of the air effort.

The enemy was learning too and used a number of 'low-tech' ruses to frustrate their airborne assailants. One was to burn trees and bushes to create smokescreens and another was to stretch wires across the expected flight path of attacking aircraft—roads, railways etc.—in the hope of snaring a low-flying attacker. This sounds primitive, and it is, but it worked—as Geoff Thornton found out on 11 December while flying an armed reconnaissance sortie with Des Murphy.

Geoff thought he was hit by ground fire, so Des inspected the underside of the aircraft and saw that some rockets had been pulled off and wire was hanging from where the rocket pods had been. Geoff then put the wheels down then up and the wire fell off. The aircraft flew reasonably well and on return it was found to have a damaged aileron and coolant air scoop. In reality, it was a lucky escape. Had the wire become more thoroughly entangled it may have interfered with the flight controls or done some other serious damage.

But for most missions the dangers were the usual ground fire and terrain worries. Both were in abundance when Lyall Klaffer led a four on a close-support mission on 13 December in the Chichon-ni area. Friendly forces were halted by enemy troops dug in to a hillside with small arms and heavy artillery. The only means of attack was to fly low passes through the ground fire and rugged terrain to search out the enemy guns and troops. This they did to good effect, destroying at least three guns and an unknown number of enemy troops—without, as luck would have it, serious damage to their aircraft.[xv]

With better intelligence, the Allies were now selecting targets far and wide on the basis of what would hurt the enemy most. One campaign aimed to cut enemy communications with Manchuria and involved flights almost to the Manchurian border, into territory becoming known as 'MiG Alley'. To this end, on 17 December Geoff Thornton led a four[xvi] to within 60 kilometres of the Manchurian border to attack a double-track railway bridge at Sonchon.

Knowing there could be MiG-15s in the area, they went in over the Yellow Sea and attacked from out of the sun. The bridge had large craters from previous attacks by B-29 bombers. Anti-aircraft guns near the bridge opened up as they approached but the Mustangs pressed on, scoring many hits. The result was all you could ask—two bridge spans destroyed and approaching railway tracks torn up. They had come a long way to get there, and it was a long flight back, but with a result like that

---

xv   Lyall Klaffer was later awarded a US DFC for this action.
xvi The other three were Ken Royal, Ray Trebilco and Des Murphy.

the long transits were more than justified.

A few days later the 35th had an enforced break from flying. Mustangs were suddenly suffering engine cut-outs, one of which killed an unlucky American who crashed into the sea when his engine failed just on takeoff (the worst possible time for an engine failure). Another force landed in a paddy field and Ross Coburn's engine quit during his takeoff run, leaving him just enough room to stop before he ran out of runway.

The entire 35th was grounded while they looked for a cause. Sabotage was suspected, but when petrol from a crashed aircraft was found to contain a considerable amount of foreign matter, it looked like dirty petrol. The problem was, no one was sure, so they tightened up the quality control procedures on the fuel and began flying again on 22 December. It was just three days before Christmas, but no break in the flying was planned and the festive spirit was pretty thin on the ground.

For the Australians, it disappeared altogether when Don Ellis, who had been flying with Gordon Harvey on combat air patrol, was killed near Pyongyang on 22 December, probably by anti-aircraft fire. The area was heavily defended and Gordon saw 20-millimetre shells coming towards them just before Don Ellis called out on the radio that he was going to crash. His death brought squadron pilot casualties to six—four in combat and two in a burning tent.

Saddened, they continued on, flying through Christmas without a break. This shouldn't have affected anyone unduly, but it did. Christmas today is often called 'The Silly Season' in Australia, and that year it proved to be so for some in Pusan. Late on Christmas Day, four pilots had their sortie the next day cancelled due to heavy snow storms forecast in the target area. They decided to celebrate Christmas with 'a few beers' and retired to bed late, only to be rudely awakened at 4.30 a.m. with the news that the weather had cleared and they were going.

They were well short of the statutory 'eight hours bottle to throttle' but the operations officer fed them black coffee as

No. 77 Squadron Mustangs photographed while climbing past a USAF B-26 Bomber. (Source: Jim Flemming)

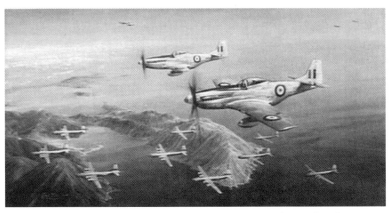

First Flight over North Korea, escorting USAF B-29 Bombers to bomb enemy airfields, 2 July 1950, the day the squadron entered the war. (Source: Jim Flemming)

A ship wreck party in Iwakuni, Japan, before imminent return to Australia, was interrupted when North Korea invaded the South. At war within a week, the squadron lost pilots Bill Harrop and Geoff Stephens (seated 4th and 5th from the left) and 38 others by war's end. (Source: Jim Flemming)

Squadron Pilots at Iwakuni in the early days of war. L-R Wally Rivers, Brick Bradford, Stormy Fairweather, (unknown),(unknown),Tom Murphy, Jim Fairweather, Bill Michelson and Jim Gray. (Source: Jim Flemming)

Japanese technicians who worked on the Mustangs before and during the war, providing loyal and professional service throughout. Note the drop tank next to starboard wheel. (Source: Jim Flemming)

Photographed early in the war, pilots (L-R) Don Ellis, Stormy Fairweather, Max Garroway and Dick Turner, are dressed in what they could beg, borrow or trade after the RAAF supply 'pipeline' shut down when the squadron was originally ordered home from Japan. (Source: Jim Flemming)

USAF B-26 bombers and RAAF C-47 Dakotas were also based at Iwakuni during the war. (Source: Keith Meggs)

Mustangs lined up on the Iwakuni tarmac. (Source: 77 Sqn website)

Russian built T-34 Tank, for which UN ground forces had no answer in the first weeks of war. On 9 July 1950, 77 Squadron destroyed the first T-34 of the war and many more were eventually stopped from the air with armour piercing rockets. (Source: Keith Meggs)

C-119 transport. One of many which flew fuel, weapons, food and other necessities in and out of Taegu each day during defence of the Pusan Perimeter in July–August 1950, keeping the vital air-base supplied despite strong enemy opposition. (Source: Keith Meggs)

Squadron Leader Dick Cresswell, who was rushed to Korea to command 77 Squadron when CO Lou Spence was killed. A strong leader, he set a fine example of courage, skill and determination during the Squadron's most trying times in Korea. (Source: RAAF Museum)

Wing Commander Lou Spence strapping in for the 9 September 1950 mission on which he was killed by ground fire. A very popular and competent leader, his death was keenly felt throughout the squadron. (Source: Jim Flemming)

Hamhung, North Korea, where freezing temperatures and nearby enemy forces made life very difficult, often dangerous and always uncomfortable for maintenance staff and aircrew alike. (Source: Lyall Klaffer)

Pilots 'Swoz' Williamson and 'Pip' Olarenshaw at Hamhung, wearing American sourced winter clothing. The RAAF could not provide this essential clothing and those in charge of such things seem to have known little about Korea's severe climate. (Source: Lyall Klaffer)

The MiG-15, the sudden appearance of which in November 1950 transformed the air war and prompted the RAAF to buy Meteor jets to help counter it. (Source: RAAF Air Power Development Centre)

Des Murphy (left), pictured with fellow pilots (L-R) Dick Whitman, Keith Meggs and 'Blue' Colebrook, was chosen along with Dick Cresswell to do jet training with the USAF in preparation for the Meteor. (Source: Keith Meggs)

A Gloster Meteor flown by Kevin Foster at 20 000 feet.
(Source: 77 Sqn website)

Ces Sly bailing out of his damaged Mustang over enemy territory on 15 March 1951. The drawing is by Keith Meggs who called a helicopter and circled to help protect Ces in one of Korea's biggest rescues. Ces continued flying Mustangs and also did 24 Meteor missions before going home. (Source: Keith Meggs)

Kimpo, near Seoul, was one of the world's busiest airfields and home to the Meteors for two years. (Source: 77 Sqn website)

Readying a Meteor at Kimpo. Note the starter battery cart (foreground), ammunition belt, ventral tank, soot around the gun ports, pierced steel plating (PSP) ground cover and sandbag revetments. (Source:77 Sqn website)

Kimpo accommodation was walled tents with unturned ammunition boxes for walkways in wet weather and drums of water near each tent in case of fire. (Source: Bill Murphy)

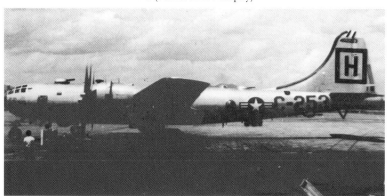

B-29 bomber. Although out flown by MiG-15s at high altitudes, the Meteors were very effective against them when escorting B-29s in conjunction with F-86 Sabres and at lower altitudes. (Source: Keith Meggs)

Meteors over typically rugged Korean landscape that made map reading a challenge and low level operations difficult and often dangerous. (Source: Bill Murphy)

Wing Commander Ron Susans, seen here with Major R.W. Gray, took command on 26 December 1951. Morale lowered by boring intercept duties and winter cold was quickly restored when he introduced the challenging ground attack role and led by example. (Source: RAAF Museum)

Ken Godfrey inspects battle damage to his Meteor sustained on a ground attack mission over North Korea in late 1952. Always dangerous, ground attack became even more so as the war progressed and target defences strengthened. (Source: Jake Newham)

Clearing snow from the aircraft in Kimpo. Note the covers on the canopy, engines and control surfaces which froze stiff and had to be removed before flight and replaced on return. (Source: 77 Sqn website)

Bill Monaghan's aircraft secured after he had an engine shot out and landed on a beach. Following later repairs, Bill did a beach take off and flew it back to Kimpo. (Source: Bill Monaghan)

The shattered canopy of Phil Zupp's aircraft, which he flew home after he was hit and peppered in the face with fragments of glass, perspex and metal. (Source: Owen Zupp)

Dave Irlam and George Hale (left) examining damage to Dave's aircraft during the air battle in which George became the last Australian to shoot down an enemy aircraft in combat. (Source: George Hale)

Squadron pilots (L-R) Viv Shearn, Ron Gilmour, Bob Turner, Don Smith (RAF) Don Arnott (RAF) and Bugs Burley (RAF) talking with Dick Cresswell (third from right) during his April–May 1953 visit. Thirty-three RAF pilots served with the squadron in Korea and six died there. (Source: 77 Sqn website)

Victory fly-past over Seoul, 1 August 1953.
(Source: RAAF Air Power Development Centre)

they showered and made sure they ate breakfast. This helped a bit, but they were still more than a bit seedy. After a thorough briefing they took off at six o'clock, in the dark, and reached the target area behind the enemy lines at daybreak. Once there they destroyed a twelve-vehicle convoy and numerous troops on the ground and returned home without incident.

It all went very well, but the truth was they were lucky to get away with it. On reflection, one of the pilots later wrote that: 'I should not have flown that day.' Nor should the other three—but they did, probably because they saw it as their duty and didn't want to let the squadron down. Like all good tales, it has a moral. The teller of this one, who still lives and so remains nameless, pondered the possibilities of their indiscretion and never pushed that envelope so far again.

Just before Christmas, the courageous and competent commander of the 8th Army, Lieutenant General Walton Walker was killed in, of all things, a motor accident. His replacement was another man of similar ilk, Lieutenant General Matthew Ridgway, who would soon win his own distinguished place in Korean War history. Meanwhile, his first big decision was to withdraw the 8th Army in the face of overwhelming odds and concede Seoul to the enemy. The capital had now changed hands three times in six months and as the New Year began, the Communists continued to gain ground.

Ridgway, having withdrawn and regrouped south of Seoul, began to plan a counteroffensive. As he was doing so, some of MacArthur's staff began contingency planning for a complete evacuation of the peninsula, much to the chagrin of ROK forces who heard of the plan. To ease their concerns, on 20 January, MacArthur publicly declared that: 'No one is going to drive us into the sea.' This turned out to be true, for although there was still little evidence of it, a UN fightback had already begun.

It was as well Ridgway's steady and professional influence was available, for once more these were critical times. On the last day of 1950 the Communists had thrown some half-million Chinese and North Korean troops into the second invasion of South Korea. With UN ground forces still retreating, regrouping, planning and positioning for the fightback, much of the initial response fell to the air forces.

The air effort was directed at both Communist troops and supply lines. The squadron joined with the 5th Air Force to attack bridges, trucks, pack animals (of all kinds, including Bactrian camels), villages housing troops, and anything else that would retard the enemy. Attacking villages raised all the old emotions about shooting people directly, but it was part of the job as villages were favourite hiding places for Chinese troops.

On 2 January, Pip Olorenshaw[xvii] attacked a camouflaged Chinese camp near a village about 30 kilometres north of Seoul, scattering running troops in all directions and killing many. They then attacked the nearby village, which was housing troops, and destroyed it before returning to Pusan. Three days later, a similar attack was made on two villages south of the capital, causing Chinese soldiers in their distinctive quilted uniforms to run from burning buildings. 77 Squadron was not alone in inflicting this level of damage on the Chinese Army, which was now losing many men to air attack.

The air forces did not have it all their own way, however. The fall of Seoul and the Communist thrust south created two million refugees who were now on the move, often near battle areas. Many suffered horribly from hunger and starvation, and from exploitation by ruthless officials, criminals and brigands. For many who saw it from the air, the sight was unforgettable.

Les Reading was one, and said recently that one of his most enduring memories of the war was the seemingly endless streams of wretched refugees who were pouring south in the hope of escape. It was a scene of mass despair, but to the Communist troops, who mingled with the refugees whenever they could,

---

xvii Retired as a Group Captain OBE DFC.

they were a godsend. From the air one person dressed in winter clothes looked very like another and few attacks were made on enemy troops mixed in with refugees.

Also, as it was now mid-winter, most rivers and creeks were frozen. The Communists crossed whereever they wished and destroying bridges did little to stop them. As before, they used white camouflage clothing and moved at night to avoid detection. All of which meant that worthwhile targets were sometimes hard to find, especially when rapidly changing front lines ruled out close support. None of this rendered the air effort impotent, but it did make it more difficult to hit the advancing enemy as hard and often as the Allies would have liked.

In early January, the squadron's pilots were told that policy regarding tours of duty had changed. Those who had done 100 missions and nine months in Korea could now, if they wished, do either an extra three months or a full second tour of nine months. Those who volunteered for a full second tour would get six weeks leave back in Australia before beginning the tour. Dick Wittman and Geoff Stephens volunteered on the spot for a second tour, but only Dick got the leave in Australia.

Geoff Stephens was killed on armed reconnaissance operations the very next day, 6 January. His leader, Ray Trebilco, did not see what happened, apart from a flash behind him, and saw only the burning wreck when he turned back. The probable cause was ground fire, and Geoff Stephens became the squadron's seventh casualty of the war.[xviii]

The same day, Donald 'Brak' Brackenreg almost became the eighth when he finished up in Pusan harbour after becoming the first Australian to ditch a Mustang. The Mustang was a difficult and dangerous aircraft to ditch because of the large air-scoop on the underside, but this ditching went well and he escaped by inflating his Mae West as the aircraft sank under him. His

---

xviii Geoff Stephens was posthumously awarded a commission, and a US DFC and Air Medal.

luck continued when he was hauled from the water in just three minutes, blue with cold and shivering violently, by a South African tug boat that wrecked its engine governor in its haste to reach him. Much longer in the freezing water and he may well have died.

In time they would get immersion suits, but now if they finished up in the water all they could hope for was to be hauled out in double-quick time before dying of cold. The very cold weather also created another problem for the pilots, who faced freezing to death if they bailed out without extreme-weather winter clothing, but were often uncomfortably hot in the cockpit if they wore it while flying. Not wishing to freeze to death, they sweated it out in sub-zero temperatures, no doubt reflecting on the irony of being so hot because the weather was so cold.

As the Communists mounted their second invasion of South Korea, Pusan became a pivotal part of the UN air effort. As well as the 35th, a US Navy Panther jet squadron was based there, and as a transport hub the base had a constant stream of every transport type in Korea. Every serviceable building was occupied and improvisation commonplace—an example being the use of a badly damaged C-119 Packet as a popular snack bar. Personnel from all 21 UN nations passed through at one time or another, and places like mess halls were a babble of accents and languages.

The Americans identified all Korean airfields with a capital K followed by a number. Pusan was K9 and so universally known as Dogpatch after the then immensely popular cartoon series *Li'l Abner*, which, along with the buxom Daisy Mae, had contributed the 'triple whammy' to the vernacular of the day.

Having provoked China into the war, General Douglas MacArthur now looked much less wise. For him, a triple whammy that floored the enemy and restored his reputation was a highly desirable thing. He began to contemplate the advantages of going out with a bang instead of a whimper, of maybe using the atomic bomb, the ultimate, real-world triple whammy.

It was not a new thought—MacArthur had considered using nuclear weapons soon after the war began and on a number of occasions since then. The US Joint Chiefs of Staff always opposed the idea, arguing that there were no targets that rated such a massive explosion and the use of atomic bombs could escalate the war. Despite their conclusions, the nuclear option was not entirely ruled out by President Truman. With the Chinese in the war and things looking pretty grim, in late November 1950 he publicly acknowledged that he had been considering the use of atomic bombs since the war began.

The reaction from other world leaders was swift and united in protest, and Truman quickly assured them that while he had considered nuclear weapons, he had no plans to use them. He did, however, keep some nuclear forces on alert—presumedly to be used as a last resort, if all other options were exhausted. MacArthur was always more hawkish, and in post-war interviews outlined contingency plans he had considered for use of up to 30 bombs—plans which, fortunately, he was never allowed to put into effect.

Meanwhile, he continued throughout January 1951 with conventional weapons, especially his air forces. As well as the usual sorties, some big efforts were mounted. For the Australians, none came bigger than their attack on the Chinese Army HQ at Pyongyang on 19 January. The plan was that twelve aircraft would make the attack. Dick Cresswell would lead two flights of three with bombs, and Gordon Harvey the other six with napalm.[xix] A dive bombing attack would be followed by a napalm attack at roof top level. The first six would machine-gun and rocket any anti-air guns as soon as their bomb run was done.

The weather report was marginal, with snow showers and poor visibility forecast. To prepare, the pilots pored over aerial photographs, memorising target positions and other salient features,

---

xix The others were Ralph Dawson, Ron Mitchell, Geoff Thornton, Ron Howe, Cec Sly, Les Reading, Allen Frost, Fred Barnes, Tom Stoney and Richard Turner.

especially the river that runs through the city. The early morning weather was unfavourable, and only after some tense hours of waiting were they able to fly. Gordon Harvey's aircraft wouldn't start, so he took the spare (having ordered the spare pilot out) and all twelve arrived over the target, as planned, at 1300 hours.

Four bombs scored direct hits and four more near misses. On the napalm run, Gordon Harvey reported his engine was losing power and Fred Barnes saw smoke and occasional flame coming from it. Gordon pressed on, dropping his napalm and firing his rockets before calmly announcing he was going to 'belly-land this aircraft'.[30] Some minutes later they saw him do a safe belly landing on an island in the middle of the river, about 7 kilometres from the city, and climb out.

He was unharmed, but almost 300 kilometres from the nearest UN forces and so in deep trouble. Allen Frost climbed to 16000 feet (4800 metres) and tried to call a rescue helicopter, but to no avail. They then had to leave, having just enough fuel to reach a friendly airfield. Later in the day, an American Mustang dropped him a note saying a helicopter was on the way, but night closed in and no helicopter arrived.

The next morning, Jack Dale and Dick Cresswell organised a rescue, beginning with Dick leading a four, with long-range tanks, to the area where Gordon had belly landed. Once there, they could provide protection and guide a rescue helicopter in. If need be, other Mustangs would follow during the day to provide continuous cover.

It was a good plan, but it didn't help Gordon Harvey. When Dick's four arrived they saw tracks all around the aircraft, but no sign of Gordon. Reasoning he had either left the area or was a prisoner, they did not call the helicopter. As it happened, he had been taken prisoner, 77 Squadron's first POW and its eighth pilot killed or captured.[xx]

---

xx   Gordon survived, stayed in the RAAF post-war and retired as a Group Captain DFC.

By 24 January the Communist advance had ground to a halt some 100 kilometres south of the 38th parallel, thanks to a combination of failing supply lines and increasing UN opposition. UN ground forces then went on the offensive, progressively gaining ground during the first half of 1951 until they reached what eventually became the Demilitarised Zone (DMZ), near the 38th parallel.

Optimistic once more, MacArthur favoured driving the Communists from the peninsula and expanding the war into China. His president disagreed, preferring containment along the 38th parallel. Most of the UN Allies agreed, and the UK and USA both publicly expressed the wish to avoid unlimited war with China, or do anything that would bring Russia into the war.

This much reduced the threat of world war, but made little difference to those involved in the Korean War, which continued unabated with both sides fighting determinedly. In seven months of war millions had died or suffered injury, abuse, hunger and homelessness. This carnage continued until mid-1951 when everything was back to square one, with the country again divided much as it was pre-war.

But as 1950 ended, all indications were that there was plenty for 77 Squadron to do for some time yet. The entry of the Chinese MiG-15 jets had made the Mustangs obsolete for air defence, and the Australian Government had decided to buy a jet fighter to replace them. The British Meteor twin jet was chosen. Controversy surrounding the selection process and the Meteor's suitability began almost immediately and continued unabated for many years to come.

4

Mustangs to Meteors

The RAAF bought the Gloster Meteor because it was the best jet fighter they could buy at the time. The options were actually very limited. Jet fighters are specialised machines; in an emergency you can't just buy a squadron like you buy a fleet of cars or trucks. If you want new fighters, you have to join the production queue. Even if you are happy with existing ones, you still have to find some for sale that suit your needs.

The new American F-86 Sabre was the RAAF's preferred buy, not just for Korea, but to eventually re-equip the entire RAAF fighter force.[i] The Americans couldn't sell them any until 1954, but this wasn't a problem until Chinese MiG-15s appeared in strength. Now any fighter Australia bought to use in Korea would have to be able to take on the MiG-15.

This was a big ask. Whatever way you looked at it, the MiG-15 was an impressive machine. Of Russian origin, it had a swept-back wing design (based on data captured from the Germans at the end of World War II) and was powered by a copy

---

i   In fact, the Commonwealth Aircraft Corporation was negotiating plans to build Sabres in Australia as the Meteors were being bought.

of a Rolls Royce Nene engine (acquired from the British in happier times). Its low wing loading and powerful engine gave it outstanding manoeuvrability and a top speed of well over 1000 kilometres per hour. At the time it was the benchmark, and in skilled hands outclassed the earlier straight-wing US F-80 and F-84 jets that then made up most of the USAF fighter force.[1]

Fortunately, the F-86 Sabre was arriving to re-equip USAF squadrons. A second-generation jet fighter, it had swept-back wings, strong construction and similar performance to the MiG-15. Although not quite as manoeuvrable as the MiG, its better gunsight and greater ability to absorb damage could make it more effective in competent hands—a very important factor as the Chinese Air Force was expanding fast and had many inexperienced pilots. USAF pilots, on the other hand, were well trained and included many World War II combat veterans.

Along with the North Korean Air Force, the Chinese were being trained by Russian fighter instructors, many of whom were also World War II veterans. Some Russians had flown unofficially with the North Koreans when the war began. Others were now playing leading roles in China's fledgling fighter force, both as pilots and as fighter commanders. Russia denied this at the time and the Allies then had only well-founded suspicions with no hard evidence.

Although the Mustangs were doing much more attack work than air defence, Australia wanted 77 Squadron's long-term role to be air defence—an area in which the MiG-15 totally outclassed the Mustang. The performance difference was very significant, and Alan Stephens tells us that: 'Air Marshal Jones [the RAAF chief] claimed it would be 'suicidal' to pit No. 77 Squadron against the Chinese jets in air-to-air combat. Little argument was needed to convince the government, and consensus was quickly reached to replace the Mustangs with jets as soon as possible.'[2]

Australia already had a jet, the single-engine De Havilland Vampire. A first-generation jet, it was quickly ruled out, being smaller and slower than the Meteor which, just five years before, had held the world speed record at 975 kilometres per hour. This was a time of rapid development in jet aircraft design, however, and since then swept-back wings were producing even greater speeds from the next generation of fighters.

A swept-back wing can go faster than a straight wing before shock waves build near the speed of sound and cause the well-known 'sonic boom'. In early jets shock waves could also cause severe buffeting and loss of control from the greatly

Meteor area of operations, showing MiG Alley and Kimpo airfield, where they, and many other UN aircraft, were based.

disturbed airflow over the wing and control surfaces. The effect is also termed 'compressibility' and effectively determines the maximum speed for the fighters under discussion.

Because the speed of sound varies with height, fast aircraft are fitted with Mach meters on which Mach 1 is the local speed of sound, and Mach .5, for example, is half the speed of sound. Early jets have limiting Mach numbers in the Mach .78 to .84 range, above which severe buffeting and control problems occur. Put simply, the MiG-15 and the F-86 Sabre experienced compressibility at a higher Mach number than straight-wing aircraft like the Meteor. The Meteor had a limiting Mach number of .84, the MiG-15 of .90.

As yet, however, only two swept-wing aircraft were being made in large numbers—the MiG-15 and the Sabre—and no other allied swept-wing fighter was available. With no Sabres available, this made the Meteor the best choice at the time—despite its World War II origins and first-generation straight wings that limited its top speed to 100 kilometres per hour or so less than the MiG-15.

The speed differential actually varied with height but was always in the MiG's favour. There is more to it than just speed, however, when fighters are compared. Acceleration, turning ability, best operating height, weapons fit, gunsight type and such things were also all important in 1950 fighters—and mostly still are. Everything that makes the aircraft an effective fighting machine has to be considered. When bundled together these factors produce the 'envelope' within which the aircraft can be flown—or, if best performance is sought, must be flown.

Thus, when comparing fighters, it is much more meaningful to say that one had a better performance envelope than another, rather than just compare speeds. And even then, this will have to be qualified by things like operating altitude and weapons load, which change the parameters of the envelope. In general, the MiG-15 had a better performance envelope at height than most rivals, especially the straight-wing ones, but lost some of its advantage at lower altitudes.[ii]

This performance was a major advantage to MiGs operating in MiG Alley—the area paralleling the Yalu to its east as far as the Chongchon River. Before entering MiG Alley, MiGs could climb to great height within their sanctuary behind the Yalu, and then swoop down at superior speed on the opposition. There is an old fighter saying that 'he who commands the height, dictates the fight' and the Russians in charge of the MiGs would no doubt be drumming this into their Chinese students.

As a result, the Meteor was undeniably a compromise to fight the MiG-15 on its home turf. Critics soon asked if Australia should have held out for Sabres and pressured the Americans to make some available sooner. The South Africans did this, and continued to fly their Mustangs in attack roles until receiving Sabres in January 1953. Some argued then, and some still do, that Australia could have done the same and finished up with Sabres instead of Meteors.

There is no doubt that Mustangs could have continued doing useful work with ground attack. The current problems were more in air defence, however, and made worse by the geographical limits the UN countries imposed on the war—in particular, the bans against operating across the Yalu River which allowed the Chinese to sweep into and retreat from MiG Alley almost at will.

This gave the MiG force such a significant tactical advantage that the UN faced losing air superiority in parts of northwestern Korea. Should that happen, the Communists could then build airbases in North Korea with MiGs protecting them. Early attempts to counter the MiGs had achieved only limited success and it soon became obvious that more and better UN fighters were needed. Not surprisingly, General Stratemeyer welcomed 77 Squadron's re-equipment with jet fighters, and knowing the Sabre was not available, supported the Meteor.

---

ii   Altitude is height above sea level.

The Royal Air Force's senior man in the BCOF in Japan, Air Vice Marshal C. A. Bouchier, also supported the decision— even though the only aircraft available were currently earmarked for RAF squadrons and would leave the RAF short. Australian purchases, however, brought in export income for Britain and provided a chance to prove the Meteor in combat. These factors, along with a wish by Britain to further assist in the Korean War, helped win the day.

For a decision of this importance though, the time frame was amazingly short—less than two months. The first Chinese MiG-15 flew in from over the Yalu on 1 November 1950. Soon after, the Americans confirmed that they could not sell Sabres to Australia until 1954. The British were then approached and agreed to supply Meteors. Finally, in December 1950, the Australian Government decided to buy them.

And once that was done, the British acted with commendable speed. On 24 February 1951, the Royal Navy aircraft carrier HMS *Warrior* arrived in Japan with fifteen single-seat Mk8 Meteors and two dual-seat Mk7s for 77 Squadron. Twenty-two more Mk8s were delivered just four weeks later, on 23 March. Another 58 Meteors, including more duals, were bought in two batches later on. Meteor-trained RAAF technical staff also arrived in Japan, along with four experienced RAF officers.

The only immediate effect of all this on 77 Squadron was the attachment in late January of Dick Cresswell and Des Murphy for jet experience with the USAF, flying F-80 Shooting Stars at Itazuki fighter base in Japan. The original plan included Gordon Harvey, now a POW, but no replacement was selected. The two trainees were well chosen. A proven performer himself, Dick Cresswell described Des Murphy as 'a highly successful, highly trained instructor in the air and an excellent pilot. He'd flown Vampires so was jet trained'.[3]

The attachments were for a month to Nos 35 and 36 Squadrons USAF, both part of the 35th Fighter Group. The decision to train in separate squadrons created some friendly rivalry between the squadrons to see which could get their Australian into operations first. It was also something of a relief for Des Murphy, who had not relished the thought of a month working at close quarters with his tough-talking CO.

Dick Cresswell's direct manner and at times abrupt speech did not endear him to all, although everyone admired his operational leadership and organisational skills. The situation was seriously exacerbated by the RAAF's strange and thoughtless decision to make Dick the CO, in extraordinarily challenging times, with only the rank of squadron leader and no other senior officer to help him run the squadron. Every other 77 Squadron CO during the war was a rank higher at wing commander and had a squadron leader operations officer[iii] to assist him.

This arrangement spread the leadership and management workload and allowed the CO to concentrate on the broader issues while his Ops O worried about the day-to-day things like flying rosters, standards and procedures. If a young pilot needed some special encouragement or training, or a 'fatherly' talk about his shortcomings, this was usually the Ops O's job, along with some of the operational leadership in the air.

Dick, in effect, had to do both jobs and do them during the most trying times the squadron faced in the entire war. To do them he worked long and hard and, when pressed for time, often issued orders and admonishments without discussion or much tact. At the time, some who received the rough side of his tongue resented it and Dick acquired a couple of uncomplimentary nicknames. But on reflection, the great majority from those times now see him as a man doing an extraordinary job in the most demanding conditions, and sympathy and admiration have replaced any resentment felt at the time.

In the circumstances, a month working in separate USAF squadrons was no doubt good for both pilots, especially for

---

iii Sometimes also called the Deputy CO or Executive Officer, but Operations Officer was usually the RAAF name for the job.

Dick, who seems to have proved the old adage that 'a change is as good as a holiday' during his time with the USAF. They each converted onto the F-80 and flew ten missions with their respective squadrons. Des Murphy's squadron got their Australian into combat first by getting him airborne at six o'clock one morning, three hours before his CO took off, having previously done some cunning undercover work to find out when Dick was scheduled to fly.

Both learned a lot and had some interesting moments. On one flight, one of Des's wing-tip tanks didn't feed, unbalancing the aircraft. After lengthy discussion with the others in his flight, they decided the best solution was to put a hole in the tank with a .45 pistol and let the fuel out. This was no easy task with the air rushing past the tank at over 500 kilometres per hour, but they worked out how to do it, shot a hole in the tank and the fuel escaped, rebalancing the aircraft. This was good thinking, but the official flight manual never endorsed it as an accepted way to deal with this emergency.

Dick's most memorable experiences were two long flights in cloud with ground assisted let-downs at the terminal airfield. The first was with an emergency that began as a rattling noise at the rear of the aircraft and a partial loss of power. It turned out to be a fire that burnt out the rear part of the aircraft, which fell off shortly after landing and would have killed him had he not got on the ground when he did.

As it was, he flew for an hour through snow cloud to Taegu, where he was told that he would have to wait his turn while they dealt with an emergency. Dick tersely replied that he was the emergency and he was given a VHF let-down to below the cloud base for landing. The other memorable experience was the flight from Taegu back to the squadron's base at Itazuki, again in snow clouds all the way, but this time with a radar system called Ground Controlled Approach (GCA) providing the let-down and approach to land.

In both cases, transit navigation was done using the F-80's

Automatic Direction Finding (ADF), usually called a radio compass. The ADF, a directional radio receiver providing the pilot with a bearing to a radio station or beacon, was standard equipment in USAF fighters. Along with the electronic airfield location and let-down aids, it gave the USAF a bad weather capability the Australians could not remotely match with visual navigation.

Operating jets would also take them higher, into the world of jetstream winds that can blow with hurricane force. These winds can create huge navigation errors for those who don't know they are in one, or who have no way of measuring how strong the wind is. They are often encountered in clear air, and apart from turbulence sometimes felt on the edges of the jetstream, provide no other clues to their existence. With such winds, something like ADF to help pilots keep track of their progress during flight is highly desirable, at times essential.

Realising ADF was essential for jet operations with the USAF, Dick wrote back to Australia, related his experiences and requested the Meteors be fitted with radio compasses. The first response, even from his past ally, Air Vice Marshal Scherger, was negative—probably because no one running RAAF HQ in Melbourne had sufficient understanding of the Korean operating environment to fully appreciate what Dick was telling them.

In some ways this is understandable. Their roots were in the days of open cockpit biplanes, clear skies and top speeds of 250 kilometres per hour, and their latest flying experience was probably in a Mustang at best. Dick was talking about something altogether different—flying in a sealed and pressurised cockpit, in cloud, 10 kilometres high at 750 kilometres per hour, and possibly with a 200 kilometres per hour jetstream to affect your navigation. Technology had changed the concept of operations and those in charge hadn't all changed with it. Understandable, but not excusable—when you're in charge, you have to keep up.

In fairness to those then running the RAAF, they were working with the aftermath of inexcusable post-war indifference and indecision from the government about defence. The sudden and unexpected surrender of Japan caught the government with no plan for a peacetime RAAF. To get ex-servicemen into civilian jobs and solve labour shortages, rapid demobilisation was encouraged. RAAF strength plunged from about 180 000 in mid-1945, to only 8025 in 1948 before growing to 15 000 or so in 1950 when the Korean War began.[iv] For most of this time, there was no firm plan for the shape of the post-war RAAF.

This shambles left the 1950s RAAF with an unbalanced workforce whose skills did not meet needs everywhere; too many bases; a wide range of aircraft to maintain and operate; and woolly defence guidance from which to shape the future. To save money, most aircrew had been kept on only if they could operate the post-war aircraft. Operational training was all done on the respective squadrons—which now numbered sixteen, including six fighter squadrons. Basic training was up and running again, but dedicated operational training units were only now being re-established.

Instilling order into this post-war chaos was a demanding task, and Dick Cresswell, a hemisphere away in Korea, had to compete to be heard. But, as usual, he persisted and eventually won when the USAF demanded ADFs be fitted as a prerequisite for combined operations. The USAF experience also highlighted for him the importance of good instrument flying skills, and the need to properly understand how to use the ADF and do GCA approaches.

Clearly, there would be more to transitioning to the Meteor than simply learning to fly it—they would also have to learn to operate it, and that was another thing again. The Meteor Orientation Flight Dick later set up owed much to his USAF experience and related conclusions, and was often the only such training given to many of the pilots who did it.

---

iv   Including WRAAF, then often counted separately.

Dick and Des left for Japan on 26 January, leaving Pip Olorenshaw in charge for the next month, but even before then it was obvious things were on the turn again. General Ridgway, in charge of the retreating 8th Army and determined to turn its fortunes and spirit around, told his commanders that 'holding ground was not important ... The main objective was to destroy the Red armies'.[4]

He planned and acted accordingly, in concert with the air commanders. Taegu was becoming a better and more permanent base, and secondary airfields for transport aircraft were being established near key towns and as near to the front line as possible. In the first 24 days of January 1951, this airfield program allowed '5041 tons of men and material to be air lifted for the Fifth Air Force and 7445 tons for the Eighth Army'.[5] Over 2000 tons were also air dropped to 10 Corps troops in the field.

This airlift capability allowed Ridgway to quickly position the 8th Army, and 10 Corps and the 5th Air Force to prepare for battle. The UN counterattack soon followed and kept the squadron very busy, flying mostly in support of troops and against enemy concentrations and supply lines. With time, the air effort broadened to attack all targets that aided the enemy's ability to wage war. This was a broad charter, and as in earlier times they found themselves flying thither and yon against a wide range of targets.

Until the UN counterattack began in earnest on 25 January the squadron's tasking was irregular due to weather and the quickly changing situation on the ground. They spent much of the time on standby, which was stressful for the pilots who began each day ready to fly and often just stood around, and for the ground crews who had to fit and detach drop tanks and change weapons loads as the potential missions changed. At such times, someone invariably reminds the group of the unofficial RAAF motto, 'Hurry up and wait', and this old saw no doubt did the rounds.

Those sorties flown were mostly reconnaissance or interdiction. On 15 January, Fred Barnes led a flight to do armed reconnaissance along roads the enemy could use for resupply once fighting intensified, only to lose track of the roads in the deep snow. While trying to relocate the roads they found a large supply dump in a depression off a minor road, with stores scattered over a 200-metre area.

They attacked for 30 minutes, causing numerous explosions, starting fires and doing considerable damage to complete a very successful, if unplanned, strike. With results like this they were clearly hurting the enemy, and news some days later that Chinese POWs had told UN interrogators that air strikes were inflicting severe casualties confirmed the fact.

Pip Olorenshaw almost didn't get his month running the squadron. Two days before he took over, he led four Australians, in company with four Americans, to check a North Korean airfield. There were signs of recent activity but no aircraft present. They were met by some anti-aircraft fire and shortly after, while attacking the nearby village, Pip's engine cut out and started up again seconds later.

They were a long way from home, so he quickly used up his ammunition and headed back to Pusan, arrived safely and took over the squadron as acting CO two days later. A few more seconds without power, and he could have finished up behind enemy lines and either dead or a POW.[6] Instead, three days later he led twelve aircraft as part of a 35th Group mission of 40 aircraft to attack a bulge in the Chinese lines below the Han River, near Seoul.

The idea was to soften up the bulge so ground troops could push the Chinese back to the river and establish a bargaining line for future diplomatic negotiations—now seen by most UN leaders as the way ahead. The first of many peace-talk meetings began at the old capital, Kaesong, then in neutral territory, on 10 July 1951—but until then the emphasis was on holding ground and gaining bargaining points.

In this case, the squadron's first bargaining-line raid was a success, with many buildings destroyed and troops killed. Later on they got the bad news: many Koreans had stayed in their villages and almost certainly died along with the Chinese soldiers hiding among them. No war is nice, but this one was particularly nasty.

The air effort continued throughout February, and despite bad weather they flew most days—as did just about every UN aircraft available. The effort was considerable, though in some cases not as successful as hoped. Too many trucks were getting through and a conference was held at Taegu to discuss the problem.

As always, the enemy was inventive. One successful ruse was to cut a hole in the wall of a house, drive a supply truck in to hide it during the day, and cover the hole with canvas. At night, the truck could be taken out and driven to the next hiding place. Knowing what to look for, the squadron soon had better success.

On 19 February, Pip Olorenshaw and Dick Bessell found some trucks hidden in houses with canvas draped to hide the holes. The canvas, however, was dirtier than the snow and showed out clearly for what it was. They attacked, destroying six trucks. Later on, Ray Trebilco and Kevin Foster found some trucks hidden under canvas and bushes, which when attacked produced red flames and black smoke, suggesting they were loaded with fuel and oil.

This much better success rate against camouflaged trucks helped a little to lift morale, recently battered by the deaths of two more pilots, Keith Matthews and Sinclair 'Sinc' Squires. They were reported missing, probably dead, after a mission on 14 February in support of UN troops near Wonju, in the middle of the peninsula to the east of Seoul. Part of a four that could not penetrate heavy cloud and had headed for the east coast, they split from the others to climb out as a pair through some very thick cloud.

A radio call from one of the pair said that he was spinning and was going to bale out. No more was heard of the caller or his companion. A little later, the other pair broke out of cloud to fly out over the sea, jettison their napalm and return to base with the sad news. Nothing more was heard and they were presumed dead, bringing the squadron tally of killed or captured to ten. Less than two weeks later Ken Royal became number eleven when he went missing on 26 February during an armed reconnaissance flight north of Seoul.

It was his 97th mission and just days after he was awarded a US Air Medal.

He was flying with Des Murphy when he called that his oil pressure was dropping, and Des saw him climb out to the south. He called again, saying the oil pressure had dropped right off and he was going to abandon the aircraft. Des did not hear him speak again, and he obviously changed his mind as his aircraft was later found force-landed near a paddy field, damaged and upside down. His body was recovered some days later and buried in the UN Military Cemetery in Pusan.

As always, the difference between living and dying was often just sheer luck—ground fire would hit one aircraft, bringing it down with a few rounds, and significantly damage another yet leave it flyable. Dick Bessell was one of many who could have died, but didn't. His good luck occurred during an armed reconnaissance mission with Lyall Klaffer when they attacked a camouflaged object which looked like a tank or a big vehicle.

They attacked with machine guns only to see the rounds ricochet off in all directions. A further attack with rockets blew off the camouflage, revealing a huge rock. It was a clever trap, for as Dick recovered from his attack, a nearby gun pit opened fire, hit him and kept firing until the Mustangs took it out with machine gun fire. Luckily, nothing critical was hit and he flew back to base without trouble.[7]

By contrast, the last man to die on Mustangs, Harry Strange, was particularly unlucky. On 19 March, he too was flying with Lyall Klaffer along a railway line between Wonsan and Pyongyang, which was known as the 'cutter route' because of the concentration of anti-aircraft batteries protecting North Korea's only open rail route across the country ... We immediately encountered ground fire and anti-aircraft fire, but continued ... About 15 minutes later Harry called up and reported his oil pressure was dropping.

Lyall could see oil streaming from Harry's aircraft so they turned towards the coast where they knew some US Navy ships were located. Once there they contacted the ships and Harry prepared to bail out as Lyall watched, to later write:

He jettisoned the canopy, disconnected his radio lead ... undid his seat harness and climbed out of the cockpit and jumped off the wing. I started a turn to keep him in sight, but to no avail. His green flying suit merged with the green sea and I lost sight of him, but I wasn't worried, because as soon as his parachute blossomed, I would see him again. I saw his aircraft hit the water, but there was no sign of Harry's parachute.[8]

In fact, Harry was never seen again. A helicopter from a USN carrier found his flying suit, badly damaged, but he wasn't in it. One possibility is that instead of pulling the rip cord, he had hit the quick release button on his parachute harness (which he would have done almost automatically after every flight to take off the parachute). This would account for him falling 300 metres without a parachute and hitting the water so hard the impact tore his flying suit from his body. Alternatively, he was heavily built and may have been flying with his harness partly undone, which he sometimes did for comfort, and had not done it up properly before bailing out.[9] Either way, the unlucky Harry Strange was the twelfth No. 77 Squadron pilot to be killed or captured in Korea.

Meanwhile, the UN counteroffensive had made steady progress, driving the Communists north towards the 38th parallel. Seoul was recaptured on 14 March 1951—the fourth and last time it changed hands in the war—and by April UN forces had established a front roughly aligned with the parallel.

The UN policy, and that of President Truman and the US Joint Chiefs of Staff, was for limited war in Korea. Accordingly, the advance stopped in mid-July after having pushed on another 30 kilometres or so in the east. The resultant front line became the border until the end of the war and the DMZ until the present day.

Chinese MiG-15 numbers continued to grow and would reach 450 by mid-year—with about 300 positioned to fight in MiG Alley and the rest for training and back-up. In response, in early March the USAF moved F-86 Sabres into Suwon, about 30 kilometres south of Seoul. The extensive recent damage inflicted by UN air power was still being repaired, making operations difficult, but the need to get Sabres operating near the Yalu was urgent, and the first patrols began on 6 March.

In some ways the war was approaching a stalemate, but the fighting continued unabated. MacArthur found the restrictions of limited war very frustrating, and sought permission to strike Chinese sanctuaries across the Manchurian border and use Chinese Nationalist forces. 'When Truman and the Joint Chiefs rejected these options, MacArthur told several editors of *US News & World Report* that he was being forced to fight under "an enormous handicap, without precedent in military history."'[10] He then cabled United Press, complaining that the UN limitations allowed the enemy to carry out 'offensive action without defensive retaliation'.

President Truman and the Joint Chiefs were appalled by this public criticism of their policies by someone under their command. Two days later, President Truman issued an order that: 'No speech, press release, or other public statement concerning military policy should be released until it has received clearance from the Department of Defense.'[11] This should have ended the matter—the president and commander-in-chief had spoken—but it didn't and the two men were now poles apart.

With South Korea liberated, Truman wanted to end the war. MacArthur disagreed, believing the job was not yet done. He maintained his public criticism of US Government policy, continued to support the lifting of the UN limitations and openly rejected the idea of negotiations before any further military advance north. Refusing to stay silent, on 24 March he issued a communiqué that asserted the Chinese attempt to take over Korea had failed, and offered to confer with his opposite number on the Communist side.

This was not only provocative to the Chinese, but it totally disregarded his president's directive to 'abstain from any declaration of foreign policy'. A war of words ensued, and on 11 April, Truman sacked MacArthur, installed General Ridgway in his place and appointed General James Van Fleet to lead the 8th Army. MacArthur had failed to respect where the ultimate power lies in a democracy, publicly disobeyed his commander-in-chief and been dealt with appropriately. It was a sad end for a man whose decisive generalship was a major factor in repelling the North Korean invasion and saving the South, but he brought it on himself.

Formal training on the Meteor began the same day, with some people reasoning that the war might now be over before they got their shiny new jets into the fray. After all, with the hawkish MacArthur gone, no one was now pushing to invade the North. Furthermore, Korean geopolitics were back to square one and the Americans and other UN Allies were ready to negotiate. There was every reason to think the fighting would soon be over. Though seemingly logical, such thinking proved wildly optimistic, underestimating as it did the capacity for devious and ruthless behaviour by the Chinese Government, and Mao in particular.

As a result, the war had more than two years to run, and

pilots like Keith Meggs, who had been posted in with three others[v] in December 1950, would see plenty of it. Following familiarisation training he joined the squadron on 15 December and flew his first mission on the 28th of that month. He then made it through to Meteor conversion despite a very close shave and some fierce enemy resistance.

The close shave was on 15 March[vi] when his Mustang was hit by ground fire and he belly landed at Seoul's airport, Kimpo, which was still in no-man's-land—pulling up within 50 metres of a USN Corsair that had previously done the same thing. Climbing out, he saw two soldiers approaching and stood on the wing with his pistol out, only to find to his relief that they were South Koreans. He was taken by jeep to a casualty clearing station, which found he was unharmed despite the belly landing. From there he flew by helicopter to Suwon, by C-47 Dakota to Taegu, on to Pusan by a C-46 transport and went flying again the next day.

Just five days after surviving the forced landing in no-man's-land, he was under fire again, helping fellow pilot, Cec Sly, survive in hostile territory. Cec was hit by ground fire, and with his engine on fire and smoke in the cockpit, bailed out, only to have enemy troops shooting at him as he descended. Keith called for a helicopter and while it was underway, he and four US Mustangs circled Cec, keeping the enemy troops at bay.

Fortunately for Cec, help was readily at hand and the weather favourable. No effort was spared to get him out in what became one of the biggest rescues of the war. Mustang numbers grew quickly to sixteen, all circling Cec to drive back the enemy troops. Many were American, and as one section of four ran out of ammunition it would be replaced by another. In all, he counted three interchanges and at least 28 Mustangs involved.

---

v   Dick Bessell, Ron Mitchell and Ron Hunt.
vi   Ron Howe was also shot down on 15 March in the same area. He belly landed on an island in the Han River near Seoul and was picked up 20 minutes later by helicopter.

As he later put it: 'Mustangs had six guns, so I had 96 guns protecting me' throughout most of his time on the ground.

After about twenty minutes, the helicopter[vii] arrived and hovered at 900 metres—probably, Cec believes, because 'I was not easily seen, having taken cover to avoid stray bullets.' A Harvard control aircraft had arrived and when Cec 'broke cover and waved to the observer in the Harvard' the helicopter descended to about 20 metres. Unfortunately, the enemy was in strength and, despite constant attacks from the circling Mustangs, was able to damage the helicopter, forcing it to return to base.

Another helicopter arrived 60 minutes later, braved the ground fire and hovered just above the ground near Cec, who broke cover and scrambled aboard. Once on board he directed the pilot away from the ground fire and they got away unscathed. Taken to Suwon, he was treated for bruises, and later on for internal injuries caused by a heavy landing from his low-level parachute drop. The helicopter crew were unharmed despite the audacious rescue under fire, but the Harvard's observer was injured. This was not work for the faint-hearted.

The dramatic rescue was reported in the Australian press, one newspaper writing that after the first helicopter had been forced to leave, another 'arrived half an hour later. It was piloted by Captain Lynden E. Thomasson, and was led to Sly's position by a T6 spotter aircraft. Disregarding the ground fire, Thomasson descended immediately, landing within 10 yards of Sly, who ran from cover and was quickly dragged aboard the 'chopper by the crew.'[12] The Australian public were still receiving incomplete news from Korea—but at least in this case what they did get was reasonably accurate and well put.

While at Suwon, Cec's internal injuries made him ill and he was placed on a stretcher in the first-aid post next to the Harvard observer, 2nd Lieutenant Brown, who had been shot

---

vii   Flown by Captain Oz McKinzie.

in the leg. Fortunately, no bones or arteries were hit and Brown recovered. Cec later took the medical evacuation train to Pusan where he spent some time in hospital followed by recuperation leave in Japan.

Two weeks after the rescue he went back in action, flying Mustangs. When Dick Cresswell asked if he would stay on and fly the Meteor he gladly accepted, converted to the Meteor and flew 24 missions in it to complete his Korean tour before returning to Australia.[13]

The squadron was glad to get Cec back in one piece, but had few regrets about losing his Mustang, which, Keith Meggs recalls 'gave a lot of trouble to a few pilots in aborted missions. I aborted one take-off in it on 2 February after others had previously done so. It had changes to plugs, leads, carburettors etc and gave the ground staff many headaches.' During this phase of the war 'engine reliability was very much needed with the surrounding mountainous terrain' and it is unlikely anyone shed tears when their least reliable Mustang was gone for good and they were about to get Meteors.[14]

Three aircraft downed in a week was troubling, but on the positive side recent arrivals had the benefit of working with what was now a very experienced group. In February, Fred Barnes and Ross Coburn had each completed 100 missions and Pip Olorenshaw and Tom Stoney were close behind them. Pip broke his wrist cranking a jeep, but flew with his arm in plaster to complete his 100th mission two days after Fred Barnes. This brought his lifetime total to 226 when his World War II sorties were added.

His feat did not pass unnoticed and the US forces newspaper, *Stars and Stripes*, ran a front-page story headlined 'Plastered Aussie Pilot Flies Hundredth Korean Sortie'. Some days later the Melbourne *Argus* sent a reporter to interview Pip's wife, who said that 'his most important mission is to see for the first time his four-month-old son, Peter'.[15] One hundred missions did not automatically mean a pilot was headed home, but it did mean he would be when a replacement was available, and most went home soon after (unless they elected to stay).

The Mustang era was nearly over when Dick Cresswell led nine aircraft against truck convoys and supply dumps north of Pyongyang. The enemy was still fighting furiously, and they flew through intense small-arms fire to destroy twelve trucks, a tank and two large guns, and attack many buildings. Just days later, eight squadron aircraft joined others from the 35th Group to attack main access roads directly behind enemy lines. Each aircraft carried two bombs, to be dropped every few hundred metres or so along the roads at points where detouring would be difficult or impossible. After the bombing, they did armed reconnaissance and returned home.

The 35th continued in this vein, but after 6 April it did so without 77 Squadron who flew their last Mustang sorties that day. In nine months of war they had flown 3872 sorties, varying in length from 25 to 30 minutes at the Pusan Perimeter to six hours plus for escort and interdiction sorties well behind enemy lines. Overall, the sorties averaged out at about three hours each.

This meant that they had averaged 430 sorties per month (or more than fourteen per day) and flown over 11 000 hours in all. Quite an effort, and a tribute to the ground crews who fixed the aircraft up at night and readied them early each morning, and to the men who flew them in harm's way.

Feelings were mixed. The Mustang was a wonderful aircraft and it was sad to say goodbye, but this was the jet era, and they were about to become part of it. Tomorrow, they would fly the Mustangs back to Iwakuni and take a break from the war to find out what the Meteor was all about.

There was no Meteor training in Australia, so all training had to be done at Iwakuni. A thirteen-man technical team had been sent to the UK for training and arrived in Iwakuni in February. As well, there were two UK field service engineers— one from Rolls Royce for engines and one from Gloster (the aircraft manufacturer) for airframes. They became known to the ground crews as Mr Rolls and Mr Gloster and provided invaluable expertise and training.

The RAAF Meteor maintenance team in Iwakuni was managed by an officer, rather than Flight Sergeant Darby Freeman who had run things in Korea, and the entire set-up was a good deal larger and more like Australia in peacetime. There was less call to work all hours in terrible weather, but that gain came at the loss of some of the camaraderie the fitters had felt as a close-knit team under the charismatic Darby, bonded together by common hardship, stress and danger.

Air training was in two general stages. The first, the basic phase, was to learn how the aircraft worked and how to fly it around safely. The next, the applied phase, was to learn how to fly it in combat as a fighter. Both stages had their challenges. For many, the Meteor was the first twin-engine aircraft they had flown. The two engines made it a powerful aircraft for its time and provided added survivability in case of a single engine failure. But having two engines meant that they had to learn to fly it on one in an emergency.

The engines were well out on the wings, and with one out of action the aircraft yawed towards the dead engine. To counter this, rudder was applied, but this was no simple task as the Meteor lacked a powered rudder and strong legs were needed to push on one rudder pedal and pull back on the other. (The rudder pedals were fitted with stirrups for this purpose.)

As a result, single-engine operations at low speeds could be dangerous. Overshoots after a missed approach or engine failures on takeoff were potentially the most dangerous of all. Safety speeds were set and each pilot had a personal single-engine 'minimum control speed' below which he was unable to control the yaw, and below which he would normally not fly on one engine unless committed to land.

With overshoots, the pilot had to deal with power that built up slowly and then came with a rush as the engine neared maximum revolutions. In inexperienced hands the sudden power rush could yaw the aircraft towards the dead engine, causing it to roll, sometimes with fatal results.

The limited yaw control was a particular problem on takeoff, which in the Meteor occurred at 10 to 20 knots below minimum control speed on one engine. When faced with an engine failure just on takeoff, the pilot had to control the aircraft until he reached the minimum control speed. To do so he often had to reduce power on the good engine until the undercarriage and flaps were retracted and he had reached safety speed. With a heavily laden aircraft, such as one with full fuel (and later on, sixteen rockets), this phase of single-engine flight was very critical, and the pilot had to work very hard just to keep the aircraft in the air.

As a result, single-engine operations required both knowledge and judgement. 'Asymmetric approaches'[viii] were an important part of early training and good instructors were a must. In this regard, the RAF did 77 Squadron proud. Two experienced Meteor pilots, Joe Blyth[ix] and Frank Easley, arrived soon after the first Meteors were landed.

An adventurous pair, they quickly got themselves to Korea from Iwakuni and talked their way into flying combat missions in Mustangs (which was against the rules for them). Shortly after, Max Scannell and Reg Lamb arrived to make up the four-man RAF pilot-conversion team. They too flew combat missions in Mustangs whenever they could, again in complete disregard for the rules.

Dick Cresswell later referred to them as 'excellent instructors from the UK—especially Max Scannell,[x] the leader' and often spoke highly of their contribution. Max made another important contribution that no one expected. He was an aerobatic pilot for the RAF and brought with him a set of larger engine air intakes

---

viii Single-engine approaches.

ix Retired as a Squadron Leader, DFC and Bar, AFC and Bar, US Air Medal.

x A New Zealander, Max was a WWII Corsair pilot with the RNZAF before joining the RAF.

that greatly boosted power. Dick Cresswell took one look at them, realised 77 Squadron should have them, and arranged for larger intakes to be sent out from the UK—which they soon were in a Hastings transport aircraft. The larger intakes were then progressively fitted to the fighters, but not to the dual-seat trainers.

With the experienced RAF instructors, the basic business of learning to fly the Meteor went very well, usually proving to be an exciting experience for the pilots involved. So much so, in fact, that some who were not earmarked to fly Meteors in Korea still managed to get checked out before going home. Lyall Klaffer was one. With 105 missions behind him, on 23 March he was sent to Iwakuni, to eventually go back to Australia. He spent a couple of weeks there test flying Mustangs and on 2 April 1951 had his first flight in a dual Meteor with Joe Blyth. Then:

> one week later I flew with Joe again, and he sent me off on a solo flight in the single seat Meteor. It was a great thrill for me … The first thing I noticed was the almost complete absence of noise, once the engines were running and the canopy closed. Then, of course, when it came time to taxy out for take-off I could actually see where I was going, without swinging the nose from side to side, as I had to do in the Mustang.
>
> Once airborne the aircraft handled beautifully, and was of course, far more powerful than the Mustang. I climbed and zoomed and dived and experienced a wonderful new step in my aviation experience. On landing, it was wonderful to be able to see the runway all the way down to touchdown! In a Mustang, the runway disappears under the nose at about 200 feet above the ground, and re-appears either side of the nose at about fifty feet.[16]

Lyall had one more Meteor flight and then went home on posting to fly Mustangs again with 24 Squadron, at Mallala, near Adelaide.

They also had to learn to live with the Martin Baker ejection seat, which was new to most pilots and ground crew. The seat, which incorporated the pilot's parachute and survival pack, was set on rails and could be fired out of the aircraft by an explosive charge. Once the seat was ejected, another gun fired out a small drogue parachute which slowed and stabilised the seat.

The first charge was powerful enough to fire the seat and the pilot well clear of the aircraft, and a seat fired accidentally on the ground would almost certainly kill anyone it hit and do considerable damage. Safety pins with large red tags were used to make the seat 'safe' before the pilot climbed out after landing, and were only removed again just before he closed the canopy to taxy. All ground-handling staff, as well as the pilots, had to be trained before anyone went flying. The procedures were simple, but it was something everyone had to know.

The 'bang seat', as it was widely known, was a major advance in pilot safety. To bail out of a World War II fighter like the Mustang, a pilot often had to deal with hurricane-force airflows which, in some cases, could pin him into the aircraft. With jets, the speeds could be twice as high or more, making bailing out in the traditional way virtually impossible.

The only way to get the pilot out, in most cases, was to fire him out in his seat, complete with oxygen and his protective clothing to deal with the thin and incredibly cold air at high altitudes, if need be. The time taken to escape was also much reduced, and a pilot could be clear of his aircraft in seconds after deciding to eject.

The Meteor fighter was also pressurised so the pilot could operate comfortably in the very thin air 12 000 metres up. (The dual-seat Meteor had no pressurisation or ejection seats and less fuel than the fighter. This made it quite a bit lighter, and, in one pilot's words: 'It went like a cut cat.') The pressurisation, though welcome, added to the complication and caused some initial problems.

One was with the filter on the valve that regulated cockpit pressure. It easily clogged with dust and was located under the ejection seat, which had to be removed along with the canopy to get to the filter. Once that laborious task was done, the filter took only five minutes to change, and the seat and canopy could be just as laboriously refitted. Rain that laid the dust must have been a welcome event for the fitters who serviced the pressurisation system.

With its twin jets, higher speeds, shorter flight times, bang seat, pressurisation and such, the Meteor was a quite different proposition from the Mustang. Despite that, the basic flying phase was all pretty straightforward, with expert instructors passing on tried and proven knowledge. This was not so with the applied phase of air training. Here, their job was to learn to fight MiG-15s—something no one had ever done with a Meteor. Indeed, very few pilots had even practised fighting any other fighter with it. Alan Stephens summed up the situation thus:

> The Meteor had been conceived and designed as an interceptor fighter; that is, as an aircraft that would be scrambled to intercept high flying bombers under the guidance of a ground radar. Air defence in Korea, however, was more likely to involve combat against the MiG-15 in the classic 'dog-fight', in which speed, manoeuvrability and acceleration were more important qualities than those needed for a radar controlled intercept. Very little information was available from the RAF regarding the Meteor's capabilities as a fighter as compared to an interceptor.'[17]

To add to their problems, only two men in the squadron, Vic Cannon[xi] and Dick Cresswell, had been involved in real-life

---

xi   Vic had flown Mustangs in Europe and Kittyhawks in the Pacific in WWII and later retired as a Group Captain DFC.

aerial combat, and that was against bombers, not fighters. No. 77 Squadron was called a fighter squadron, but it had become a ground-attack outfit, and a very good one at that. With the Meteor, they now had to forget about ground attack and become fighter pilots—very specialised work they knew almost nothing about.

The inherent difficulties with the complete role change seem to have been ignored in Australia, where those in charge continued to demonstrate little understanding of what was happening in Korea. No RAAF fighter instructors were sent to Iwakuni to teach the basics of fighter tactics and manoeuvres. Nor was help obtained from the USAF, which now had many fighter pilots with MiG-15 experience and would almost certainly have loaned a couple of experienced men to help train their Aussie allies. As a result, in these early times 77 Squadron did not fully understand what it needed to do to become an effective fighter squadron in MiG Alley.

This ignorance was a serious problem and they quickly set out to rectify it as best they could. Once again, they were lucky Dick Cresswell was there. He used his connections with the USAF and in mid-May they lent him a Sabre and a pilot for two weeks to fly against Max Scannell in a Meteor, using the Sabre as much as possible as a MiG-15. From this they found that the Meteor was: 'OK for patrol at 35 000 feet,[xii] but our best fighting height was about 15 000 to 25 000 feet,[xiii] as far as we were concerned to have a crack at a MiG.'[18] In fact, the Meteor had shown it had a better turning radius than the Sabre below 25 000 feet and a higher rate of climb at lower levels.

The problem was at the higher levels where it would not be able to match the MiG-15. Its good performance at mid levels, however, indicated that it would be more than useful if used in combination with Sabres at height and the Meteors lower

---

xii   About 10 500 metres.
xiii About 4500 to 7500 metres.

down. This was something to go on at least, and they planned their future operational training accordingly.

The first batch of Meteor trainees varied in experience from recent arrivals to second-tour men like Les Reading. Les was one of a number who had earlier volunteered for a second tour. The volunteers had a range of reasons, but all shared a disdain for Communism in action, with its callous human-wave fighting tactics, millions of wretched refugees, and widespread suffering and destruction in the name of Utopia.

Communist theory then appealed to millions in the West, but the reality in Korea was horrible and something that had to be opposed. Les subscribed to what later became known as 'the domino theory'; that if Korea fell the Communists would not stop there, but would try again somewhere else and progressively take over East and South East Asia and ultimately the world.

He knew that by fighting on he would help contain the spread of Communism with its vicious disregard for human life. After volunteering, he had gone on leave to Australia, and found out about the Meteor only when back in Korea. He had actually come back to fly Mustangs, but found the idea of now flying jets an exciting prospect.

The later part of the course owed much to the specialist knowledge of the RAF pilots and Dick Cresswell's aim to produce a squadron trained for 'combat against the MiG-15s and working with the Americans with their Sabres'.[19] That is, the training was for work in concert with the Americans, not as an autonomous unit operating independently. In this respect, the knowledge Dick and Des Murphy had gained while working with the USAF was a key factor. The need to compensate for deficiencies in RAAF training, especially instrument flying, was also a key influence.

Nevertheless, the operational training was necessarily limited because their knowledge was limited. Fighter combat with jets was a new thing and in some ways still evolving. The Sabre versus Meteor trials, and the time Dick and Des had spent with the

USAF, were a big help. Nothing, however, could fully compensate for the lack of RAAF and USAF input from specialist fighter instructors. And, without practical Meteor combat experience, they could not create individual and group tactics specifically designed to fight against MiG-15s. Not surprisingly, Les Reading remembers his Meteor training as 'learning to fly and operate the aircraft, some GCAs but not enough on tactics'.[20]

The course began with a program of lectures, followed by flying a Wirraway and a Mustang to review the basics of instrument flying and gain some practice, and a night cross-country in a Mustang. It then moved on to lectures on the Meteor and at least two flights in the dual, with an emphasis on asymmetric landings. Once in the fighter, the pilots practised all aspects of flying, including high-altitude work, night flying, aerobatics, formation flying and let-downs (using VHF and GCA), and at times an intercept sortie with a Sabre.

Some Meteors were fitted with rocket rails, and Keith Meggs's conversion course 'all did some rocket training on the island just to the east of Iwakuni. The rails were then removed.' Also, for that course: 'Night flying in Meteors was carried out from about 5 am after a night's sleep and, legal or not, a high speed, high power approach across Iwakuni village was the norm—the beautiful sound of a Meteor at high speed must have been a wonderful thing for the Japanese to wake to.'[21]

Navigation and fuel planning were also stressed. The Meteor was much faster than a Mustang, flew for much less time—an hour twenty at best on internal fuel, depending on the sortie type—and at times had to deal with things like jetstreams. Timescales were compressed and pilots could get into trouble with navigation or fuel much faster than before, and have less time to sort things out. Furthermore, as there were no navigation beacons in enemy territory, pilots couldn't use their ADF there and had to plan accordingly. To help cope with these potential problems, more and better pre-flight navigation and fuel planning was done.

In the circumstances, the squadron was now as ready as they could be to go back to Korea, but this was not to be—not just yet, anyway. The radio compasses had not been fitted. Without them, the Meteor was not ready for the Korean theatre and installation now held them up for a month at least.

The radio compass design and installation process was very slow and General Robertson told Dick he could not approve the release of the aircraft into Korea and combat until they were all equipped. At the current rate of progress, this could take months. Dick argued that when enough aircraft were equipped to ensure flight leaders always had an ADF-equipped aircraft, they could go, and General Robertson, practical as ever, agreed.

But that solved only part of the problem. The aircraft had not been designed to take a radio compass, which consisted of an antenna, a receiver, a control unit and a display. All the best places for switches and dials were already in use and the control unit and the display somehow had to be squeezed into the cockpit not designed to take them. The end result worked, but only just.

Col King, who flew Meteors later in the war, tells us that

> the location of the unit was awkward for frequency changing. This required the pilot to un-strap, wriggle around to the right as far as possible and extend the left hand into the right, rear recess of the cockpit. By exhaling and drawing in the stomach it was just possible to nudge the crank handle in small increments. Larger men declared this was a feat achievable only under the impetus of sheer desperation.[22]

Nevertheless, enough Meteors were fitted with radio compasses for the squadron to officially be approved as operationally ready in that regard. (The control box was later moved to beside the pilot's seat, but as it could not be seen directly the frequency display was reflected in a mirror—which, of course, produced a mirror image and a subsequent need to do some things back to front.) To overcome tuning problems, ADFs were preset before flight whenever possible.

On the positive side, the aircraft was a good and stable platform should the squadron need to drop bombs or fire rockets—even though the RAF had not yet cleared the aircraft for rocketry. These matters, of course, would only be relevant if the tasking changed from air defence to attack, and there was no suggestion of that at the moment.

Until now, they had relied heavily on the Americans for almost everything. This was no longer possible—the only thing in common between the Meteor and the US aircraft was the fuel. Everything else was different—ammunition, bombs, rockets, spare parts, the lot. They would no longer be able to trade spares and expertise with the USAF or simply plug into their logistics system as in the past. Their aircraft was unique in the theatre and they would have to create unique training and logistics systems to support it.

While these problems were being sorted out, training continued, and not without incident. Dick Bessell once more proved that he was born under a lucky star. Sent to practice takeoffs and landings, although the airfield was closed, he finished up in cloud and sought a GCA approach to get him out of the cloud and lined up on the runway for landing. Unfortunately, the Iwakuni GCA radar produced false echoes from the nearby hills, sometimes making it difficult for the operator to track an aircraft. This happened to Dick, who had done only limited GCA work and flew too fast for the GCA controller to keep track of him. After 50 minutes trying to relocate Iwakuni, he finished up running out of fuel and had to ditch near the coast about 15 kilometres south of the base.

He ditched the aircraft cleanly, inflated his dinghy and got into it without even getting his feet wet. Once ashore, he rang from a nearby railway station, and when Des Murphy answered the phone said: 'Guess who?' Des found this reply somewhat frivolous, but an alternative explanation could be that Dick was in shock—running out of fuel and ditching, even if you escape unharmed, would do nothing to settle the nerves for most people, and Dick Bessell was probably no exception. But in shock or not, the important thing is he lived to tell the tale. The aircraft was later salvaged by 491 Maintenance Squadron and flew again.[23]

Not everyone had such luck. Roy Robson was killed during a Mustang night cross-country training flight over nearby Shikoku Island, on 17 April, to become the thirteenth squadron pilot killed or captured during the Korean War. Tom Stoney could well have become the fourteenth in a bizarre incident that remains unexplained. He was flying at about 5000 metres when he suddenly found himself hanging in the air with his aircraft disappearing below him.

The ejection seat had fired for some unexplained reason, but having done so it worked perfectly, deployed the parachute and drogue and left him dangling safely in the air. He detached himself from the seat and floated down to the ground. His back was injured, and after time in a local hospital he was sent home to Australia for treatment and a later return to Korea.[24]

In April, once the squadron was reasonably organised, General Partridge visited from 5th Air Force headquarters. Dick Cresswell took him for a flight in the dual, after which he flew the Meteor fighter. The flight confirmed for him the known shortcomings like the lowish top speed, limited manoeuvrability at height and restricted rear vision, but General Partridge nevertheless ruled it good enough to fly in the air-to-air role.

This would not happen, of course, until many of the problems previously outlined were solved. Once that was behind them, the squadron would join the 4th Fighter Intercept Wing, at Kimpo, near Seoul. This was good news. Kimpo was being developed into a proper operational airfield, with a 2000-metre runway, good tarmac and maintenance areas, and reasonable living and working accommodation. And importantly, it was close to the border, and within easy striking distance of the Yalu where things were really hotting up.

The spring thaw was melting the ice on the Yalu, making the international bridges important again and vital targets for US bombers. Also, North Korean airfields were being repaired and rehabilitated, and the USAF was conducting an airfield neutralisation campaign against them. In the vigorous response from the Chinese, the USAF F-80s were proving too slow to match the MiGs, the F-84s were of some use and the Sabres were being confirmed as worthy opponents for the MiG-15.

Sabre numbers were still limited, but as they grew in strength the USAF began using them as top cover for F-84s flying with bombers. This evened things up and suggested that as Sabre numbers grew, the UN air superiority picture would improve. It also suggested that the plan to operate the Meteors lower down in conjunction with higher flying Sabres was sound.

They wouldn't prove it, however, until they joined the USAF in combat. They were ready to do so in June, but the radio compasses held them up until late July. The first peace talks had been held and gone nowhere, the spring thaw was now well and truly over, it was summer again in Korea, and the war had been going for more than a year when they moved to Kimpo and began fighting in MiG Alley.

5

Air to Air

The Chinese Air Force continued to grow rapidly in 1951. When 77 Squadron arrived in Kimpo in late July, the Chinese had over 1100 aircraft, some 700 of which were fighters. Two new airfields were being built to augment their main fighter base of Antung, just over the Yalu. These three airfields would soon be home to more than 300 MiGs, and other construction work suggested that the Chinese might be planning a further build-up in the border area.[1]

In unlimited war—as World War II had mostly been—these airfields would be juicy targets to the UN air forces and would not have been built right next to the border. But this was a limited war—with limited aims and limited geographic boundaries—and allied aircrew were prohibited from crossing the Yalu. Frustrated UN fighter pilots watched enemy aircraft taking off and landing in complete safety just a few kilometres away. Apart from waiting for the MiGs to come to them, all the UN airmen could do was bomb the North Korean airfields, supply lines and industrial base to suppress the Communist air effort.

And bomb they did. By mid-1951 the airfield suppression campaign in North Korea was largely successful, continually pounding to pieces airfields the Communists were putting considerable effort into building. Attempts to hurt the enemy's industrial base were much less successful—for the simple reason that most of it wasn't in Korea.

In fact, much of the industrial support base for Communist efforts in North Korea was in Russia and the rest of the Soviet Union as far back as Eastern Europe. The Russians were careful not to drag the Soviet Union into the war, but they gave wholehearted support to others doing the fighting against what they saw as a common enemy. This Russian support allowed China—then still wretchedly poor after decades of war and occupation—to create a very large, modern air force and run a huge army.

Much material went via rail, but a surprising amount was airlifted. Indeed, 'the Soviet air corps provided a vital link between the Chinese and North Korean armies in the field and their principal sources of re-supply in the rear, all the while protected by the sanctuary status which operating out of Manchurian bases provided'.[2] Stalin gave only reluctant support when China first entered the war, but once Russia realised its transport aircraft could operate safely, they provided vital air logistic support to both China and North Korea.

As a result, 77 Squadron arrived at a time of increasing and well-supported enemy air capability. In response, the US put as many aircraft as it could into Kimpo, which was only about 50 kilometres from the border and 200 or so from the southern end of MiG Alley. This made Kimpo one of the world's busiest airfields and produced accommodation problems that forced 77 Squadron back into tents with floorboards and head-high internal timber walls.

As it was summer, the tents were fine, except when summer rains turned part of the base into foul-smelling mud that stuck to boots and was tramped inside. In response, they used upturned ammunition boxes to make elevated pathways, which kept the occupants out of the mud and water during wet spells.

Five USAF C-54s[i] flew an advance party over on 20 July 1951 and by the 25th the squadron was assembled. Kimpo was effectively an armed camp, ringed with barbed wire, armed guards and anti-aircraft pits. Security was a priority everywhere and the aircraft were soon parked, facing out, in sandbag revetments to protect them from attack and to contain damage should there be a fuel or weapons mishap. The 'tarmac area' was the ubiquitous PSP, without which much of the air war in Korea would have been impossible. With time, the squadron got dedicated buildings to house workshops and store things like spares and the battery carts used to start the aircraft.

Kimpo was crowded and extremely busy and they were thankful that their tents were near the flight line with everyone close to work. Their first priority was to learn how to operate from the almost frantically busy airfield and to help protect it if need be. There was much to learn for the ground crews as well as the pilots, but they soon got the hang of things. By the 27th they were flying training sorties with the Ground Control Intercept (GCI) station nearby whose call sign 'Dentist' would become part of their new world.

They flew in flights of four with Dentist, and practised approaches and landings under the very tight rules designed to cater for the extremely heavy air traffic. The high-quality air traffic control was reassuring, and they quickly grew used to landing before the aircraft further down the strip was airborne, and doing many other things simply not done in peacetime. With time, things got worse, not better. Within eight months, Col King tells us, there would be:

> touch down rates as much as one each fifteen seconds for prolonged periods. Take-off runway occupancy was frequently six aircraft at a time; two rotating into lift-off, two in mid-runway, and two just rolling. These were 'busy-

---

i   DC4 equivalents; four engine transports.

period rates' and the place was almost always busy by day …
With battle-damaged aircraft making unusual arrivals or not
quite reaching the runway, and with occasional cases of fuel
exhaustion during landing or taxy, there was no shortage of
drama.[3]

At times, aircraft were landed from both ends simultaneously,
under strict instructions that 'everyone keep right'. This wasn't
normal routine, but the airfield was always extremely busy and
no place for the timid or indecisive. Just learning to operate
effectively out of Kimpo and stay alive was a task in itself.

That said, 77 Squadron were there to fight and soon got
on with the job, with their first operational Meteor mission on
29 July 1951. It was a fighter sweep along the eastern side of
the Yalu, beginning to the south some 50 kilometres in from the
river and intended to establish air control by a show of force or
a successful fight.

Dick Cresswell led the squadron, divided into four flights
of four and using their new call sign 'Anzac'. The other flight
leaders were Geoff Thornton, Vic Cannon and Dick Wilson, a
squadron leader and World War II veteran posted in recently[ii] to
be operations officer.[iii] They were to fly in two groups of eight,
one at 35 000 feet and the other at 30 000 feet with USAF F-86
Sabres at 25 000 and 20 000 feet.[iv]

Like much else in life, the flight turned out to be interesting
but unimportant. Some ill-directed flak opened up as they
passed Pyongyang, and when they got further north they passed
Antung and saw some MiG-15s with their distinctive swept-

---

ii   Others posted in with him were Cedric Thomas, Ron Guthrie, Bill Middlemiss,
      Don Armit and Allan Avery.
iii   Just weeks before Dick Cresswell was due to go home, and after the toughest
      time of his command was past. It was, however, appropriate manning for the
      squadron then, as it always would have been.
iv   35 000 feet = about 10 500 metres, 30 000 feet = about 9100 metres, 25 000 feet
      = about 7500 metres and 20 00 feet = about 6000 metres.

back wings parked on the airfield. And that is where they stayed. Safe in their sanctuary across the river, the Chinese were not enticed to get airborne and check out this new twin jet, and the Meteors returned to Kimpo without sighting the enemy in the air.

The Chinese were treating the newcomer with caution, which was very frustrating for Dick Cresswell, who was due to go home soon and had only limited combat missions on the Meteor. He recalled later that while he was there 'we never really proved our ability against the MiG-15 ...'. He felt that there was no doubt that the Chinese were giving them 'a bit of a wide berth initially until they could work us out, and sort out who we were and what we were capable of'.

For someone with limited time and an aggressive spirit, he found it annoying that 'on the first two or three missions up MiG Alley, we were flying up and down the Yalu River and the Chinese on the other side were flying ... to check us out. We were about ten miles apart. We turned into the sun, they'd turn into us, and that sort of thing—just checking us out, that was it.'[4]

That certainly was it, although just what was happening wasn't known until 40 years later when Russian records became available. 'Unknown to the Australians, the pilots at the controls of the MiGs were Russians ... studying the newcomers. Air to air photographs were taken using a special automatic camera installed in a MiG ... and the film rushed to an intelligence officer ... The Russians, before long, were able to confirm that British jet fighters had in fact, been committed to the Korean War.'[5]

This explains the cat-and-mouse game that went on until well into August, with MiGs approaching but not engaging the Meteors. On 14 August, the unproductive sweeps up and down the Yalu ended and the squadron escorted 22 B-29 bombers to Pyongyang where mass raids were being carried out. The task was a mixed bag. On one hand, speed is a basic asset for a fighter and defending the much slower bombers meant flying slower than they would have liked. On the other hand, the bombers might attract some MiGs. The current impasse, which must end one day, would then end and the waiting would be over.

Defence-in-depth was provided for the bombers by an outer F-86 Sabre screen with the Meteors closer in. Their task was to engage any enemy aircraft that penetrated the screen and 'draw the MiGs away from the bombers with whatever it took, be it front-on attacks or passes'[6] while always staying as close as possible to the bombers. To do so, the Meteors formed in three flights of four, 1000 metres or so above the bombers, with one flight ahead, one on top and one behind the bomber formation. To keep up speed and widen their scan, the Meteors continually flew a weaving pattern.

Some tactical freedom was lost by the need to stay close to the bomber formation and concentrate on keeping station rather than looking out. On the plus side, the bombers usually flew a little below 7000 metres, close to the Meteor's best fighting height. Normally, the MiGs would not concede their height advantage and come down to 7000 metres to fight Meteors. Now, if they wanted to attack the bombers, they had no option but to come down to near the Meteors' best fighting height.

Their three-flight arrangement also provided highly visible fighter cover to bomber crews who had been taking a beating from MiGs in recent times and needed some good news. And in this case, the bombers got a much-needed morale boost when no attack occurred; either because the Russians were still not ready to fight Meteors, or the fighter escort was seen as a good deterrent.

Les Reading flew on a number of B-29 escort missions after the MiGs had started to fight and believes that they achieved their brief 'to draw the MiGs away from the bombers' with 'good success'. He cites one occasion when 'a B-29 was hit and recovered to Kimpo with a hole the size of a large door in its side. Its pilot, a colonel, made a point of visiting 77 Squadron to compliment them on their effectiveness and tell them: "You guys are great."[7] This wasn't just friendly chat. Although the colonel's aircraft was damaged, attacks on many others in his squadron had indeed been 'drawn away from the bombers' by 77 Squadron Meteors.

Some days after the first B-29 escort mission, they did their second, this time to Sinanju, near the mouth of the Yalu. When one of the B-29s was hit by flak and badly damaged, Des Murphy led four Meteors to escort it home but the badly damaged aircraft couldn't make it and the crew bailed out just north of Pyongyang. F-80s and Mustangs were diverted to give them cover until a helicopter could arrive and the Australians, running low on fuel, had to leave without learning their fate.

This pattern continued for the first eleven missions, with the squadron sending aircraft into enemy territory and the MiGs avoiding close contact. Ironically, although the enemy was reluctant to fight during August, two pilots still died that month following a collision during a formation change. They were returning from a fighter sweep and changing from battle formation[v] to line astern before approaching Kimpo for landing. Both were experienced men, but neither was able to eject after the collision and Reg Lamb, one of the RAF pilots, and Ron Mitchell became the fourteenth and fifteenth pilots from 77 Squadron killed in Korea.

In the previous week fate had dealt a different kind of blow when Dick Cresswell was posted out on 16 August 1951. The timing could not have been worse for the aspiring jet fighter squadron. Dick had seen them through conversion onto the Meteor, instilled some fighter lore into them and got them going in Kimpo. All that remained was the crucial last step—to lead them into combat against the MiG-15s. But this was not to

---

v   A 'battle formation' of four aircraft is the basic fighter combat grouping. Two
     aircraft are called a 'fighting element' and in both cases the leader looks ahead
     and leads to the combat area and those behind cover the sides and rear.

be, and he left on posting at a time when his presence with the squadron would have been invaluable.

The bad timing was no one's fault. His departure date was planned months before to allow time for his replacement to convert onto Mustangs and Meteors and otherwise prepare himself for command. Had the radio compass not delayed them for a month, Dick would have had a month more of combat flying with the squadron before handing over to his replacement—Wing Commander Gordon Steege, 'a man with an illustrious record as a fighter pilot and wing leader in World War II.'[8]

As it was, Dick left with his outstanding World War II reputation further enhanced. Throughout their time in Iwakuni, the nightmares of Pohang and Hamhung, the repositioning to Pusan and the transition to the Meteor he had led the squadron with an unparalleled mixture of drive, skill, energy and courage. In recognition, the Americans had given him a DFC and Air Medal and Australia a DFC; all richly deserved.

But in the case of the Australian DFC, there was a whiff of damning with faint praise, of not fully rewarding him for his magnificent work. In this regard Alan Stephens wrote:

> Many who were familiar with his performance thought the higher Distinguished Service Order would have been more appropriate. There were suggestions that his occasional flamboyance, confidence and impressive combat experience were resented by more pedestrian senior RAAF officers, who were sometimes said to have 'reached high rank but not high altitude'[9]

Wally Rivers, who flew 319 missions with the squadron in Korea, rated Dick as 'the best and most experienced Commanding Officer under whom I served' and added 'Why he was never made a Wing Commander and decorated with a DSO whilst in Korea, Christ would not know'.[10] Retired RAAF Chief and

Korean veteran, Jake Newham, agrees that Dick was poorly recognised, and in a contribution to his obituary in December 2006 wrote that it was 'an insult to the squadron and to Dick that he was not given a higher award'.

Had he worked for the USAF, Dick's treatment might have been different. They regarded him very highly and before he went home invited him to fly with them. He accepted and flew ten combat sorties in Sabres, during which he had a number of encounters with MiG-15s and damaged one. He also flew other US aircraft, including a secret spy plane on (an illegal) mission deep into Manchuria (which would no doubt have pleased MacArthur had he known). This brought his official count of combat missions flown in Korea to 144: 110 in Mustangs, 10 in F-80s, 14 in Meteors and 10 in Sabres.

On 25 August the MiGs ended their sparring and began fighting Meteors. They started with eight Meteors led by Max Scannell to cover RF-80s doing reconnaissance south of Sinanju, near the mouth of the Yalu. Kevin Foster saw the four MiGs first and called the break as tracer passed near his wingtip. They then attacked Bill Michelson, just missed and dived through the Meteor formation to seek safety over the Yalu.

The short attack took place at about 7500 metres—a reasonably good height for the Meteors. But by using only high-speed passes the MiGs had maximised their speed advantage and negated any chance the Meteors might have had to engage them in close combat. This suggested that the MiGs were still feeling them out a little, but had already decided to use their height and speed advantage whenever possible, and to exploit their sanctuary over the Yalu once the height advantage was gone. It was logical behaviour from pilots with the initiative, and the MiG pilots usually had it.

They also had the advantage of having fought against the straight-wing USAF jets, the F-80 Shooting Star and the F-84 Thunderjet, which had similar performance to the Meteor. This was especially so for the F-84, as Les Reading found out soon after arriving in Kimpo. Along with Lieutenant John Gregorius of the USAF's 67th Photo Reconnaissance Squadron, he did an informal, limited comparison between the twin-jet Meteor and the single-engined F-84.

The more powerful Meteor out-accelerated and out-climbed the Thunderjet up to 25 000 feet (7500 metres) and could out-accelerate the F-84 at that height. The Meteor deceleration with power off and speed brakes out was also markedly better. Top speeds were similar, but the F-84 gained an edge in climb performance approaching 35 000 feet (10 500 metres), at which height both aircraft had similar acceleration—except in a full power dive where the F-84 out-accelerated the Meteor. An impromptu dogfight was held and both pilots felt that the Meteor had the upper hand at the lower heights and the F-84 was a little superior higher up.

In short, the two aircraft proved to be similar in performance and the Meteor's good characteristics below 25 000 feet were confirmed.[11] With regard to fighting MiGs, this simply reinforced that the Australians had much to gain by fighting lower down, but just how this could be achieved was not clear. The fighter sweep, where they went out looking for MiGs, was a partial answer as they could go in strength and select speeds and heights to suit their expected tactics. As always, however, the MiGs could choose not to fight if the conditions didn't suit them and cross the river to safety.

As a result, the fighter sweeps were best done at a height that allowed the Meteors to perform reasonably well while also enticing the MiGs to fight. When this wasn't possible, the Meteors would opt for height, which is more logical than it first seems. Surplus height can quickly be shed and converted to speed, whereas being too low and having to climb is a major disadvantage to a fighter. Thus, when given the option, fighter pilots will usually choose to patrol higher than their best fighting height.

On 29 August, eight Meteors and sixteen Sabres were at

10 500 metres when they sighted twelve MiGs cruising west at about 12 000 metres and decided to attack. Dick Wilson, who was leading one four, then saw two MiGs below and also decided to attack, but found himself alone when his wing-man spun out. Soon after he was hit by enemy aircraft coming out of the sun—the two MiGs below were probably there as bait—and had to break off and head for home with a badly damaged aircraft. Two Meteors attacked his assailant, driving it off but not apparently damaging it.

The UN aircraft broke formation and engaged in individual combat during which a number of Meteors fired at MiGs without appearing to hit any, and Ron Guthrie's aircraft was badly damaged, forcing him to eject. By so doing he made the first combat ejection using a Martin Baker ejection or 'bang' seat[vi] and became the sixteenth 77 squadron pilot to be killed or captured. He was not seen to eject, and his survival and capture was confirmed only some months later by the Communists during an exchange of prisoner names.[vii]

Dick Wilson's aircraft had taken quite a battering, with the port aileron virtually destroyed, a hole in the wing big enough for a man to stand in, and his main fuel tank punctured from above with the bullet still in it. That he had been able to fly it home was a tribute to the toughness of the aircraft and reassuring to all the Meteor pilots.

Less reassuring was the fact that to some the MiGs had passed like 'greased lightning' and the speed of the enemy and the aerial combat had surprised some, despite their training jousts against each other. This reaction is understandable with the speeds involved. At full speed, Mach 0.9, the MiG-15 is doing more than 250 metres per second.

---

vi   The seat type fitted to the Meteor, variants of which were widely used then and still are. For years, an ejection was often called 'a Martin Baker letdown'.

vii   Ron's writings on his time as a POW leave the reader wondering how he survived the ordeal, and would make all but the most ardent Communist apologist disgusted that human beings can treat a fellow human so brutally.

At such speed, high-speed passes could be over in a flash, giving the impression of great speed and feeding the early belief that the MiG-15 was even faster than it actually was. In practical terms it is the overtaking or closing speed that is important, not the absolute speed. And if the Meteor was just cruising, a MiG at top speed could achieve a high closing speed, even if it was coming from behind the Meteor.

As a result, in most encounters with MiGs the impression of extreme speed and compressed timeframes resulted. Few of the Australians had experienced anything quite like it before. No one had expected it to be easy, or for the Meteor to star, but with one shot down and one damaged, and no hits on the enemy, it was clear they and their aircraft had been out-fought.

It was a sobering experience, even though it was evident that they had fought at a tactical disadvantage, the pilots were still pretty raw and it was early days. With experience, they assured one another, they would improve. That said, by any honest appraisal they clearly still had a lot to learn about the fighter business. Fortunately, they now had World War II fighter veterans like Dick Wilson and other recent arrivals from whom to learn.

A week later they found out just how much they needed to learn when Vic Cannon led six Meteors[viii] to escort two unarmed F-80s on a photo reconnaissance mission and was attacked by 12 MiGs. George Odgers' description of the MiG attack tells us that:

> Six of the MiGs came in first in well disciplined passes. They followed the Meteors in pairs. Two would fire then pull up. A second two would fire then pull up, and a third would go in, all in formation. The first two MiGs had come in very fast and passed ahead of Dawson and Michelson, who drew

---

viii The others were John Myers, Joe Blyth, Don Armit, 'Smoky' Dawson and Bill Michelson.

a bead on one and opened fire. As he did so Dawson saw …
two more MiGs behind them firing at Michelson.'[12]

Bill Michelson's aircraft was hit badly and flipped on its back,
but he was unhurt and managed to recover and fly back to base.
On reflection, they realised that the attack had been done with
surgical precision and was the result of highly developed tactics,
coordination and skilful flying. In other words, they had been
out-thought as much as out-flown, if not more so. With time
the picture of what they were up against emerged and slowly
clarified. It was a highly professional effort, clearly conceived
and coordinated by men who were not just fighter pilots, but
fighter controllers.

They soon suspected direction was coming from controllers
who stayed above the fighting, and this (much later) proved to be
true. This direction, plus the tactics and discipline, produced what
Les Reading recently termed 'paired attacks, well co-ordinated,
using height to initiate and maintain the offensive—quite advanced
stuff. By comparison, we were mostly on the defensive with
limited experience and knowledge of fighter tactics, especially in
the beginning.'[13]

It was also apparent that they were up against two classes of
pilot: the leaders who were experts and all the rest who were
not. As the Chinese Air Force was embryonic, this suggested
that the leaders were from elsewhere and Russia was the most
logical choice for Australian suspicions. There was also evidence
that the Meteors were being specifically targeted, and Les
Reading recalls that sometimes the MiGs would 'deliberately
by-pass USAF Sabres and F-84s, in numbers as many as 45 to
50, to have a hack at us'.

These deductions and suspicions all proved to be true—
although not known for decades in some cases. We now know
from the Russians themselves that they operated not just as
instructors but also as fighter leaders and coordinators and did,
indeed, target the Meteors. None of these disclosures surprised

Les Reading, who suspected at the time that they were up against something special when

> my wing man, Phil Hamilton-Foster, was shot up and had to return home. Normally I'd have shepherded him, but I was then a straggler and four MiGs set upon me. They worked me over very, very professionally, carrying out co-ordinated individual attacks beyond our capacity. We started at about 30 000 feet, and I turned into each attack pulling over 6G to thwart their gun-sight gyros until they broke off at low level. I stayed among the trees until I was sure I had lost them and then rubbernecked my way home—somewhat relieved.[14]

The Chinese pilots, on the other hand, were pretty raw. Some had received as little as six months' training and, according to later Russian accounts, were often too poorly fed to withstand the physical stress of fighter operations.[15] These accounts explain why some MiG pilots were timorous, many seemed inexperienced and occasional attacks looked more like training exercises to the Australians than serious combat efforts.

Whatever the reason, sometime later a MiG attacking a bomber they were escorting passed right in front of Les and Wally Rivers, presenting them with an excellent target as it swept away. Although it was drawing away, Les was able to attack and damage the MiG. (In recent times, Les's attack has been confirmed as a kill, making him the first Australian to down a MiG in Korea.[ix] Until this confirmation, Bruce Gogerly's kill on 1 December 1951 was listed as the first.)

All of which tells us that there was no one factor for the early supremacy of the MiGs over the Meteor. The Meteor's poorer performance at height and in top speed was just one factor—and

---

ix   The kill was confirmed from three pieces of evidence—following the attack, Les and Wally Rivers saw a MiG burning in the distance; a B-29 pilot who had to land at Kimpo sought Les out to thank him for 'clobbering the MiG', and, decades later, Russian records showed that one MiG did not return from that sortie.

maybe not the main one. The Russian pilots who devised the MiG tactics, coordinated the attacks, flew brilliantly and picked out stragglers were a major contributor. So too was the fact that they targeted the Meteors in the early days and usually made sure they outnumbered them by big margins before attacking. And when they did attack, they did so with tactics that exploited their height and speed advantage and the lack of an equivalent coordinated, tactically sophisticated defence from the Meteors.

But much of this was not known at the time. Russian involvement, it must be remembered, was still only suspected and their full contribution was not known until recent times. Also, 77 Squadron's picture of enemy tactics and their own potential was still building and by no means complete. Without such a picture, development of Meteor tactics relied partly on informed guesswork and for some time yet would be a work in progress. As the retired US Secretary of Defence, Donald Rumsfeld, might have said, 'They had known unknowns and unknown unknowns' to grapple with, and plenty of them.

Such is the 'fog of war'. Few military commanders ever know all they would like to know about their enemy, their operating environment, or even their own forces. Those fighting this fight were no exception, and had no option but to do so with the knowledge and skills they had, while trying as hard as they could to build that knowledge and those skills to competitive levels. (Les Reading's recent thoughts on MiG-15 tactics are included at the end of this chapter.)

From 1 September on, the enemy had 'upped the ante' in the air war, at times massing as many as 90 MiGs against UN fighters. This allowed them to use the type of tactics Les Reading experienced and which produced the attack that badly damaged Dick Wilson's aircraft. It also meant that the number of MiGs available for combat in MiG Alley was growing, and the tempo of fighter operations was growing with it.

This was unwelcome news for the new CO, Gordon Steege, who already faced two major problems—an enemy that was outclassing them in the air, and low squadron pilot numbers, now at 21. In trying to solve these problems he would have known that the enemy would probably get stronger, not weaker; that 77 Squadron could not magically improve overnight to counter them; and that new pilots could not be created fast enough to replace those killed, captured or gone home at the end of their tour.

The low pilot numbers were a problem not just for the squadron, but for the RAAF. Fighter pilots need comprehensive training and it then took about eighteen months for a raw recruit to become a raw fighter pilot. Those graduating in the next few months were recruited before the war began. Their numbers were set to meet peacetime needs and were now too few to meet the increased demand with war in Korea. Pilot training numbers had since been increased, but would take time to filter through. To build up 77 Squadron pilot numbers in the short term, extra pilots would now have to be taken from Australian squadrons and trained on the Meteor—which would still take some months.

This complex problem, involving far more than just raw aircraft performance, gave the new CO plenty to exercise his mind. On the plus side, he had wide command experience from World War II, having commanded 260 and 450 Squadrons in the Middle East and later on 73 Fighter Wing and 81 Wing in the Pacific. A fighter ace, he had ended the war with a personal score of eight enemy aircraft destroyed and two probable, the rank of Group Captain and a DSO and a DFC.[16]

He left the RAAF in 1946 and worked in New Guinea until rejoining in 1950. He had not previously flown Mustangs or Meteors, but converted to both types after arriving in Iwakuni in May 1951. Instead of then being given the opportunity to gain experience on the Meteor, he was sent to an Air Power Symposium in Britain. Delayed there for several weeks due to transport problems, he had returned to Japan only on 5 August to take over from Dick Cresswell on 16 August.

In the next three weeks Ron Guthrie was shot down, and Dick Wilson's and Bill Michelson's aircraft were badly damaged in one-sided encounters with MiG-15s. They were clearly not doing well, and although he had flown very few operational sorties, Gordon Steege concluded that the Meteor was outclassed and so unsuited to its role. At the RAAF's The War in the Air 1914–1994 Conference in 1994, he gave a clear indication of his thinking when he stated that:

> The Meteor was purchased by the RAAF for the air-to-air role, but you didn't have to be a Rhodes Scholar to know it just wasn't going to cope with the MiG-15. I was quite convinced of the aircraft's inadequacies even before it went into operations, but of course my opinion wasn't well received either by Air Force Headquarters in Melbourne or by the Royal Air Force representatives who naturally had their own ideas about the value of a British aeroplane.
>
> But the critical difference is that the RAF intended using it as an interceptor, not for air combat, and it was suitable for air defence in the UK in those days. But to put it into air-to-air operations against the MiG in Korea was just asking for an entire squadron to get knocked out. Having had some experience with fighters during the Second World War, that was not my way of doing things.[17]

The decision has been controversial ever since. Supporters agree with him that the Meteors were being outclassed by the MiG-15s in the battles then being fought and the RAAF could, in fact, have had 'an entire squadron knocked out'. To continue in the air combat role, they argue, would have contributed little to the UN air effort and cost many lives and aircraft.

Critics say that he seems to have arrived in Korea with his mind made up, and after only a couple of sorties placed far too much blame on the aircraft for their problems in the air. It was not the Meteor's fault that they were continually outnumbered, or that they still lacked a full and clear understanding of the MiG's *modus operandi* and Meteor tactics to counter it. With time and the right effort, considerable improvement was possible.

Bill Simmonds'[x] thoughts add to the debate. One of five[xi] RAAF Meteor pilots to shoot down a MiG-15, he stated in 1996 that:

> History records, unfairly in my view, that the Meteor 8 was no match for the MiG-15. At high altitudes it was no contest, but at lower altitudes it was a different proposition. I suspect that the MiGs shot down or damaged by 77 Squadron were all below 25 000 feet where our aircraft had equal or even superior acceleration and sustained rates of turn. Contrary to popular belief, the MiG-15 was not a supersonic fighter, although it did have very effective weapons … USAF evaluation trials later confirmed that its performance had been overrated.[18]

Other experienced Meteor pilots, some with experience against the MiG-15, some against the Sabre, also believe the aircraft was harshly judged. All point to its performance below 25 000 feet (7500 metres) and limited opportunity to perform on equal terms with the opposition. Steege clearly saw things differently—and importantly in this case, he was the man in the hot seat, making the decision on the evidence as he saw it.

Having decided that the Meteor 'wasn't going to cope with the MiG-15' he then decided to act and on 6 September held discussions with the Director of Operations, 5th Air Force, in Seoul. At those talks, George Odgers tells us, 'the role of the Meteor was modified. Everest, the commanding general, agreed that they should no longer operate further north than the Chongchon River. Their job would be to escort B-29s and

---

x   Continued to fly fighters and retired as an Air Vice Marshal.

xi   Updated from four to five with the recent confirmation of Les Reading's previous 'damaged' as a 'kill'.

fly CAP [combat air patrol] over fighter bombers attacking the main supply route as far north as the river. They would no longer be included in the first line of fighter screen defence.'[19] As well, they would now provide airfield air defence at Kimpo, and later at Suwon, which consisted of standby on the ground and vectored GCI intercepts from Dentist or another controller onto unidentified targets.

This change of roles was a major decision. It took 77 Squadron out of MiG Alley despite the increased tempo of Chinese fighter operations there and the pressing need for UN fighters. They were no longer a front-line fighter squadron in there mixing it with the best of them. A reduction of their profile and standing in Korea would almost certainly follow. Nevertheless, the RAAF Chief Air Marshal, George Jones, endorsed the decision soon after on a visit to Kimpo. The matter, however, did not end there.

The RAF had delayed equipping their squadrons to supply the Meteor to the RAAF. Their local representative, Air Marshal Bouchier, who had earlier recommended the aircraft, was very annoyed. He believed the decision was hasty and resulted from brief combat experience, the inexperience of squadron pilots in air-to-air operations and the fact that 'Wing Commander Steege did not fly regularly, if at all, on operations'.[20] Bouchier went on to cite Max Scannell who 'believed no Meteor pilot should be shot down by a MiG-15 below 9150 metres unless he made a mistake, because the Meteor was more manoeuvrable'[21] and recommend that the RAF send a dozen or so high-performing jet fighter pilots to Korea to lead and teach 77 Squadron pilots.

Whatever the merits of this suggestion (and there were some) the ongoing debate had the potential to ruffle a good many RAAF feathers—including those of RAAF chief, George Jones, who had endorsed the role change. Aware of this, the RAF chief, Sir John Slessor, decided that the RAF, which was happy with the aircraft in its interceptor role, would from now on stay out of the debate on RAAF Meteor employment in Korea.

This defused the issue and was no doubt a wise decision in the circumstances. It is interesting, however, to speculate what an injection of a dozen experienced RAF fighter pilots would have done for the squadron and the air war—which continued unabated while all this high-powered discussion went on. After all, the new changes had not taken the Meteors completely out of the air war. Their participation in aerial combat would now be more limited, but it was by no means ended. Indeed, during the next 21 months they would have many more fights with MiG-15s and score four kills against them.

Their new roles included airfield air defence, which put eight Meteors on immediate alert, pilots strapped in ready to go, at Kimpo each morning from one hour before dawn until one hour after. Another detail of two was on five minutes' standby from 30 minutes before dawn until 30 minutes after dark, with three changes per day at meal times. 'Scrambles' were initiated by Dentist, with whom they had been working since day one at Kimpo.

Dentist was just one of a number of GCI stations using long-range radars to detect aircraft and vector fighters to intercept them. These radars reached well into North Korea and were an integral part of the air defence of South Korea and the area around Seoul and Kimpo. Many of the controllers were ex-fighter pilots from World War II and so understood the rudiments of intercepts very well. As the radar could not tell one aircraft from another, a transponder system, called Identification, Friend or Foe (IFF) was used, but it was not fitted to all Allied aircraft and did not always work if it was.

When MiGs were detected entering MiG Alley, GCI would tell pilots that 'a train is leaving the station'. One especially aggressive MiG commander was nicknamed 'Casey Jones' after the legendary American locomotive driver, and when GCI detected MiGs peeling off for his characteristic diving attacks they would broadcast that 'Casey Jones is at the throttle'[xii]—a warning usually followed by a well coordinated fast attack on some unfortunate Allied fighter group.

But in this case MiGs were seldom involved. Because IFF was not fitted to all Allied aircraft, Dentist often detected unidentified aircraft that were probably Allied transports or something equally harmless, but might not be and had to be checked the only way possible—with an interceptor. The first Meteor pair scrambled was Des Murphy and Keith Meggs, who were vectored to intercept various aircraft, all friendly. This was the usual outcome and they came to suspect that some of the 'scrambles' were to provide training for the GCI controllers. Along with the boring periods of waiting on the ground, this did nothing for morale.

Fortunately, their bomber escort role was a complete contrast, being most useful and a test of their skills and knowledge. On 8 September, they had their first task under the new arrangements, escorting B-29s attacking the North Korean airfield of Sunan with twelve Meteors led by Dick Wilson. No enemy fighters were seen, and with the Meteors patrolling above, the unhurried bombing was impressively accurate, giving the 77 Squadron pilots the feeling that their presence had contributed to the success of the mission.

The MiGs, meanwhile, were exploiting their superior numbers by operating as pairs in groups of seven or eight, often stacked at two levels, at times using new tactics to attack in trail or circling at height to suddenly attack and then zoom to height again. While to some extent variations of existing themes, these new tactics indicated the treatment the Meteors could expect on their next, inevitable, meeting with the MiG-15s.

---

xii   Casey Jones was a real man. A Russian Fighter Commander, he was one of the guest speakers at a USAF Korean Air Power seminar Dick Cresswell attended in Hawaii many years later.

Apart from CGI scrambles, their next combat mission was two sections of four sent to find and strafe targets of opportunity on the main supply routes into Pyongyang. Max Scannell led one four which hit a building that exploded, a jeep and two pairs of trucks. Dick Wilson, leading the other four, found a truck convoy which they attacked despite heavy anti-air and small-arms fire. On the second pass an armour-piercing shell hit Dick's aircraft on the left side below the canopy line, passed through the cockpit, hit a beam on the right of the cockpit and disintegrated, making a loud noise and wounding him in the arm and shoulder.

The worst wound was a painful one to his right bicep, but his arm still worked and they immediately returned to Kimpo where he landed safely. The airman unstrapping him got his hand covered in blood 'and nearly fainted' as a result. Having climbed out of the damaged aircraft, he was taken at reckless speed by ambulance to a US Army hospital in Seoul—a ride which, for Dick, was 'the most terrifying part of the day'.

Once there he was treated for some 50 small shrapnel wounds in his right forearm and shoulder,[xiii] soon recovered and was flying again in October. Ground attack, it seemed, could be just as effective in a Meteor as in a Mustang, and every bit as dangerous—especially for anyone rushed to hospital by Dick's ambulance driver on return.[22]

MiG Alley had meanwhile widened to a boulevard as extra MiG numbers allowed the Chinese fighters to extend their operating area to the east and south. The Chongchon River— which under the new arrangements was as far north as 77 Squadron would operate—was no longer the border of MiG territory but somewhere near the middle.

This much larger area meant that Meteors—without ever going into the original MiG Alley—were again flying in MiG territory only two weeks after they had been withdrawn from

---

xiii Dick had some of the smaller pieces of shrapnel in his arm thereafter.

the air-to-air war. Many of their bomber escort tasks took them into the expanded MiG territory and, while officially not supposed to go out looking for MiGs, in reality they flew fighter sweeps on a regular basis. A new version of the MiG versus Meteor air war had begun.

In this new war, the Meteors would eventually get to operate on a 'level playing field' and more than hold their own. Unfortunately, this level playing field took some time to emerge. The Meteors continued to be out-fought until it did, but in the end some basics of fighter operations told on the MiG force. Firstly, as the MiGs operated further and further east of the Yalu, some of their tactical advantage was lost. When flying deep into North Korea their ability to quickly dart back over the Manchurian border to safety was reduced and they could spend less time on patrol or actually fighting.

Furthermore, North Korean airfields were not sanctuaries. MiGs operating from them could be attacked any time—be it on the ground, while climbing out after takeoff or when returning to land. Additionally, to protect airfields and other assets, the MiGs had to fly at the level of the Allied attackers—normally below 25 000 feet (7500 metres) and into the Meteors' best fighting altitude band.

All these factors eventually curtailed MiG effectiveness, but not yet. Sheer numbers initially allowed them to maintain their earlier tactics—including choosing when, and when not, to fight—over a larger area. As a result, 77 Squadron never knew just what to expect. On 18 September, Des Murphy led twelve Meteors escorting B-29 bombers on a radar bombing mission against enemy supply lines, but no fighters were seen. The next day fourteen Meteors, again with Des Murphy leading, did a fighter sweep at Anju near the mouth of the Chongchon River with the same result.

They were planning more thoroughly now and approached Anju arranged in three flights of four, with two aircraft positioned further back and higher to act as a relay for the GCI controllers—whose radar could still detect high-flying MiGs but not the lower flying Meteors now below their radar horizon. As it happened they saw 40 or so MiGs above them before the radar operator detected them.

Expecting to be jumped any minute they prepared to fight. The MiGs had other things in mind, ignored them and attacked some nearby USAF fighters instead. The MiGs were still playing cat and mouse with them, being deliberately unpredictable, hoping, one assumes, to catch them by surprise one day.

This unpredictability became a fact of life and the Meteor pilots often did not know if they would be attacked or not. A week later Vic Cannon led twelve aircraft tasked to escort B-29s to bomb Pyongyang. Soon after takeoff the GCI controller changed their task to a fighter sweep over Anju where previous sweeps had been ignored by MiGs. But this was another day, and on arrival they were attacked by fifteen MiGs.

After the initial confrontation, Don Armit's aircraft was hit but still flyable, so he rejoined his leader, Ray Trebilco, and continued to fight. Max Colebrook and Smoky Dawson engaged two MiGs and Smoky hit one with a long burst of cannon fire, producing a stream of liquid from the wing, but not downing the aircraft. The MiGs used their usual tactics of high-speed passes in pairs, often coordinated, but the Australians now knew better what to expect and managed to make some attacks of their own, but without obvious results.

Cedric Thomas and his wingman, Vic Oborn, had just survived a head-on attack when another enemy pair appeared in their attack zone. The two Meteors made a firing pass at the leader who broke and headed for the Yalu. His companion broke the other way by mistake and Cedric and Vic were able to drive him south away from the Yalu but not catch him. They made frantic radio calls alerting other UN fighters in the area that a lone MiG was heading south, but to no avail, and the MiG eventually did a climbing turn into the sun and headed for home.

By then Vic Cannon was calling for them to break off and head back while they still had enough fuel to do so, and they returned to Kimpo. They had, however, driven the MiG well south and doubted he had enough fuel to get back over the Yalu. If so, the pilot would have had to abandon his aircraft, which would then be lost to the enemy just as much as if they had shot it down. Unfortunately, they never knew the lone MiG's fate and could only class it as a maybe (which doesn't count).

The MiGs continued to choose when and where to fight. That afternoon, twelve other Meteors saw 49 MiGs in the Anju area, but for no obvious reason none attacked. The Communists were now mounting a campaign to establish air superiority over an expanding area of North Korea and were in greater numbers over a larger area. Most MiGs seen were in large groups, and the Meteors were invariably outnumbered when they fought. Superior numbers was obviously part of their tactics, but when 49 aircraft choose not to attack just twelve of their enemy, it is clear numbers alone are not the full story.

The Communists were not trying to establish air superiority just as an aim in itself, but as part of the bigger picture. Ideologically, it was a chance to demonstrate their superiority over their capitalist opponents. In Korea, pragmatism and military strategy modified the ideological aims but never enough to take the politics out of the war. Peace negotiations were still stalled, with disagreements over everything from the meeting site to how prisoner exchanges could be arranged.

The main issue with prisoner exchanges was that many Chinese prisoners wanted to go to Taiwan, now run by the Nationalists under Chiang Kai-shek. This embarrassed the Communist Chinese, who wanted them all back and refused to compromise. Eventually a new site was agreed and 25 October selected as the date to resume talks. Until then, continued Communist success in the air would strengthen their bargaining position and they acted accordingly, intensifying the pressure wherever they could.

Not only were MiG numbers up—more than 2500 were sighted by UN forces in October—but many were an improved variant with a more powerful engine and improved ability to out-accelerate and out-climb the opposition. The situation was serious. In response the USAF rushed 75 Sabres from the mainland, despite the need for them to travel as deck cargo through rough winter seas. These aircraft left the US in early November and were flying in Korea by the end of that month, adding to the Sabre numbers already being boosted by existing plans.

Sabre numbers took time to build and as they did MiG numbers also increased, keeping the Sabres fully occupied with air-to-air work during the last months of 1951. With no Sabres available for escort work, the USAF had to abandon interdiction bombing in MiG Alley. Interdiction now shifted to the rail network north of Pyongyang where there was no lack of vital targets.

Communist airfield repair and construction work previously halted in MiG Alley was now able to begin again under the cover of their better air umbrella. This was an ominous development and the Sabre force mounted a maximum effort to wrest back the initiative, sparking some of the greatest air battles of the war during October 1951.

As a result, 77 Squadron pilots saw plenty of MiGs during October. The MiGs, however, continued to be unpredictable. When not specifically targeting the Meteors, they seemed to be concentrating on the Sabres—which they no doubt saw as a greater threat to their air superiority. Whatever the reason, the Meteors saw many more MiGs that could have attacked them than actually did so. Sometimes it was obvious the MiGs chose not to fight. At other times the MiGs seemed not to have seen them—possibly because they where looking higher up for Sabres.

As previously, the Meteor pilots often geared themselves for attacks that didn't come. This happened to the eight aircraft Max Scannell was leading to escort RF-80s doing reconnaissance just to the west of the mouth of the Chongchon River. Two groups of twenty MiGs were seen but neither attacked, either because they did not see the UN aircraft, or they chose not to.

That afternoon, more Meteors escorted B-29s bombing a railway bridge near Pyongyang. The GCI radar reported MiGs in the area, but again none attacked. Two escorted raids some days later to the same area were also ignored—possibly this time because some fierce fighting was going on elsewhere and even the numerous MiGs couldn't be everywhere at once.

Such good luck couldn't last forever and later in October 77 Squadron fought two big air engagements. Dick Wilson had recovered from his injuries and was once more in the air, providing senior leadership, experience and determination. On 24 October, in company with ten USAF F-84 Thunderjets, he led sixteen Meteors escorting eight B-29s bombing at Sunchon, some 40 kilometres north of Pyongyang. As they neared Sunchon, they saw a dogfight to the northwest between some Sabres and MiGs.

The Sabres were trying to keep the enemy fighters away from the bombers, but with only partial success.

As they closed, some MiGs approached, threatening the B-29s, and Dick ordered an attack to repel them. The attack succeeded, but Phil Hamilton-Foster was hit in the wing and fuselage and the starboard engine flamed out, sending him into a spin. He recovered and headed for Kimpo on one engine. His fuel tanks had been holed and the good engine ran out of fuel and stopped at the end of his landing run. Luck was with him that day.

The B-29s were less lucky and took a pounding. The attack was 'very advanced stuff' and the 40 or more MiGs put all the UN aircraft under great pressure. The battered bombers headed east, hoping to drag the MiGs outside their combat radius, and the fighting continued almost to Wonsan on the peninsula's east coast.

Three days later the squadron fought another large-scale engagement. Thirty-four F-84s and sixteen Meteors, again led by Dick Wilson, escorted eight B-29s to attack a rail bridge at Sinanju on the Chongchon River. Once there, they were attacked by a large force of MiGs. The fighting was furious. No Meteors were lost, but Bill Middlemiss had a close shave, finishing up in a vertical dive at Mach .84 to shake off an assailant, finally recovering below 2000 metres, all alone, and eventually recovering to Kimpo in company with an equally lonely USAF F-84.

In both encounters the Australians had fought well, better understanding now what to expect and what to do about it. So much so, indeed, that Dick Wilson later said that he could not recall the Meteor screen around the bombers being penetrated in either fight.[23] On reflection, Les Reading believes 'bomber escort was a good role for us, and we were good at it', thanks in part to their tactic of 'not being drawn off into dog fights, but staying with and protecting the bombers whenever possible'.[24]

But in the end, being good at it didn't matter. They couldn't escort bombers if there were no bombers to escort, and that was soon the case. The next day Geoff Thornton led sixteen Meteors on the squadron's last B-29 bomber escort mission. The mission, to bomb a bridge at Songchon some 30 kilometres northeast of Pyongyang, was also the last daylight bombing mission for the B-29s. GCI radar reported MiGs in the area, but none attacked and the historic mission was uneventful.

The reality was that although aircraft like the Meteor could give effective close-in protection to B-29s, overall success depended on a large screen of Sabres further out to first oppose the mass MiG attacks now occurring. Extra Sabre squadrons were arriving in the area, but they were urgently needed to counter the extra MiGs air-to-air. Sabres could not be spared for bomber escort, leaving the bombers so vulnerable during daylight that they were switched to nighttime bombing.

This ended the bomber escort role for the Meteors, which as day interceptors lacked the radar and other equipment needed to work effectively at night. It did not, however, in any way diminish their achievements so far. These were recognised by the presentation of a Presidential Citation to the squadron by Dr Syngman Rhee, president of the Republic of Korea, on 1 November 1951. The citation stated that the squadron had 'earned the highest reputation' while flying Mustangs and when re-equipped with Meteors had 'continued its fine record'. Part of the politics of war, for sure, but well earned and welcome nevertheless.

The change of role did not leave 77 Squadron unemployed. Almost everything that could fly was needed. MiGs now ruled the skies north of Pyongyang for much of the time and would do so until the extra Sabres got going, and the MiG airfields in North Korea, such as Sinuiju and Uiju (which now housed 90 MiGs between them), were neutralised.

This concentrated much of the November 1951 UN air effort into the area around Pyongyang and northwards up to the Chongchon River. Fighter bombers attacked the main supply routes and Sabres took the fight to the MiGs wherever possible. All available UN air power was put to work, including 77 Squadron, which in November did fighter sweeps south of the Chongchon River to provide air cover for fighter bombers in the area.

Apart from the intercept tasks, the agreement reached only two months ago was now quite meaningless. There were now no bombers to escort and the squadron's main tasks were airfield protection and fighter sweeps into the expanded MiG territory as part of the increasingly successful 'Operation Strangle'—an interdiction campaign aimed at key supply routes, especially railways, in the northwest.

They saw MiGs on most sweeps, making the sweeps tense affairs even if they didn't fight. When an attack came, it often came quickly, was followed by frantic action and was over as quickly as it began. Like many others, the 2 November sweep by sixteen Meteors, led by Dick Wilson, began uneventfully when the dozen or so MiGs they saw heading southeast ignored them. Suddenly, twenty MiGs attacked and some Sabres joined in. The Meteors gave as good as they got, attacking when they could and watching each other's tails in the many individual fights that made up the bigger battle.

Scotty Cadan fired at a MiG attacking Les Reading, missing but driving it off. Joe Blyth fired at three MiGs and two began smoking, one from the engine and the other from its wing. He was then confronted by two Sabres lining him up for an attack, but stopped them with a hasty radio call. Ray Trebilco got away a long burst at two enemy fighters, drawing smoke from one. More MiGs joined in and the melee went on for some time, during which Max Scannell saw tracer all around his canopy but was not hit. Luck, as usual, was a good thing to have on your side.

This was also true for two of the Sabres who almost fell victim to the split-second decision-making done in air battles. During the melee, Scotty Cadan fired at what he thought were two MiGs, but a post-flight look at his gun-camera film told him they were Sabres, and that he had hit one, fortunately doing little damage. But in all, it had been a good day. No Meteors were lost and post-flight analysis gave Joe Blyth a 'damaged'—a good result in the circumstances.

Intelligence was now confirming 'Operation Strangle' aircraft were destroying North Korean railways faster than they could be repaired. Not surprisingly, Strangle pressure was kept on, despite MiGs being seen almost daily, at times in numbers as high as 60 to 80. The squadron flew another sixteen-aircraft fighter sweep the very next day. It too was attacked, but this time the Meteors took hits. Don Armit's port engine was hit, but he was unhurt and managed to get back to base. Don Robertson was also hit and on the way back found he had lost hydraulics and had a fire in the port wheel well (which, luckily, soon put itself out).

Robertson belly landed his aircraft, which was later used for spares, having been made unrepairable by a combination of battle damage, fire and the belly landing. Don Armit's aircraft was in much better shape, and was patched up and flown back to Iwakuni for repairs. This was clearly dangerous work, but they kept on. Max Scannell led twelve Meteors escorting a photo reconnaissance mission on 5 November and two days later Vic Cannon led a fighter sweep into the now familiar Anju area.

On 8 November, Joe Blyth and Wal Rivers flew their 100th Meteor missions, and Dick Wilson learned his wife had been involved in a car crash and he was returning home as soon as possible. This was not just bad news for Dick's family, but for the squadron to whom he had brought experience and operational leadership in tough times and done so with energy and spirit. He was told the next day that he would be awarded an immediate DFC in recognition of his efforts—the first British Commonwealth DFC awarded this way during the Korean War and a popular decision.

The activity level remained high, and two sweeps were flown the next day. This type of work continued throughout November. Despite many brushes with the enemy, the only losses in the air were from an accident between Ken Blight and Don Robertson on 11 November when they were returning home from a fighter sweep and collided while regaining formation.

Don's aircraft flicked onto its back, and spiralled down with no sign of him ejecting. Les Reading broke off, followed him down, confirmed he had crashed and then turned for home. Ken spun twice but regained control. Although damaged, he headed for Kimpo but was forced to eject before reaching the base. By sheer coincidence, Les also saw the ejection, called rescue services and Ken was picked up by a helicopter.

A recovery party sent to Don's crash site later that day found a dead Korean farm labourer nearby who had been killed by crash debris. Much of the aircraft was already salvaged by the local people, who were very poor and for whom the metal in a crashed aircraft was manna from heaven, and little information about the collision or the crash was gained. Don Robertson was the seventeenth squadron pilot killed or captured in Korea.

The previous week the Chinese had introduced another element into the air war by sending Tu-2 light bombers to bomb islands in the Yellow Sea contested by ROK troops and Chinese marines. Unopposed by fighters, they returned unharmed, but later in the month twelve bombers, with an escort including 16 MiGs, were intercepted by Sabres, which destroyed eight of them. This showed that the Tu-2s were little threat in themselves, but it introduced the possibility of the Chinese getting better bombers which could threaten UN airbases in South Korea.

The success of 'Bed-check Charlie'—Chinese light aircraft that penetrated the Kimpo GCI some nights on nuisance raids and had bombed and (slightly) damaged some Sabres—added to these worries, as did the appearance of occasional MiGs near Seoul. There was no evidence of Chinese bombers in the offing, but the Tu-2, 'Bed-check Charlie' and the south-flying MiGs all highlighted the issue of airfield protection.

Bed-check Charlie was immortalised in the TV series *M*A*S*H* and merits further comment. Mostly just a nuisance—apart from one very successful raid—Ross Glassop recalls a

> Russian aircraft similar to our Tiger Moth [a biplane training aircraft] that flew just as slow. He would fly over Kimpo and pour out a bucket of hand grenades hoping to cause damage. In June he struck pay-dirt elsewhere when he destroyed 5 500 000 gallons of aviation fuel on another base. Jet aircraft tried to shoot him down but he was too slow for them. Subsequently the Navy—God bless them—using Firefly aircraft shot down four of them.[25]

November 1951 continued much as it began, with intercept standbys and twelve to sixteen Meteor fighter sweeps most days that saw them in air-to-air combat more often than not. And as in the first days that month, they continued to give as much as they got, hitting enemy aircraft but not downing them, and being hit themselves but not mortally so. In retrospect, surviving so many fights with so many MiGs was good luck, and on 1 December their luck changed.

It happened over Sunchon, some 30 kilometres north of Pyongyang. Geoff Thornton was leading a twelve-aircraft fighter sweep attacked by some 40 MiGs. In the furious fighting that followed, Don Armit, Vance Drummond and Bruce Thompson were shot down. It was later found that Don Armit and Vance Drummond ejected, and Bruce Thompson made it to within 150 kilometres of Kimpo under GCI guidance and then disappeared. With time, it was confirmed that Don Armit was dead and Vance Drummond and Bruce Thompson were POWs. These incidents brought the total of pilots killed or captured in Korea to twenty.

On the positive side, Bruce Gogerly had definitely downed a MiG—then thought to be the first by a Meteor in Korea—and at least damaged another, and a number of others had scored hits, the end results of which were not known. Furthermore, given the ferocity of the attack and the fact that they were outnumbered throughout, things could have been worse.

We now know that those behind the attack claimed that it was, indeed, a lot worse. In their book *With the Yanks in Korea*, Brian Cull and Dennis Newton tell us of a written account many years later by Russian Lieutenant General Georgi Lobov who was

> responsible for a plan to ambush and hopefully wipe out the Meteors of 77 RAAF which, if successful, he believed might have serious political repercussions that would be felt not only in Australia but also in Britain and possibly the United States. Lobov's reasons for electing to concentrate on the Meteor squadron were political. In comparison to the massive US forces involved in the war it was only one squadron among so many, but it was the only non-American, UN unit operating

jet fighters over Korea … On the morning of 1 December, two dozen MiGs … were prepared for action. Sixteen pilots … had orders to attack the Meteors. The other eight MiGs were to fly top cover in order to defend the others against possible attacks by Sabres.[26]

Lobov further stated that there were two attacks, the first an unexpected assault diving in from over 9000 metres and the second as the Meteors were withdrawing.

Some of Lobov's account ties in reasonably well with Australian records of the battle, but the Russian claims to have destroyed at least nine Meteors are wildly exaggerated—even when the tendency during these frantic, high-speed battles for double counts and some wishful thinking is taken into account. This suggests that there might be an element of 'the older we get the better we were' in Lobov's writings. But even if this is so, the fact that the Russians set out deliberately to target the Meteors is now well established—the only thing in dispute is some of the detail of just how they did so and how successful they were.

Had this been known at the time it would have explained why the Meteors were sometimes ignored by the MiGs and at other times apparently singled out for spirited attack by superior numbers using advanced tactics and very skilled pilots. But they didn't know and 77 Squadron could only act on the facts before them. And those facts were not encouraging.

In the past month they had lost four pilots and six aircraft and had other aircraft damaged. It could be argued that this was an unrepresentative bad patch, that losses per month since arriving in Kimpo were nowhere near that bad (which they weren't). Or it could alternatively be argued that the recent increased tempo of MiG operations had changed their world, that from now on losses would be higher than past averages and that recent events were the more reliable predictor of the future.

The 'bad patch' argument was less convincing than the 'changed world' argument for three reasons—the MiG-15s had always held the upper hand over the Meteors and now there were more of them than ever. They were superior at height, had tactics that exploited this fact and were able to fight when it suited them. None of this would change, but their more powerful new model and higher numbers would make the operational performance gap even bigger.

Added to this, Meteor pilot numbers in the short term, if they suffered more losses, would go down, not up. They would then be fighting higher numbers of MiGs with even fewer Meteors. This all added up to a good case to stop fighting MiG-15s with Meteors—at least until USAF fighter numbers grew and the Meteors were no longer outnumbered almost every time they fought. This effectively happened, but not as a result of decisions made on the squadron or elsewhere in the RAAF. In the end, other factors determined the Meteors' fate and its change of role.

The most important thing was the (otherwise very welcome) increased numbers of Sabres, boosted by the 75 from the mainland and steady growth from other sources. These increasing numbers meant that Sabres—which were undisputedly the best choice against the MiG-15—were more and more being chosen over the Meteors for air-to-air work. This trend continued as Sabre numbers grew and took over the air-to-air war.

To this must be added the need to protect the airbases. At this stage, the need was more potential than real. However, the Tu-2, Bed-check Charlie and MiGs sometimes flying near Seoul had all highlighted the potential threat. As a purpose-built interceptor with a rapid start-up capability and strong climb performance at lower levels, the Meteor was well suited to airbase protection.

Logic pointed to much less air-to-air tasking for the Meteors and more intercept duties. This happened, and during the rest of December, '90 percent of 77 Squadron's sorties were related to the airfield defence role'.[27] Frustrating times followed, sitting on standby or launching to check an unidentified 'bogie' that invariably turned out to be a friendly. Morale dropped at the prospect of a future doing this and the feeling that fate had treated them unkindly.

They had fought an enemy who invariably had the initiative, superior numbers, a height and speed advantage, high-quality leadership and a sanctuary to retreat to if things went bad. And in doing so they had usually managed to hold their own, despite their initial rawness as fighter pilots and the limitations of the Meteor. It had, in fact, been a strong performance, but one for which their only thanks seemed to be their present frustrating and unrewarding duty.

Their understandable low spirits were not helped by the onset of winter. November had begun so mildly the airmen's club ran a sweep on the date of the first snowfall, but by December the Korean winter was in full force, once again demonstrating that tents, even if fitted with internal walls and oil heaters as these were, are not suited to weeks on end of sub-zero temperatures. The cold affected almost everything they did, and maintenance in particular was now more difficult as well as more unpleasant.

Special covers protected the canopy, engines and tailplane and along with accumulated ice and snow had to be removed before flight. Clambering about the icy wings was no fun and taking off the cover to the high tailplane was more than a bit hazardous, with a nasty fall awaiting anyone who slipped on the frozen surface while doing so. Ice and snow had to be cleared off everything left outside, including weapons and battery carts if they were left uncovered.

It all added up to the feeling that they had been dealt a bad hand they didn't deserve—boring, undemanding work in freezing, unpleasant surrounds and no prospect of change. Luckily, this feeling was overly pessimistic and things soon improved when the squadron was taken over by Wing Commander Ron Susans. A decorated World War II veteran more interested in what they could do than what they couldn't, he soon acted accordingly.

MiG-15 Tactics as seen by Les Reading, Group Captain DFC (retired)

The Meteor/Sabre comparison at Iwakuni, using the Sabre to simulate a MiG-15, showed that up to its best fighting height of 20 to 25000 feet the Meteor had the edge on the Sabre, whereas above that height band the Sabre was significantly the better in all respects. It was thus decided that in Korea the Sabres should patrol at 35000 feet in combination with Meteors at their best level of 20 to 25000 feet. Oddly, tasking was reversed: Meteors at 30 and 35 and Sabres at 20 and 25 thousand feet.

At all levels the MiG had advantages over the Meteor of greater level top speed by up to 150 kilometres per hour; higher critical Mach where compressibility takes over; greater numbers by far; and ready access to the Manchurian sanctuary over the Yalu River with its twin advantages—refuge, and safe climb to height. At the higher levels the MiG also had better manoeuvrability and rate of climb. Pilot capabilities aside, protracted combat at height should therefore have been disastrous for the Meteors. In the event, the MiGs did not prolong early engagements, but broke off and scooted across the river to safety.

In our early sweeps along the Yalu the MiGs in their sanctuary shadowed us, back and forth, assessing. Later, when they were ready, they used their refuge to gain vital height advantage and attack us with quick thrusts, then hightail it at great speed over the border.

Soon, the MiGs came in greater numbers, 30 or 40, and more at times, at superior height. Some would break off and coordinate pairs attacks on us, the majority remaining above. As we broke into their attacks, they might yo-yo for second passes while we recovered from the breaks. It was as though controllers were demonstrating tactics to those on high: 'this is how we do it; that is how the enemy responds'. Our suspicions that the controllers were Russian pilots were later confirmed.

Before long, controllers sent the Chinese down to deal with us, directed the fight from above, and pounced on stragglers. Later tasking included B-29 bomber escort. The Chinese were by now able to mix it for longer and press home their attacks, and B-29 escort missions were hectic affairs. Our job was to stay with the bombers and protect them at all costs from the very determined attacks. We were not to be drawn away, as the Russians wished, into dogfights that would leave the bombers unprotected.

We flew in sections each of four Meteors, weaving above the bombers to maintain control speed and effective look-out. The Chinese coordinated pairs attacks in rapid succession on the bomber formation, coming in very fast and seemingly endlessly. Our aim was to intercept them or fly across their bows and briefly engage them when we were able, to deter and deflect them, and that we did. But it was a dangerous business. The MiGs were armed with 23 mm and the monster 37 mm cannons meant for attacking bombers, and they used them whenever they could, with some success. But we were not deterred. And when a MiG broke off an attack without great care we were able to get fleeting fire on him. We looked after the bombers very effectively, heavily outnumbered though we were.

Of the United Nations fighter units, 77 Squadron was the foremost target, probably for both political and operational reasons. We were certainly a handy tool for the Russians in their combat training of the Chinese pilots, and the controllers did their work well.

6

Ground Attack Meteors

When Ron Susans took command on 26 December 1951, 77 Squadron had suffered almost a month of intercept duty and winter weather. In combination, these two things could make life pretty miserable. The intercept duty was mostly at Suwon, 30 kilometres south of Kimpo. This meant crack-of-dawn takeoffs from Kimpo and long, cold waits for tasks that seldom came—and when they did come they were either friendly UN aircraft or occasional MiGs flying so high they were no threat and couldn't be intercepted.

The Suwon strip-alert in sub-zero temperatures posed special problems. The covers to prevent ice forming had to be hastily removed with frozen fingers with each scramble call. A quick engine start and taxy could then blow snow and water everywhere, which froze on contact and had to be scraped off the canopies of parked aircraft and anything else that had to be kept clean.

Taxying on frozen PSP was difficult and sometimes hazardous. The Meteor was steered during taxying by differential braking and variable engine power, and on PSP areas that were not dead flat—and there were many—much sliding occurred.

Surprisingly, despite the potential, no serious taxying accidents on frozen PSP occurred.

Although the aircraft were scraped clear of ice in the lines, it was sometimes so cold more ice formed again during taxy. As this could affect the aircraft's flight characteristics, when taxying they would move into the jet exhaust of aircraft ahead of them to keep ice-free whenever they could. The leader, of course, was unable to do this and had to add a little extra speed on takeoff to compensate for any ice he may have accumulated since leaving the lines.

Pilots and maintenance staff weren't the only ones with problems; the cold affected everyone and almost everything they did, at times in the most unexpected ways. On one occasion, when a fire started in a tent, the fire extinguishers were frozen and wouldn't work and the fire barrels kept inside each tent were frozen over. Something that could have been anticipated perhaps, but what Australian would expect the cold to prevent him fighting a fire?

In fact, there were many effects of the cold that would not occur to someone from a warm country. Bill Murphy, a photographer with 77 Squadron at Kimpo, recalls that on arrival he was taken to the Ground Crew Club in the evening where 'a case of Asahi Beer was opened and we had to hold the bottles over the space heater because the contents were frozen'. He also remembers that the tents were heated with stoves burning JP4 jet fuel and that

> although we could not have survived without the heating it created enormous pollution. The base had about 700–800 tented structures each with at least one heating stove ... The soot would permeate into every crevice of your clothing and exposed skin. Nose ears and eyes were the most vulnerable ... Body cleanliness was always a problem in winter. Water pipes would freeze and it was impossible to get a shower, sometimes for days on end. Jerry cans of water had to be

heated on the stoves and you would top and tail … The cold
was unbelievable … Outside one morning the thermometer
read minus two Fahrenheit—34 below freezing [about −19°C]
and sometimes only reached 8°F [about −13°C] during the
day.'[1]

The cold even defeated the Meteor's heating system, which was
normally quite effective, and pilots had to wear bulky winter
dress to keep warm in the air and to survive if they were forced
to eject. This made the already tight cockpit cramped, and for
some larger men the full backward movement of the control
column was restricted. Normally, such things were accepted as
part of the job, but distaste for their current work now added
them to a growing list of morale-sapping factors.

On 18 December 1951, POW lists were exchanged. The
UN listed 132 472 prisoners and the Communists 11 559,
including Gordon Harvey and Ron Guthrie. Vance Drummond
and Bruce Thompson were POWs but had not yet made it
onto the list and their fate was still unknown.[2] The news served
as a reminder that one in four pilots who had flown with 77
Squadron in Korea was now either dead or a POW. The boring
hours spent sitting and waiting gave the pilots plenty of time
to think of such things. While each man no doubt had his own
thoughts, the collective effect was declining morale.

One happy note was the postings of Max Scannell, Vic
Cannon and Les Reading, who had survived 107, 102 and 188
Korean missions respectively. Each had a DFC in the offing.
They had done their share, and more, but in a squadron with
little to cheer about their example and experience would be
sorely missed.

This was especially so for Les Reading, who had become
something of a fixture. He was in the squadron when war broke
out and flew 98 Mustang missions, including the last one flown.
He then flew 90 Meteor missions (including the first) and,
although he did not yet know it, had scored the first Meteor

kill of the war. A friend later worked out he had spent 444 days in Korean combat zones.

But for most, December 1951 was an uncomfortable and frustrating month. As Christmas neared, frustration became humour and they sang 'all I want for Christmas is my wings swept back' in place of a popular novelty song. News that their work in November had produced positive results would also have lifted spirits a little. Operation Strangle had, they heard, 'shattered the North Korean rail-transportation net, had resulted in the destruction of some 40 000 Communist trucks and had prevented the Reds from building up for a future offensive'.[3]

This was good news, but the rest of the story was a bit depressing. The peace talks were still bogged down, the war was still stalemated roughly along the line established in mid-1951, and the Communists had again refused an armistice. This impasse gave the enemy ample opportunity to repair the damaged supply routes and use other ways to fortify their front lines. No end appeared in sight. The struggle by each side to prevent the other from building up to push over the *de facto* border would continue.

That ongoing struggle would include continued air interdiction—first as an intensified Operation Strangle and then as another operation to replace it. The interdiction was pounding much of North Korea to pieces, greatly increasing the suffering of its people who were now mere pawns in the game, victims of the Chinese wish to prolong the war. Unfortunately, the UN air forces had no other option. Unable to take the attack to the Chinese over the Yalu, the only way to stop a major Communist build-up was to attack the supply lines in North Korea to the front line.

Operation Strangle was doing this, and on a large scale. Communists supplies were still getting through, however, thanks to a massive repair effort that rebuilt key bridges and roads virtually overnight and kept the supply lines open. The effort was immense; by one estimate a million workers were employed to keep just the North Korean railways open.[4]

With no alternative, UN planners fought fire with fire and increased the interdiction effort during 1952. Under current plans, 77 Squadron would not contribute to that interdiction, but these were changing times. Few of their plans so far had stayed current for very long—especially when there were good reasons to change them.

Ron Susans soon found such reasons. He quickly saw that their degraded role had badly affected morale and the Meteor's full potential was not being exploited. He was well placed to make such judgements, with previous command experience and time flying the Meteor during a specialist fighter course with the RAF earlier that year. As well, having just left Fighter Operations at RAAF HQ, he was familiar with the Korean situation.

The RAF course had included ground attack with rockets and proved the Meteor to be a stable and effective platform for such work. He also knew the aircraft to be suitable in other ways, being easy to maintain and, with two engines and a tough airframe, able to absorb punishment and still fly. Furthermore, the makers, Gloster, had been stressing the Meteor's suitability for ground attack and had produced the necessary modifications. All 77 Squadron needed to do ground attack was a supply of weapons, some simple aircraft modifications and official approval.

That done, the squadron would have a challenging role and the Meteor would again be making a proper contribution. Morale, hopefully, would then also improve. Having satisfied himself that the logistics system could provide the required weapons, he discussed his ideas with the squadron pilots and Group Captain Tony Carr, now the 91 Wing commander at Iwakuni. He then contacted General Frank Everest, the man in charge of the USAF 5th Air Force and with it 77 Squadron's tasking.

The timing was opportune. General Everest was unhappy with 77 Squadron's limited contribution and was considering moving them to Suwon to make way for a Sabre squadron in Kimpo. He welcomed Ron Susans' proposal to turn the Meteors into a ground-attack squadron that could fly precision strike with rockets and cannon, and approved the new role. The attack missions would be in addition to air defence patrols and standbys and would focus on special targets selected by 5th Air Force operations staff. The rate-of-effort was agreed at a challenging 750 sorties the first month and 1000 sorties per month thereafter.

On return, Ron called the pilots together and told them the news. 'Butch' Hannan, the Operations Officer, prepared lectures on strafing and rocket-firing and they set about learning these skills, which were new to most of them. The necessary rocket bits and pieces were sent from Iwakuni and four aircraft were fitted with rocket rails, allowing each aircraft to carry eight rockets and a full load of 20-millimetre cannon ammunition. The four cannons could be loaded with a mix of high-explosive and armour-piercing shells, and normally were.

Things moved quickly and on 8 January—just two weeks after he had arrived in Korea—Ron Susans led Butch Hannan, Phil Hamilton-Foster and Dick Wittman (experienced men all) to attack a water tower at Chongdan, to the west of Kaesong. The attack left the tower leaning and seriously damaged, proving the Meteor to be an excellent rocket platform well suited to the new role. The only negative was some ground fire that hit Butch's aircraft, reminding them that ground attack was dangerous work—especially in the now static war that gave the enemy ample time to put in effective defences around potential targets.

Having proved the concept they then began fitting rocket rails to more aircraft and getting ready for further sorties, confident of the way ahead. The wheel had turned full circle. They had come to Korea to do ground attack and eighteen months later were doing it again. The difference now was that the Mustang had given way to the Meteor with its extra attack speed, ability to climb quickly away from targets, tough airframe and two robust engines. These factors gave the Meteor better survivability against current anti-aircraft systems than the

Mustangs of the USAF and the South African Air Force, which were now experiencing ever-increasing losses from more and better enemy weapons.

As always the squadron did other work too, including fighter-bomber escort and air defence with standbys and airborne patrols. This meant that they were never entirely out of the air war, although in early 1952 MiG activity slowed down for a number of reasons. Firstly, main North Korean airfields seriously damaged by B-29 night bombing were still not all adequately defended or under repair. Next, an improved Allied GCI system was making better use of available Allied fighters.

Also, Communist leaders, apparently judging the recent intense MiG activity not worth the high cost, had begun a partial pause. Airfields near the Yalu were maintained and defended, but those well within North Korea were no longer repaired when bombed. And the overall MiG effort was cut back so pilots could be given more training before they went into combat. MiGs still flew, of course, and usually in good numbers, but less aggressively than previously, and so without their earlier dominance.

During the lull the UN forces stepped up the interdiction effort and honed close-support skills in preparation for the next, virtually inevitable, enemy offensive. The Communists too used the time well. By April–May 1952 a Communist GCI-equivalent radar system was covering much of MiG Alley, and reinvigorated MiG pilots were acting aggressively once more.

As a result, 77 Squadron began its Meteor ground-attack operations in a very fluid air environment. This made regular intelligence updates an important part of the thorough mission preparation now standard in the squadron. New arrivals were introduced to this fast-moving world with comprehensive briefings on things like the enemy's order of battle and capabilities (especially anti-aircraft weapons) and search and rescue arrangements if they were shot down. The potential dangers of the very busy airfield were also stressed and airfield and safety procedures (especially if returning with weapons 'hung up') were covered in detail.

Col King arrived in these times and recalled directions that also included:

> Radio discipline ... no chatter. No flying on an empty stomach ... you will not skip breakfast.[i] Wear your regulation gear in flight. String vest, warm underwear, thick gabardine trousers, warm shirt and flying suit. American combat boots with rubber snow shoes firmly laced over and 38 mm service revolver secure and, of course, the 'Mae West' life-jacket.

Tasks were received the previous day at about 4.30 p.m. Planning began soon after for maintenance staff to ready and arm the aircraft and for pilots and operations staff to prepare for the mission. Some preparation was general and some was mission-specific. In the briefing room, Col tells us,

> there was a large relief model of the whole of North Korea, perhaps fifteen feet square. We spent much well-used time intent on that model, memorising the rugged landscape with its steep-sided valleys. Particular attention was paid to the snaking MSRs [Main Supply Routes]—our main hunting grounds ... For the most part we were leaving the MiGs to the Yanks ... but occasional clashes occurred.'[5]

All pre-flight briefings covered intelligence, relevant meteorology, IFF settings, airfield status, weapons and fuel loads, emergency and alternate airfield states and a host of other information, with specifics for either air defence or ground attack. Briefings always finished with the minimum fuel needed to return to base, known as 'Magpies', and synchronising of watches.

---

i   A contemporary joke defined a fighter pilot's breakfast as 'a cigarette and a slow look around the airfield', which sometimes drew a laugh, but did nothing for blood sugar levels and other important physiological things their task demanded.

These briefings usually lasted 30 minutes or more. Thorough debriefings on return added to squadron knowledge and the UN intelligence picture. For many missions, pilots spent considerably more time in individual preparation, briefing and debriefing than in the air.

Throughout the rest of January they flew a number of ground-attack sorties and began flying airborne patrols from Kimpo instead of sitting on tarmac alert at Suwon. The airborne patrols were mostly in the Haeju–Singye region about 100 kilometres northwest of Kimpo near the coast and well over the border. The patrols were flown in pairs, began half an hour before dawn and lasted until half an hour after dark. As patrol time-on-task was usually less than an hour, 30 or more individual flights per day were often needed.

Chiefly from these airborne patrols, they flew 769 sorties in January and 1005 in February. A useful number of ground-attack sorties were also flown. The pace for the Kimpo maintenance crews was hectic, fixing, testing, refuelling and rearming aircraft. At one point, no tankers were available and the refuellers worked 48 hours straight refuelling from 44-gallon drums. Some losses and damaged aircraft reduced the numbers available, making the maintenance task more difficult. Nevertheless, throughout January–February 1952 serviceability rates were seldom below 90 per cent and during the last three days of February 142 missions were flown.

Iwakuni maintenance people were also kept busy, doing major servicings and readying eight new Meteors recently arrived on HMS *Unicorn* which needed to have their corrosion inhibitors removed and other work done. Battle damage repair was an ongoing task and would be for as long as the Meteors did ground attack. Tactics minimised time in the target area, but the sheer amount of ground fire, even if poorly aimed, meant that hits were inevitable.

Two vulnerabilities were soon apparent. The Meteor's ventral tank carried additional fuel on the underside of the aircraft. Aerodynamically much better than the more common drop tanks, it was also much more costly and was usually only jettisoned for safety reasons. Its placement made it vulnerable to even small-arms fire. An empty tank still contained fumes which could ignite if hit by ground fire. On a number of occasions the resultant fire spread to the aircraft before the tank could be jettisoned, with fatal results. The other problem was that, unlike bombs that fell away under the aircraft, rockets streaked ahead and on detonation could throw debris up into the aircraft's flight path.

This could be a serious problem and on two occasions Ron Susans was surprised to see his rocket heads whizzing past overhead as he climbed away. There was also the chance that a target might explode just as the aircraft overflew it, and this happened in one case. Tactics were designed to minimise the associated danger. A dive angle of between 25 and 30 degrees was used and a release height of above 300 metres AGL—but when you deliberately fire explosives ahead of you onto your flight path, there is only so much you can do to avoid flying though the aftermath.

During rocket attacks, Meteor pilots could also fall victim to the inertia that prevents fast-moving aircraft from quickly changing direction. This was always a factor but was most evident when the aircraft carried extra weight, such as a full ventral tank, which added about 10 per cent to aircraft weight and adversely affected the Meteor's responsiveness, turning ability and dive recovery.

Thus, with a full ventral tank an aircraft took longer to pull out of a dive than an aircraft without the extra weight. Pilots had to plan their attacks accordingly. Training and experience helped, but every attack was different, if only subtly so, and key decisions were often made while under fire. As a result, dive recovery was at times not only a trap for young players; experienced pilots could also be caught out if they failed to allow enough for the weight of extra fuel or weapons.

But as always, the biggest threat was from ground fire and it accounted for Mark Brown-Gaylord and Bruce Gillan in separate incidents, both on 27 January 1952. Mark was hit by ground fire, but what followed is something of a mystery. Thirty minutes after takeoff, he radioed that he had been hit and lost his airspeed indicator and altimeter but was not otherwise seriously damaged. He was not heard from or seen again.

Bruce Gillan was on an armed reconnaissance mission with five others and had just strafed Chujin airfield. He was heading towards another target when he called that he had been hit on the starboard side and was trying to make base. He pulled up and headed southeast towards Kimpo and made no further radio calls. His aircraft began to lose height and trail smoke. Allan Avery flew alongside the Meteor and saw that there was no one in it and the seat was gone—he had ejected.

In both cases they looked for parachutes, but the snow-covered ground made spotting a white parachute very difficult. Having stayed as long as their fuel allowed, they returned to base. Neither pilot was ever seen again. They were both classified as killed in action, bringing the total of pilots killed or captured in Korea to 22.

Shooting down an enemy aircraft was no doubt cause for celebration from those being attacked, but in this case the Communists made the most of it via their strictly controlled news outlets. George Odgers tells us that: 'Moscow Radio broadcast news of the shooting down of the Australian pilots and attributed this result to ground fire from guns of the army of the Korean "People's Government."'[6] In a war as politicised as this one had become, propaganda was more important than ever.

Indeed, the Communists had become masters of the 'big lie' and used it with practised ease in Korea. One claim was that the Americans had used biological warfare by dropping infected insects into North Korea and China, and another asserted germ warfare, which led to General Ridgway being tagged the

'Bacterial General' by Communist supporters when he took over NATO after Korea. Again, access to Soviet records in recent times has proved both claims completely false, although they were widely believed at the time by Communists and their many sympathisers in the West.

Another 'big lie' compared Communist prison camps to 'Swiss holiday camps' when they were in fact very brutal. Torture was commonplace and death a daily event. As many as 12 000 ROK and 6000 US POWs died in Communist prison camps.[7] But such was the quality of the propaganda that even when the facts emerged, support for Communism barely waned among Western theorists and stayed strong into the 1980s.

The squadron pilots, on the other hand, had almost daily reality checks of the yawning gap between Western theory and Korean reality and so saw the propaganda for what it was. It remained part of the background noise, but they had many bigger and more immediate problems to deal with, including the consistent killer: ground fire. Always a worry, it was even more dangerous now than in their Mustang days.

With much of the war fairly static, the Communists had been able to build good defences around likely targets. As before, the ground fire came from purpose-built radar-controlled anti-aircraft guns, light arms like machine guns and rifles, and everything in between. And as always, being predicable was deadly and they dived in on targets with different approaches and made quick getaways in as many ways as possible.

'Flak traps'—the fake targets positioned to draw aircraft into hidden anti-aircraft guns—were still being used and were not always easily spotted in the short time available. The wide range of targets didn't help, providing plenty of scope for deception. In these times, Col King found that

the types of targets assigned us were quite variable and included storage and barrack buildings, ammunition dumps, camou-flaged revetments, anti-aircraft gun-posts, general military fortifications, factories and mine buildings. Locomotive sheds, fuel depots, and all other railway installations received our enthusiastic attention. When returning from rocket missions we would search for likely targets. Fast moving, low flying aircraft had many successes in surprising the enemy troop concentrations before they could take shelter. Vehicles along the main supply routes were prime targets and sometimes exploded under the impact of our 20 mm shells.[8]

His description of his first mission gives some feel for the physical and emotional factors involved. On each attack, as his leader

recovered from each strafing dive I was intrigued to see sheets of steamy vapour envelope the wing surfaces and vortices curling behind his wingtips as he pulled the machine into a tight climbing turn. In time I came to realise this was a common sight with high speed attacks, as pilots hauled their aircraft into gut-wrenching pull-outs ...

Setting course in a tight orbit we looked down on the untidy aftermath of our activities—towers of smoke rising from a dying inferno of cars burning like torches in the morning sun.

On return he 'arrived home with my first bullet hole and my first stirring of guilty conscience. Those were my introductory 'shots in anger' but there was no anger. Perhaps 'anguish' would be a better word—no one likes to kill.

Like the Mustang pilots before them, they found that attacking people in the open could be emotionally difficult. Even if the people were the enemy, or obviously helping the enemy, attacking them often produced feelings seldom experienced from attacks on buildings and machines like trucks, tanks and aircraft. And always, the flying could be physically demanding as well as emotionally challenging.

The Meteor was not fitted for 'G suits' that apply pressure to the lower body and help a pilot withstand the 'gut-wrenching pull-outs' Col King mentions or the manoeuvres of aerial fighting. All the pilots could do was tense their bodies, especially the thighs, to reduce the pooling of blood into the lower body and legs that drains blood from the head and causes 'blackout'. In air-to-air work this could make a pilot vulnerable or result in an opportunity lost. Pulling 'G' could be tiring work and two sorties in a day were usually enough to aid a sound night's sleep and three to guarantee one.

Unless MiGs were encountered, the airborne patrols were usually not as physically demanding or dangerous as ground attack, which continued to take its toll during February. Butch Hannan was the first victim that month. While leading four Meteors on a strike he was hit in the ventral tank and began streaming smoke. He headed for home, but the fire spread and he had to eject, which he did safely, only to be lost in the white, snow-covered mountains.

Ray Taylor and Phil Zupp began an immediate search. While investigating what looked like a distress panel, Phil was hit by ground fire that shattered his canopy and buckled his goggles as the round ricocheted around the cockpit to finally lodge near the instrument panel. His face was peppered with fragments of glass, Perspex and metal, which produced a good deal of blood but no serious damage. An ex-World War II commando, Phil stayed calm, flew back to Kimpo[9] despite his injuries and went on to complete 201 missions. They flew patrols in the area all day and alerted rescue services, but to no avail and Butch became a POW, and the 23rd squadron pilot killed or captured in Korea.

In just two weeks they had lost three pilots, but they kept at it, busy on airborne patrols and attacking enemy facilities and supply systems whenever tasked to do so. As always, trucks were targeted, but increasingly in smaller numbers as the interdiction efforts bit. But on 14 February their luck was in when a large convoy was found in a ravine. Wally Rivers (now back on another tour) and three others[ii] attacked in company with two USAF Mustangs. They made full use of their rockets and cannon fire, destroying 28 vehicles and damaging eight others without serious damage to any of the UN aircraft.

Richard Robinson was not so fortunate only two days later when he became the second squadron pilot shot down in February and the 24th lost in Korea. He was hit while attacking a target in the now familiar area near Haeju and began to climb with his ventral tank on fire. The Meteor was tough but in this case his luck was out, the tail section of his aircraft broke up and it crashed into a hillside and exploded. He was not seen to eject and was assumed killed.

These were testing times for the squadron, with high sortie rates, dangerous work and fatalities; but morale remained good, helped greatly by the fact that Ron Susans had led from the front on arrival and continued to do so. In a six-month tour as CO he did 110 operational sorties, 100 of which were rocket and strafing missions into North Korea, mostly against heavily defended targets.

Always ready to innovate, he did the first operational trial with the napalm rocket developed at RAAF Williamtown in Australia and further tested in Korea. The rocket was developed to overcome the need to fly slow and straight over a target to deliver conventional napalm. Ron's operational trial on 8 February against a North Korean barracks block was disappointing due to the relatively small amount of napalm, but the rocket was later used with success against more combustible targets—despite unrefined ballistics that saw some rockets fly wildly off-target.

He also maintained close relations with the tasking staff at the 5th Air Force and visited them regularly, on one occasion accompanied by his Operations Officer, a hard-to-obtain bottle

---

ii   Zupp, Hamilton-Foster and Hill.

of Scotch and a wish for more of the action. Once there, a signal arrived stating that 600 Chinese troops were camped near Yonan, just over the border near the west coast. Having persuaded the 5th Air Force taskers that they were the men for the job, they rushed back to Kimpo and got things moving.

The strike had to be made before dusk, and some frantic activity followed to get twelve aircraft armed and airborne in time. They arrived in the area with just enough light left to see their target. The rocket attack lasted only 90 seconds for all twelve aircraft, producing an impressive fireworks display in the gathering gloom and doing considerable damage. Tracer flashed past them as they attacked and two were hit by ground fire, but all returned safely to Kimpo, which was only eight minutes' flying time away. Things could happen fast in the jet war and this fine example of surgically applied air power took less than an hour from start-up to shut-down.

The pattern of operations of the first two months continued into March and April, but with more attack sorties and, as fate would have it, four more fatalities and an end total of 28 pilots lost in Korea. The first was Ian Cranston, who on 9 March was hit during a second rocket pass and caught fire before he could eject.

Then, on 30 March, Lionel Cowper died in a burst of flames, probably because he was hit by ground fire. Col King was there and wrote that 'little black puffs and flickering lights were part of the local scenery' and that 'I vividly recall a great sheet of flame tumbling across the countryside …'[10] Next to go, on 13 April, was the experienced Max Colebrook, who was hit in the ventral tank by ground fire. He jettisoned the tank, called that he was heading home, but never arrived.

All such deaths were tragedies for the individuals, their families and friends, but Bill Purssey's death on 22 April was especially so. Unlike most of the others, he was not a career RAAF pilot. He had flown with the RAAF in World War II in North Africa with the 'Desert Harassers' and then in Italy before resigning at the end of the war to study medicine in Brisbane. When Citizen Air Force squadrons were formed in the main capital cities in 1948 he joined 23 Squadron in Brisbane and flew Mustangs at weekends and on yearly camps as a part-timer.

Knowing they needed experienced men, he re-joined the permanent air force in mid-1951 to fly in Korea. He was on his 110th and last mission attacking buildings near Chinnampo when hit in the ventral tank by light anti-aircraft fire. On fire, he was advised to jettison the tank, but the wing burnt though before he could do so and, although he ejected, he was killed. His mother accepted his posthumous DFC on behalf of the family at Government House in Brisbane some months later.

At such times it is not surprising some men become superstitious or believers in fate. Jim Kitchenside was selected for the Chinnampo mission and was twice strapped in ready to go. On both occasions his aircraft was unserviceable and the second time Bill Purssey took his place. Sheer luck, destiny or a guardian angel can all explain Jim Kitchenside's good fortune, but all produce speculation that can affect morale if left to run unfettered. Ron Susans seems to have known this and acted accordingly, for the record shows consistently good morale despite the squadron's travails.

The high activity rate also helped, keeping everyone busy and allowing little time to mope around feeling sorry for themselves. Some were up before dawn for air defence patrols and others were flying ground attack, which along with the rest of the interdiction effort was doing considerable damage. It was not, however, permanently cutting key roads and railways, which the industrious enemy was repairing almost as fast as they were damaged—albeit with huge effort.

In response, in March Operation Strangle was replaced by Operation Saturate, aimed at doing greater damage to fewer targets. It concentrated on severely damaging short lengths of railway line, selected for their importance and low level of defences, making them difficult to repair. Follow-up night bombing then disrupted repair gangs. The initial success was high, but the enemy soon responded. By the end of April, all significant railway lines were well defended and the MiGs—reinvigorated by the lull in activity and some extra training—were back with their old aggression.

The USAF fighter-bombers flying Saturate missions now faced ground fire on every attack and an air threat from the resurgent MiGs. If Saturate was to continue, the fighter-bombers would have to be protected from MiGs. In May, the squadron found itself again flying to protect bombers; combat with MiG-15s would almost certainly follow.

Their tasking was fighter sweeps, mostly at 15 000 to 25 000 feet (about 4500 to 7500 metres) out over the main supply routes (MSRs) which were still getting priority treatment from the bombers. At this height the Meteors were well matched to the MiGs and actually did quite well against them, beginning with an encounter on 4 May when John Surman and Ken Murray were attacked by two MiGs while patrolling near Pyongyang.

John Surman later described what happened next, saying that:

> I was flying wingman to Ken Murray. We saw nine MiGs above us. They broke and two came down to us. One cut across in front of me and started firing on Ken. He gave me a perfect target, dead ahead. I fired and hit him. I must have hit the pilot as he didn't take evasive action. I pulled out about thirty yards from him and broke away, otherwise I would have run into him.[11]

John Surman was a December 1951 graduate of the first course from the RAAF College formed in 1947.[iii] Four days later his coursemate, Bill Simmonds, also tasted success on one

---

iii   Which later became the RAAF Academy until being absorbed into the Australian Defence Academy.

of the busiest days in the squadron's history. In the biggest single attack since the war began, 485 fighter-bomber sorties concentrated on an important supply depot at Sunan (now the site of Pyongyang airport). To help protect them, the squadron that day flew 70 fighter sweeps along the MSRs and near Sunan.

Bill Simmonds was in a flight of four Meteors attacked by MiGs from behind and learned of the attack when tracer bullets passed over his wing. His attacker then passed only a few metres below him and Bill was able to get behind the MiG and in a good attack position. He fired a long burst and hit the aircraft, which went into a spin. The pilot abandoned his aircraft and parachuted down as his aircraft crashed to earth. That made it two MiGs in four days, without loss—and from a squadron taken off air-to-air work because their aircraft couldn't match the MiG-15.

The result was very satisfying, but in some ways remarkable when the training of the newer pilots is considered. The shortage of pilots suitable for 77 Squadron was now acute and pilots were being rushed through their Meteor familiarisation courses to replace losses—eight so far this year—and returnees on completion of their six-month tours. Bill Simmonds later recalled that with Meteor training

the Mustang pilots who returned to Japan for their three months conversion were mostly quite experienced and all flew about 50 hours during their transition. On the other hand my group's flying time averaged less than sixteen hours. We had only four live air-to-ground gunnery and rocket firing sorties. There was no air-to-air gunnery, very little instrument flying and no night flying. Furthermore, when we joined the squadron there were no pilot attack instructors to brief us on air combat tactics—useful knowledge should we ever be confronted by MiGs.[12]

Dick Cresswell had identified the need for good instrument flying skills, and night-flying competence, before the first conversions to the Meteor were done. These had been built into the course he, Des Murphy, Max Scannell and others had put together, along with some rudimentary fighter work. Even then, their first meeting with MiG-15s had found them wanting—by a fair margin. The need was clearly for more and better preparation on the Meteor before going into combat, not less, but the abbreviated training Bill Simmonds described was now the norm and had been for some months.

John Parker was a few weeks ahead of Bill in the new-pilot pipeline. In later life he became a RAAF fighter combat instructor and a Department of Civil Aviation examiner of airmen, experience that drove home to him how poorly prepared he was for combat in Korea. In 1998 he provided some written comments for *The Part-Timers* with which he 'relates how he was sent into combat in Korea with only 30 hours on Vampires, 21 on Meteors, very limited experience in air/ground or night flying and no instrument training on type. Four of his course mates fought in Korea with similar scant preparation and died there.'[13]

There was no single reason for this sad state of affairs. Some blame rests with the post-war indecision by government that left the RAAF unable to set up comprehensive operational conversion units until 1950 and later. But most blame must lie within the RAAF, with those who sent such poorly prepared pilots to Korea and those who then whisked them through the abbreviated Meteor course. By the last year of war, better training was in place in both Australia and Iwakuni—but that was too late for men like Bill Simmonds, John Parker and their contemporaries who had every right to expect better of their air force.

And there was more to it than just the operational training. Unlike the present-day RAAF, there was no formal continuation training during the squadron's time in Korea. Nor were there qualified instructors at the squadron who periodically checked standards and corrected weaknesses and faults, especially among the new pilots. As a result, bad habits and weaknesses sometimes went undetected and unchecked.

How much this inadequate preparation and supervision contributed to the fatality rate cannot be quantified—it may have been only one factor among several that tipped the scales against some unlucky pilots. All that can be said for sure is that eight pilots lost in four months did not go unnoticed back in Australia. Dick Cresswell, now in charge of Fighter Operations in RAAF HQ, discussed the matter with the current RAAF chief, Air Marshal Sir Donald Hardman (RAF), who agreed to give Korea every priority.

This eventually led to a high-quality fighter Operational Conversion Unit (OCU) in Australia and other changes, but little could be done to give 77 Squadron more and better prepared pilots in the next few months. This inability owed much to the Australian Government agreeing to commit 78 Wing Vampires to Malta to release RAF assets there and, to a lesser extent, to ongoing commitments in Malaya. To plug the widening gap, in April 1952 the RAF was approached to supply pilots 'on loan' to 77 Squadron. They agreed and soon arranged for six pilots to arrive in Korea by July that year and more to follow later in the year.

The high losses of men and machines also began to worry the government, especially as the war seemed to have stalemated and a single undermanned Meteor squadron was unlikely to affect the outcome one way or the other. The Minister for Air, William McMahon, concerned by the human and financial costs, suggested the squadron be withdrawn, but was overruled by Prime Minister Menzies who was anxious to protect the strong ties with the US reflected in the recently signed ANZUS treaty.

Politically sound, though otherwise questionable, this decision meant that the squadron would fight on to the bitter end—whatever the cost and however useful their contribution. In the short-term that meant more of the same—a mixture of fighter patrols and ground attack, which now included more armed reconnaissance with pilots continually operating in the same area to get to know it. Obvious changes to roads, buildings and such could then be quickly noted and the sites of anti-aircraft gun pits plotted and avoided.

But like all tasks that required low-level flying and attacking ground targets, armed reconnaissance always carried the risk of ground fire. On 15 May, Donald Robertson, another classmate of John Surman and Bill Simmonds, became yet another victim to this scourge. Col King was number four and wrote:

> Quite early in the dive, well before normal rocket release height, Robertson's aircraft, which was ahead and below me suddenly rolled to the right, simultaneously discharging its rockets. In anguish I watched the Meteor plummeting earthwards, waiting and desperately hoping to see an ejection seat. The aircraft continued its lazy rolling motion terminating in a great ball of orange flame on the edge of the village ... Another fine young man was gone![14]

Less than a month later, on 9 June, John Surman too was killed. He was attacking trucks sighted during an armed reconnaissance mission when his aircraft was seen to 'mush' into the ground during an attack run and begin burning on impact. John was most probably another victim of the inertia of a fast-flying jet and the need to initiate the pull-out earlier than in a slower aircraft—knowledge acquired either by training or experience. Their deaths brought the total of pilots killed or captured to 30 in two years of combat.

On 26 May, Ron Susans finished his tour and was immed-iately awarded a DSO (Distinguished Service Order) for the great work he had done refocusing the squadron and restoring their spirit.[iv] He handed over temporarily to his deputy, Squadron Leader Bill Bennett, a World War II veteran who had won a

---

iv   Ron Susans continued on in the RAAF and retired as an Air Vice Marshal CBE DSO DFC.

DFC flying in Europe and spent time as a POW.[v]

He was replaced in July by Wing Commander J.R. 'Congo' Kinninmont, who had flown Buffalos in Malaya during the Japanese invasion and won two DFCs during the Pacific War. The squadron did not lack combat experience from the men at the top, even if they were somewhat short of line pilots as they awaited the first group from the RAF.

Also in May 1952, General Ridgway was replaced by General Mark Clark as UN commander-in-chief. General Clark wasted no time adopting a new air strategy that had emerged from a study of the disappointing returns for effort achieved by air interdiction so far. The new strategy, Air Pressure, aimed to apply air power more for political reasons than purely military ones. In simple terms, from now on the strategy was to achieve the greatest damage for the lowest cost and the highest political impact on the enemy.

Air superiority, interdiction and ground support were still the three main tasks, but with greater emphasis on maximising the cost to the enemy while minimising their own losses. Air superiority—a prerequisite for some of the missions planned—would be mostly provided by the increased numbers of Sabres now available. This would have a sting in the tail. Less able to control the air, the Communists concentrated more on ground-based anti-aircraft systems, with obvious implications for ground-attack squadrons like 77.

Another important change was more big missions with large aircraft numbers hitting important targets with high political as well as military impact. The first of these was a series of attacks on North Korean hydroelectric stations—until now left alone because of their high value if Korea was unified, or failing that, for post-war reconstruction. These attacks took place in late June and knocked out 90 per cent of North Korea's power generation.

---

v   Bill Bennett won another DFC in Korea. On retirement he wrote popular books about fighting in the air which featured heroic 'goodies' and dastardly villains but which took the ordinary reader convincingly into the pilot's seat.

North Korea virtually lost power for two weeks and the power available to northeast China was cut by some 25 per cent. Follow-up bombing kept the power generation low for weeks.

Militarily it was a great success, achieving the greatest damage for the lowest cost and reducing the enemy's ability to wage war. Diplomatically, things were less agreeable. Many UN Allies, including Britain, had not been consulted and protested, seeing it as an escalation of the war and a provocation to China. From then on the Air Pressure strategy was curtailed and never able to achieve its potential in what was very much a limited war. Critics of Allied air power achievements in Korea should always remember the Yalu River was not the only boundary to air operations.

With time, the squadron also flew more aircraft per mission, at times sending sixteen Meteors at a time to the same target. Some of this change reflected the new strategy and some the fact that the MiGs had been resurgent since April, seemingly emboldened by the recent diplomatic row among the Allies and the limits placed on Allied air power. Squadron missions included air patrols, usually in company with Sabres, as far north as the Chongchon River to engage any MiGs pushing southwards. Initially using fours, with the increased MiG numbers Meteor and Sabre flight numbers were soon changed to eight.

It was now summer again, at times still and hazy, at other times hot and humid with thunderstorms, torrential rain and the unpredictability that went with them. The haze came with stable high-pressure systems that trapped all kinds of air pollution under an inversion layer—including, at times, dust from the Gobi desert. It often so reduced visibility that only the ground directly below the aircraft could be seen. Everything further from the aircraft was obscured by the haze, making map reading and flying about the airfield so difficult it sometimes restricted operations.

In most cases bad weather was just a nuisance, increasing navigation or approach problems but all part of the day's work.

But when it blocked out your airfield, bad weather could be just as big a threat as MiGs or ground fire—as Wes Guy found out on 13 June when he led a four back to Kimpo, only to find that an unexpected large sheet of low cloud had just moved in over the airfield and their alternate, Suwon, to the south.

The cloud base was 200 feet (60 metres) and the local gremlins, who often appear at times like this to bedevil aviators, had rendered the GCA radar unserviceable. It would have to be a visual approach. Wes ordered the flight into line astern and headed for the Han River, about 30 kilometres away, which was not fully clouded in. Once there, he descended very low over the river and reduced to circuit speed so he could work his way back to Kimpo and arrive at the right speed to land immediately, fuel being at a premium and burning at a rate of 7 gallons (about 30 litres) a minute.

The ragged cloud base was so low the gap between it and the undulating ground was sometimes barely enough to squeeze through, but they got to Kimpo, left flaps and gear until the last minute to eke out their fuel, and all landed safely. The refueller told them later that there was almost no fuel in any of their tanks and one aircraft was actually empty. They had landed with a minute's fuel left at most. Someone said: 'Far better to be down here wishing you were up there, than up there wishing you were down here' and that pretty well summed it up.[15]

In July 1952, they continued with the now usual mix of ground attack and air patrols. Ground-attack missions were the more common of the two, continuing to hurt the enemy but just as dangerous as ever. Once more, experience counted for nothing and on 8 July Ken Smith was killed while leading a rocketing mission and became the 31st squadron pilot lost in Korea.

Air patrol was proving safer when done as part of something big like the 11 July bombing attack on Pyongyang. As the North Korean capital, Pyongyang was an acceptable political target under the now restricted Air Pressure policy. It was treated accordingly, with a range of targets bombed and 1254 sorties flown, including air patrols by the Meteors along the Chongchon River and ongoing Yalu patrols by Sabres, which were now enjoying good success against the MiGs. Considerable damage was done, with only three UN aircraft shot down by ground fire and none by MiGs—thanks to the air patrols.

August arrived, marking a year of Meteor operations and 8000 missions flown, and a continuing high tempo of operations. Interdiction was still important and on 4 August Eric Ramsay led a successful attack on a North Korean supply point. Like many other valuable targets, it was very well defended.

They flew through heavy and accurate fire, taking damage but not casualties. Despite the heavy fire, Eric calmly directed the mission to an effective end before leading them home.[vi] Once more, squadron pilots had cheated death, but the very next day death won. Slim Haslope was killed on takeoff, for reasons unclear, the 32nd pilot killed or captured in the war.

Unlike the summer weather, operations were reasonably predicable now with strikes against fixed targets, armed reconnaissance along supply routes and air patrols supporting major strikes, usually in company with Sabres. As a result, when the first batch of RAF pilots arrived mid-year, the squadron had a fairly stable *modus operandi*. Doug Hurst,[vii] a Pacific War Kittyhawk pilot, arrived at about the same time to work as the 'A' Flight commander. He remembers the RAF men[viii] well, recalling the much-needed boost to both numbers and experience they brought with them and the ease with which they fitted in.

Like many others, Doug had not previously flown jets and did 40 hours on Vampires in Australia at the training unit set up to prepare pilots going to 78 Vampire Wing in Malta. This

---

vi   This mission was an important contributor to his award of a DFC.

vii Group Captain, DFC, retired in Canberra. No relation to the author, but a friend of some years.

viii The first six were John Mellors, Martin Chandler, Butch Hoogland, Jim Cruickshank, Olaf Bergh and Bill Holmes.

was now standard procedure for pilots posted to Korea who needed jet training. His Iwakuni Meteor training too was now better matched to the squadron's tasks, with 22 training sorties covering the basics of flying the Meteor and operating it in combat.

Some pilots benefited more from this preparation than others, depending on experience and individual approach. Things like instrument flying still varied pilot to pilot and remained patchy, but in general the operational training was now better than when people like Bill Simmonds and John Parker were 'whisked through' in short time. And it stayed that way until Meteor conversions in Iwakuni ended.

As 'A' Flight commander, apart from flying Doug was in charge of mission planning once tasks came in and the allocation of pilots to tasks. They flew mostly in fours and eights, or pairs of eights for the bigger tasks. Flight leaders were, as Dick Cresswell had established, still chosen by experience and suitability, not by rank, and he happily continued this practice.

One NCO pilot Doug nominated to lead was Tom Stoney, 'a good pilot' and an excellent map reader, even in winter with snow-covered ground.[16] Good map-reading skills were especially important on dawn and dusk patrols looking for vehicles not yet hidden for the day or just emerging for the night. These missions involved either pre-dawn takeoffs or night landings, but were worth the extra effort as they often caught vehicles unawares in the half light.

Special skills were needed at the best of times, but without men like Tom Stoney who could find their way around snow-covered territory in the half light the winter missions could not have been flown. Even without snow, parts of Korea were poorly developed with few easily identified man-made features and no unique topography. In these parts, one valley with a village often looked very like the one next door, and the best map reader was usually chosen to lead in these difficult areas.

This 'best man for the job approach' meant that Doug (then a flight lieutenant) sometimes flew as flight leader, and sometimes was led by NCOs like Tom Stoney and Col King—who on one occasion led a flight including the CO, Wing Commander Congo Kinninmont, and his deputy, Squadron Leader Ian Parker.

When not under radar control, knowing where you were was a big part of leading and Col recalls that on return, Ian Parker, who was examining the big relief map intently, asked him where they had been. Ranks still counted, but flying experience counted more, and as a professional pilot Ian Parker happily asked questions of juniors when he didn't know something.

A week later, Ian was to lead a sixteen-aircraft mission against an ammunition dump in an unfamiliar area. Col was to fly as his wingman to help with the navigation, but after long discussion with the CO, Ian reversed the arrangement, put Col in charge and flew as his wingman. There was no loss of face deferring to a more experienced man, even if that man was a sergeant and you were a squadron leader. Having learned what he needed to know, that afternoon Ian Parker led another sixteen aircraft into the same area.

This commonsense arrangement served the squadron well throughout the war. At Kimpo it was helped by the fact that all the pilots ate and relaxed in the same USAF officer's mess, despite some still not being commissioned. To do so the NCOs simply removed their rank and wore no rank in the mess. The Americans knew this and happily accepted the arrangement. In Iwakuni, 77 Squadron pilots still used their respective messes and most of the NCOs had two sets of uniforms—one with rank for Iwakuni and one without for Kimpo.

The mission Col King led against the ammunition dump was one of their most successful in August. The target was a nondescript building in some rugged country. This made it something of a navigational challenge as it had to be located quickly to avoid circling around and alerting ground defences. This was done and they attacked out of the sun, diving in at a 30-degree angle and each firing eight rockets at 1200 feet (360 metres) AGL.

The 128 rockets hit hard, starting a ripple effect that suddenly turned into a gigantic explosion, sending a column of smoke high into the air. The dump was completely destroyed, but when they returned that afternoon to a nearby target the column of smoke was still rising, providing Ian Parker with a reassuring navigational fix.[17]

Sixteen aircraft missions against higher-profile targets were now reasonably common. A typical example was the attack on important Communist barracks and administrative buildings at Chaeryong, some 50 kilometres inland from Haeju. The usual heavy curtain of gunfire greeted them and Olaf Bergh, one of the RAF pilots, was hit. He ejected, almost horizontally but successfully as his aircraft tumbled to earth and was seen to land safely. Unable to help, the others marked the position and returned home. A planned attempt to locate Olaf the next morning had to be abandoned due to weather. He was later confirmed a POW and the 33rd pilot lost to the squadron.[18]

The RAF pilots were now an important part of the squadron and would remain so until war's end. John Price[ix] was one and the RAF Historical Society[19] in 2000 published a talk he gave about his experiences in Korea. Apart from the winter weather, the squadron John discussed was very like the one the unfortunate Olaf Bergh had just left. It was typical not just of the RAF experience, but that of all squadron pilots and tells us much about those times. He arrived 'in snow clad Iwakuni on Christmas eve' in company with fellow RAF pilot Bertie Booth and:

After a Meteor 7 ride and eight solo air-ground gunnery/rocket sorties ... a Gooney Bird [C-47 transport] took Bertie

---

ix   Retired in 1986 as a RAF Air Vice Marshal, CBE OBE MID. Two years after Korea
      he served with the RAAF again with 2 OTU and 75 Squadron at Williamtown.

and me to Kimpo … The tour on 77 consisted of 28 days operations followed by two days rest & relaxation back in Iwakuni. Mid-way through the tour one had a 14 day break in Japan. The tour for USAF aircrew was 100 missions; the RAAF had … a tour length of six months, during which one could fly between 100 and 140 missions … On 77 one never knew which mission marked 'going home'—the CO came up to you after a trip and said 'Right, pack your kit'—and that took much of the stress (a word not then in vogue) out of the final days on the squadron.

Like everyone else John had intensive briefings and kept 'a personal "flak" map showing the location of all known A-A[x] sites … I spent hours making and updating mine and never flew without it.' He found there was

considerable emphasis on never flying on the same heading or at the same height for more than a few seconds, apart from when tracking a target, of course, so as not to give A-A gunners a steady aim. Radar laid A-A had started to appear and as their predictors seemed to be programmed for Meteors that flew about 50 knots slower than was the case, there was powerful incentive not to lag … and get caught by the undershoots.

And like everyone else, he found there was much to keep abreast of, and before flying:

one self-started mission briefing with a check of the master flak map and updated one's personal map as necessary … A quick look at the general intelligence picture and a look at the latest survival gen[xi] followed—those friendly off-shore islands had a habit of changing hands and it would be embarrassing

---

x   Anti-Aircraft.
xi   'Gen' is a slang term for specialist information or intelligence.

to walk ashore shouting 'I'm here' only to find a different landlord. Then, about an hour before take off, the formal briefing started …

On a road-recce we operated in pairs, going around the route at about 8000 feet [2400 metres] to be above light flak and below the heavy stuff, looking for targets and attacking them as quickly as possible after sighting to reduce their chances of escape and to get in before that flak got organised. Having made an attack, you never went around again …

Strikes by 16 Meteors were quite impressive … the first eight aircraft attacked with 60lb SAP[xii] rockets to shake-up the target and the rest followed with napalm-headed ones to get fires going … In an effort to add more pressure on the supply routes some road-recces were flown at night if the weather and moon-phase were co-operative. Ground attack at night in areas with 8000 ft mountains was certainly character forming.

The route back to Kimpo passed through several 'gates' to ensure safe passage, as the IFF was not always reliable. Often the Meteors were short of fuel and intentional single-engine recovery and landing was a well practised technique. A squadron tractor or two would be at the end of the runway ready to tow in the 'empties'. Kimpo was a busy place … Air traffic handled it all with great skill and an air of competency, which was most reassuring after a hairy mission.

John finished his talk with mention of the six RAF pilots killed in Korea and the fact that he was 'somewhat put out … later when a senior RAF officer said to me: "Of course, the RAF pilots only got to 77 when the war was over and you just sat around for six months." ' If that RAF officer had asked any of the RAAF pilots there at the time about the RAF contribution, he would not have made such an ignorant comment.

---

xii Semi-Armour Piercing, with delayed fusing of the High Explosive element.

As it happened, for 77 Squadron the last few months of the war were very busy and their most dangerous time in Korea. In the preceding months, the war had stalemated, that is true, but the fighting had certainly not stopped and did not do so until the very end of the war. Much of this fighting resulted from the continuing failure of the peace talks—which had gone nowhere since late summer 1952—encouraging both sides to fight for the best bargaining position.

The talks were held in Panmunjom, a little to the east of the old capital Kaesong—and today the Joint Security Area of the DMZ. Flying near Panmunjom was prohibited and the designated restricted area was invariably called 'the holy land' by pilots.

In yet another attempt to persuade the Communists of the futility of continued war, a massive 'All UN Air Effort' was mounted against Pyongyang on 29 August 1952, involving 1407 sorties from carrier- and land-based aircraft. Airfields, power stations and factories were bombed and strafed and special attention paid to key government buildings, including the Ministry of Rail and Transport headquarters. The bombing was continued at night by B-29s. Meteors flew their now familiar air patrols along the Chongchon River to protect the 420 fighter-bombers flying that day. In all, it was an impressive show of strength and the MiG force, obviously impressed, was rarely seen.

As always, the weather could prove as dangerous as the enemy. On 1 September Alan Avery was flying the squadron Engineering Officer, Eric Johnston, from Iwakuni to Kimpo in a twin-seat Mk7 Meteor in company with Randy Green in a Mk8. Near the coast of Japan they met a very violent thunderstorm that damaged both aircraft and threw them out of control. Randy Green recovered control and limped back to Iwakuni.

Allan and his passenger tried to bail out—there being no ejection seats in the Mk7—but probably hit some part of the aircraft and were killed. Their bodies were later found on the Japanese west coast with unopened parachutes. Allan had finished his tour and was in Iwakuni doing test and ferry flights before returning home. Their deaths bought the total of pilots lost from the squadron to 34 and the overall number to 35.

Well-defended targets, which now often included troops, continued to make life hazardous during September. Three missions in particular got a warm reception but succeeded despite it. The first was on 6 September when Bob Turner led a successful attack in bad weather on a large troop concentration well defended by anti-aircraft weapons. Aircraft were hit, but there were no losses.

The next was on 22 September when Doug Hurst led a rocket attack against a dangerous build-up of enemy troops in northwest Korea. They too were met by intense and accurate anti-aircraft fire, but with a well-planned, low and fast attack they destroyed the target without loss. Two days later, 'Blue' Philp led an attack on a headquarters complex in mountainous country and by thorough planning and good navigation successfully located and destroyed the target.[xiii]

In all three cases the virtues of navigation that allowed quick target identification followed by a rapid attack were demonstrated. With anti-aircraft defences continually strengthening, a single fast, elusive attack with the flight closely spaced became pretty much the standard operating procedure for the rest of the war.

Always a political war, by now it was even more so with strategies on both sides aimed more at political than military objectives. Diplomatically, disagreement over management of prisoner repatriation was still a major barrier to an armistice. The Chinese Government was still insisting on getting them all back, whatever the prisoners wanted. The UN, naturally, wanted to give the prisoners free choice.

---

xiii The three missions described here each contributed to DFCs awarded to Bob Turner, Doug Hurst and 'Blue' Philp.

In September, in an attempt to break the deadlock, the UN had put forward three alternatives to facilitate prisoner exchanges reflecting prisoner wishes. The Communists rejected all three alternatives and on 6 October 1952, as if to drive the point home, launched an offensive which caused heavy casualties on both sides.

The American public, who were already tired of the war, faced presidential elections and elected General Dwight Eisenhower, who had promised to go to Korea if elected and, by implication, find a way to get America out of the war. He did so as president elect, talked with ROK President Syngman Rhee, General Mark Clark and other military people and created the clear impression that he was determined to end the bloodshed.

This was all very promising, but it was only the start of Eisenhower's initiatives, and the fighting continued as winter closed in for the third time in the war. The mix of US and British cold-weather gear now worn made life easier, but immersion suits—essential for survival of more than a few minutes in the local seas—were still not available and arrived only in the last months of the war. Now used to cold-weather operations, they continued on much as before, mounting spirited attacks against well-defended ground targets and suffering the inevitable hits and losses.

The toughness of the Meteor got some pilots home with damage that would have downed most other aircraft. On 29 November 1952 Ken Godfrey was one of 12 pilots attacking a heavily defended supply area in North Korea. Heavy snow made target identification difficult, delaying the attack and alerting the AA defences as they circled and descended below 10 000 feet to get a better look.

During his attack dive Ken: 'felt a severe thump on the left side of my aircraft and I knew I had been hit by flak. A 37-mm high explosive anti-aircraft shell had exploded in my port engine. With my aircraft yawing and rolling savagely to the left, I used hard right rudder, full trim and aileron and reduced power on my right engine to regain control as I pulled up steeply to gain as much height as possible. I got to about 8000 feet and found that my left engine was dead. My radio, airspeed indicator, altimeter and some other instruments were also out of action.'[20]

By now the savage treatment of prisoners was well known, and determined not to fall into enemy hands, Ken headed for home rather than ejecting from his severely damaged aircraft. The damage increased the drag on the left side of the aircraft, increasing the yawing effect and requiring full rudder at all times despite the reduced power on the right engine. This soon tired his right leg—the rudder, remember, was not powered—and when resting the leg he had to further reduce power on the right engine to maintain control.

As a result, he continually lost height and arrived at Kimpo at only 200 feet. With no radio he was unable to declare an emergency. Finding the airfield vacant—a very rare event— he simply dropped the wheels and did a straight-in flapless approach (because of damage to the left flap) and landed. The brakes worked only briefly and to stop he ground looped the aircraft, finishing up just off the end of the strip.

Two Americans came out in a control-tower jeep and helped him out of the cockpit. Somewhat incredulous, one said: 'Hey, buddy, how the hell did you get this thing back?'[21] This was a good question as Ken had flown with great skill and enjoyed more luck than most. Some feel for the damage can be gained from the photo in the picture section, which shows Ken inspecting the damage to the port engine nacelle after landing.

Not everyone was so lucky, and soon after Ken's close shave Jim Cruickshank, one of the RAF pilots, was killed while attempting to eject after being hit by a MiG. Then, on 24 December, Fred Lawrensen was killed by ground fire. And by 20 January 1953, when Congo Kinninmont handed over to his replacement, Wing Commander John Hubble, another RAF pilot, Bertie Booth had failed to return from an attack mission.

These recent losses no doubt gave John Hubble cause to reflect, but he would also have learned of some significant achievements along the way. January 1953 marked two and a half years of war, in which time the squadron had flown over 15 000 individual sorties, 11 000 in Meteors. Life continued delivering a mix of good and bad. In mid-February Don Hillier, an experienced World War II pilot, was killed in action.

Just what happened is not known. Ross Glassop[xiv] was there, having recently replaced Ian Parker as second-in-command. A Pacific War Kittyhawk pilot and Milne Bay veteran who later won a DFC in Bougainville, he was now

> flying No 3 in a section of four aircraft led by Don. Our task was to carry out a reconnaissance of a road in North Korea … It was to be Don's last mission before returning home. After dividing into pairs and commencing our task it wasn't long before Don's No 2 called me and said he had lost his No 1. We immediately stopped our task and raced down to help look for Don. When our fuel became critical we returned to base and reported his loss … We searched for days but never found his aircraft.[22]

And then some good news; on 17 February, Ken 'Black' Murray flew his 320th mission, beating Wally Rivers' total of 319, before going on to fly a Korean War record of 333 missions—an amazing achievement from both men. They knew each other well, having flown together at Williamtown and during their first Korean tour. Both were obviously highly skilled, and Wally recently wrote of Ken that 'I class him as a top pilot and friend.'

Bill Collings[xv] was flying with Ken on the historic 333rd

---

xiv Ross flew 77 missions before the war ended, mostly as leader, was awarded a bar to his DFC, retired as a Group Captain and now lives on the Gold Coast.

xv Became an Air Vice Marshal, DCAS and the Logistics Commander before retirement in Canberra.

flight and still smiles at what he considers was 'the perfect squelch'. As they neared Kimpo they heard an excited USAF pilot call up for permission to do 'a hundred mission fly past'— the traditional 'beat up' flown to celebrate the end of a USAF combat tour. Ken's following request for 'a three hundred and thirty-three mission fly past' was met with momentary silence and no doubt put things in perspective for the young American and everyone else listening in.

In February they also received a very welcome Christmas card from Gordon Harvey—the first communication from him since he was shot down on 19 January 1951. He was still a POW and now being treated less brutally than during his early days, which included 45 days kept in a small pit, and endless indoctrination sessions.

From late 1952 on things improved and he was able to write letters, which he did, telling the squadron he was well and asking for some personal matters to be dealt with. He concluded with 'I hope fate will not be as unkind to you as it has been to me', but this in no way detracted from the lift in spirits his card evoked.[23]

March 1953 brought with it much that made history for the war and the squadron. On 5 March, Stalin died and the new Russian leaders decided to end the war, take a peace dividend for the Soviet Union and ease tensions with the West. Knowing Mao wanted to keep the war going, they offered him generous aid and arms, but he resisted. In response, the Russians ended support for the propaganda about biological and germ warfare (which they believed was unsupportable anyway) and brought other pressures to bear.

Later in the month, Kim Il-sung and his North Korean colleagues—desperate to stop the destructive bombing of their country—agreed to a proposal from General Clark to exchange sick and wounded prisoners. Soon after that, Chou En lai, the Chinese Foreign Minister, made a public statement recommending that when hostilities ceased, prisoners who did not wish to be repatriated should be sent to a neutral country for processing to ensure a just solution.

This indicated that in China too, senior figures like Chou also wanted to end the war. Mao held out for more than four months, but in the end faced the reality that he could not continue without strong Russian diplomatic and military backing and full support at home, and an armistice was signed on 27 July 1953.[24]

But that was yet to come. In March, these political machinations had no immediate affect on the war, which continued with its past intensity on the ground and in the air. Interdiction was still needed, especially against truck convoys, and on 16 March the squadron found their biggest convoy of the war. Bob Turner spotted it while on a dawn road patrol with Dave Irlam just south of Wonsan on the east coast where he had attacked some trucks the previous evening. To their surprise, a line of some 140 trucks stretched almost 5 kilometres through a narrow pass between steep cliffs and sheer drops.

Bob and Dave attacked and blew up the two lead trucks and then attacked the last four, disabling them and trapping the entire convoy in the pass. Bob then called in Vin Hill's nearby Meteor section (of four) and radioed for more help from Kimpo and US units. A number of UN aircraft joined in throughout the day.

Bill Collings remembers that it was hilly country and he was hit by a ricochet from his own fire as they flew all day attacking the trapped trucks. The ricochet hit his aircraft on the nose, reduced his speed by 20 knots and damaged the air conditioning.

Jake Newham[xvi] was flying with John Hubble, the CO, and they 'joined in the gunnery circuit; as one pair expended ammunition another arrived. USN aircraft then joined in the act … This sort of target was ideal for the Meteor's 4 x 20mm cannon armed with a 1:1 mix of high explosive and armour piercing shells.'[25] Many trucks were set alight and some exploded. Jake also noted

---

xvi Became Chief of the Air Staff and an Air Marshal AO.

that: 'We were fortunate that the trucks were in an area where there were no mature anti-aircraft installations.'[26]

Quite a few enemy troops had, in fact, climbed the hills and fired down on the Meteors as they flew below them, inflicting small-arms damage that clearly came from above. One bullet hit an oil tank with serious resultant damage to the engine, but all aircraft got home safely. The Meteors alone destroyed 24 trucks and at least 90 were destroyed or damaged overall in this memorable attack.

The same day Ross Glassop had a tread separate from a retread tyre just before lift-off, jamming the wheel and preventing it from turning. Forced to abandon the takeoff, he finished up in the overrun area with a damaged front wheel and the port engine full of foam squirted in to stop it. It was a close shave, but he was uninjured and the aircraft was repairable.[27]

But as always, luck was capricious. Ten days later, on 26 March, Peter Chalmers flew into a flak trap during a high-speed dive in mountainous country and died. The 'bait' for the flak trap was a truck cleverly painted onto the road and from then on the squadron no longer attacked lone trucks. At high speed the Meteor tended to nose over and bank to the left if not prevented from doing so by the pilot. Peter was almost certainly killed by the flak because his aircraft rolled left and dived after it was hit.[28]

The very next day their fortunes changed again when George Hale downed one MiG and possibly downed another. He was flying to the southeast of Pyongyang with David Irlam and had descended to about 10 000 feet (3000 metres) to patrol a supply route when he spotted a MiG chasing two US RF-80s a little below them. Although his gunsight was not set up, he dived in to attack and saw another MiG behind the first.

Turning hard left, he fired at the second MiG and missed. Another came up beside him, so he turned towards it, popped the speed brakes to slow down and once behind it fired, hitting it a number of times but not downing it. Realising he was in for a fight, he jettisoned his ventral tank, readied the gunsight and prepared to fire his rockets to get rid of them.

The scene became a little confused as other MiGs joined in. Dave Irlam called that he had been hit and George found that despite the actual speed of events, for him things now seemed to be happening in slow motion.[xvii] Finding himself behind two MiGs, he fired two rockets between them, almost hitting one. This split the two, so he chased one, only to see two more appear on his left. He got in a shot on one, causing a massive white explosion (almost certainly large quantities of fuel), but the aircraft kept flying and the two MiGS applied power and climbed steeply away.[xviii]

Dave Irlam didn't see his attacker and was hit hard. He'd lost an engine and with over 100 holes in his aircraft headed for home, reaching Kimpo safely with the aid of radar guidance and a touch of luck. John Hubble had seen Dave being attacked and joined in, along with his wingman, Sainsbury 'Sainy' Rees, who hit a MiG but believed he only damaged it. After analysis, George Hale was credited with a kill and a probable, and became the last Australian to shoot down an enemy aircraft in air combat.

The combat report was drawn up accordingly, but later changed when John Hubble and Sainy Rees claimed that George had mistaken two MiGs for RF-80s and no USAF Shooting Stars were involved. That evening two USAF RF-80 pilots[xix] came into the mess, each armed with a bottle of Scotch, looking for 'the Aussie who saved our hides today'. The combat report was duly amended again for the second time that day.[29]

Also in March, No. 30 Transport Unit, formed out of 77 Squadron's original transport flight run by Dave Hitchins, became No. 36 Transport Squadron, equipped with additional

---

xvii At the debrief he assessed the whole encounter had lasted about 10 minutes, but on reflection believes two minutes was a much more likely time.

xviii Given the sizeable fuel loss the MiG would not have flown for long and it was assumed it would not get back to base. This was later confirmed post-war.

xix The RF-80 pilots were Charles Abbey and Jim Schnider.

C-47 Dakotas. This provided welcome extra numbers to the small force which had always been stretched, sometimes to the limits. By war's end, the RAAF C-47 units had carried some 100 000 passengers, 60 000 tonnes of freight, and more than 12 000 medical evacuees from Korea to Japan.

In a nine-month tour, crews usually flew over 900 hours, in virtually all weather—thanks to a determination to get the job done and GCA radars that allowed them to operate in weather that would otherwise have grounded them. While not officially part of 77 Squadron once the transport flight became No. 30 Transport Unit, their origins and the close links maintained throughout the war made them an important part of the 77 Squadron story in Korea.

The comments about prisoner repatriation made in March by North Korean officials and Chou En lai encouraged a resumption of the Panmunjon peace talks on 26 April. Hopes for quick action soon faded, however, as the Communists adopted their usual tactics of finding endless reasons not to give ground or to consider all options. It looked like more of the same, and in many ways it was, but in fact only some of the Chinese leadership wished to keep fighting. Everyone else at the table had more to gain by stopping than by going on. The UN delegates knew this and the Air Pressure campaign was stepped up to apply pressure in the only way available.

One Air Pressure aim was to prevent the Communists getting enough supplies to the front lines to mount an offensive. UN interdiction was doing great damage, seriously restricting the flow of supplies, but the Communists, with a massive repair effort, were still moving significant quantities. The only way to control the flow was to increase further the UN interdiction efforts. For the squadron, this meant continued concentration on MSRs and more attacks on enemy troop billets, villages and supply centres during April–May.

It also meant that the already dangerous anti-aircraft environment would simply get more dangerous as the static war allowed defences to be progressively improved around potential targets. Many aircraft were hit and returned to base, at times just making it. With a combination of luck and skill Jack McCarthy flew a damaged aircraft home and landed it with forward stick against back trim; a difficult and potentially dangerous thing to do.[30]

In particular, main MSRs were now all well defended and were becoming more so. To contain the growing danger, on 28 March 1953 John Hubble issued a CO's directive that: reconnaissance flights would be at 8000 feet (2400 metres) or above; known defended targets were not to be attacked; and targets were only to be attacked once. He also directed that efforts should aim to saturate the defences and maximise use of natural elements, like terrain and the sun, to gain surprise.

These directives are reflected in John Price's earlier description of his operations. Another RAF pilot, Don Smith,[31] wrote that in practical terms the directives meant that 'for road recce missions, we were instructed ... not to attack anything less than three vehicles and they had to be moving. We were told that because there were none of their own aircraft operating at low level or from North Korean airfields, any aircraft seen by North Korean or Chinese soldiers would be an enemy one, and they were to shoot at it.'

The directives definitely reduced the risk, but the innate dangers of ground attack remained, and three RAF pilots—Jim James, Jim Dollittle and Taffy Rosser—were killed during combat operations in the first half of 1953. Jim James went in the now all too familiar way, and Jake Newham saw him 'hit just after roll in. His aircraft exploded into dozens of small pieces. I vividly remember cowering low in the cockpit as I flew through the debris and the flak concentration. An orbit did not note anything the size of an ejection seat.'[32]

Don Smith knew Jim Dollittle well and 'was behind him when he followed his rockets in—either he got hit or misjudged his height. It was a 16-aircraft napalm strike made at dusk on

17 May '53 and what we initially thought was a secondary explosion was him hitting the target. The radio check-in after the attack revealed we had lost another super bloke.'[33]

As always, some hits downed aircraft and at other times badly damaged aircraft got back home. There was always an element of luck, but good flight leaders helped reduce the luck factor. In these last months Jake Newham pays tribute to Ted Jones, 'an older pilot ... who had a knack of map-reading and commonsense. His ability was quickly recognised by squadron executives and he led many operations, particularly when the target was difficult to find. On these strikes he put a lot of effort into planning.'[xx]

Interestingly, the fact that the CO and flight commanders deferred to Ted's skill elevated these men in the eyes of the junior pilots, who saw the decision as good leadership.[34] Indeed, through men like Ted and sensible leaders, the 'best man for the job' approach continued in the squadron not just until the armistice, but well beyond it.

The end may have been in sight for some, but the squadron had to prepare to fight on for as long as it was needed and innovation continued. In April, an AN-6 gun camera was fitted to Jake Newham's aircraft. It gave better resolution than the standard camera and Bill Murphy remembers that it 'afforded faster frame rates and more flexible exposure control. It also had a longer overrun time once the rockets were released. The downside to this was that in order to achieve maximum effect, Jake had to fly tail-end Charlie in line-astern attacks—not the best spot when the North Korean gunners started to get the range.'[35]

This was actually even more dangerous than Bill implies. Jake later wrote that

---

xx   Ted was awarded a DFM (a DFC equivalent medal for non-commissioned personnel) went on to fly the Jindivik (a pilotless drone then under development) and later on had a successful career with Qantas.

I was expected to roll in a little higher than those ahead and hold a steady dive from 8000 feet [2400 metres] with the camera running. This day the camera behaved well and we got good film which was used for PR. Later John Hubble commented that my camera work had deteriorated. My response went along the lines of 'flak makes me nervous and I feel better jinking along with the rest of the team' … I was stuck with the chore for too long for my liking.[36]

Tail-end Charlie was always the worst place to be, but when you were denied the ability to fly evasively, it was even worse. His efforts produced good results, however, which Bill Murphy says created 'some very good film. A couple of times we put together footage of the best strikes and screened it in the Ground Crew Club; this went over pretty well.'[37]

By May, most of the Meteors were fitted with modified rocket racks and could now carry sixteen rockets instead of the previous eight. This not only increased their firepower in general, but greatly assisted John Hubble's direction to saturate defences when possible. It also produced an even more impressive display with multi-aircraft attacks. With multiple aircraft strikes in summer, however, only the lead aircraft carried sixteen rockets in order to give the wingmen better performance when formation flying.

On 5 June 1953, John Hubble handed over command to Wing Commander Al Hodges, who quickly found that the war was still on. The Allied interdiction efforts were in full swing, and on the day the new CO took over, the squadron attacked an enemy anti-aircraft training battalion on the Chinnampo peninsula and destroyed twenty buildings. The strike went well and was soon followed up by a strike on a chemical factory and an electrical power station, which produced spectacular results, with vivid greens and other bright colours among the usual flames.

These were typical missions, flown by a squadron that was

as good and as busy as it had ever been. The same was true for the rest of the UN air effort, but it was still not enough to fully counter the even more effective Communist repair efforts. By mid-June, the Communists had enough supplies at the front line to mount an offensive and proceeded to do so. Allied air and ground efforts were intensified and in June the squadron flew its highest daily sortie rates of the war. Robert O'Neill tells us that: 'The squadron's operational support systems had also continued to develop' and that on one day

in ten hours from 9.45 a.m. eighty-eight sorties were flown. The ground crews laboured under a hot sun, stripped to the waist, to replenish returned aircraft while pilots waited to fly back to North Korea. Wing Commander Hodges flew five missions during the day and several other pilots flew four, spending, in the day, more then four hours over enemy territory.[38]

It was a very busy day for all, including the operations staff who were no doubt happy to see four aircraft depart on the 88th and last sortie. Ross Glassop led them, and when he, Sainy Rees, Peter Coy and John Price returned, the operations officer made a short speech and presented Ross with a bunch of flowers to mark the occasion.

The diplomats were talking in hopeful terms, but 77 Squadron continued to lose pilots. Des Nolan was killed on a training sortie on 11 June when the tail section separated in a tail chase. On 15 June, Don Pinkstone was hit by ground fire in a gunnery dive and miraculously survived an ejection over North Korea below the limits of the seat. A rescue helicopter found him but was driven off by intense enemy fire and he became a POW.

Two days earlier Bill Monaghan had almost suffered the same fate. He had already had a close call, arriving home with a load of railway ballast in his ventral tank,[39] and this time was hit while attacking a cable station. Don Smith was there too and later wrote that

> it was a noteworthy trip because it was at extreme range and we all dropped ventral tanks before the attack. The target was a fairly large square building, about five storeys high, standing in the open. The first rocket impacts created a massive dust cloud and the building disappeared. Bill was a couple of aircraft ahead of me and I saw him disappear into the dust, and emerge saying he had been hit and lost an engine.[40]

Two 37-millimetre cannon shells did the damage, but Bill's aircraft was still flyable with the good engine going strong. Being near the coast, he headed for the open water, hoping for a helicopter rescue should he need to eject, or a landing on one of the Allied islands (mentioned earlier by John Price) using a beach as an emergency airstrip. The flak was still heavy and as he flew out over the water he could see the shrapnel falling in bunches into the water below him.

A US amphibian rescue aircraft appeared and began flying along beneath him, straining to keep up despite his much-reduced speed and providing welcome reassurance of help should he need it. He reached Paengnyong-do[xxi] Island, got the wheels down, landed on the beach and was greeted by Allied personnel placed there partly for that purpose.

The US Marines captain in charge greeted Bill with an impressive salute. When Bill pointed out that he was only a sergeant the captain replied: 'Sar, any man who flies one of those goddamn rocket ships gets my salute' and saluted again.[41] A C-47 flew in a new engine and engine-change crew and flew Bill out. The engine was fitted and two days later Bill did a beach takeoff and flew the Meteor back to Kimpo.

At Kimpo it was fully repaired, but within days it was hit and

---

xxi Also spelled Pyongman-do.

badly damaged. Although still flying, it could not be controlled well enough to land. The RAF pilot, John Coleman, managed to fly it back over Allied territory and eject, to be later picked up by helicopter and returned to Kimpo.

His escape well illustrates the importance of ejection seats and helicopter rescues in Korea, which singly and in combination saved many pilots from death or capture. Without these two factors, 77 Squadron's losses would have been even higher than they were—probably by a considerable margin.

Unfortunately, the ejection seat could not—as seats now do—fire the pilot out safely from ground level, and on 16 July Len McGlinchey[xxii] was killed when his Meteor, with full rocket load and full fuel, crashed on takeoff. Bill Collings was his formation leader and, along with some others, believes that a faulty tyre had shed some tread and knocked the mudguard into the flap, locking it down. The locked-down flap then caused the aircraft to roll and crash when the flaps were retracted after takeoff.

The squadron was then using retread tyres prone to tread shedding—as pilots like Ross Glassop had already experienced—and this fact supported the theory.[42] There was, however, also the possibility of engine failure and this was given as the most likely cause in the crash report, pending further investigation.[43] Don Smith, who was first on the crash scene, also believes engine failure was the more likely cause. But like the others there at the time, he adds that we will never know for sure what caused the crash.[44]

Whatever happened, the unlucky Len McGlinchey was the last pilot killed during the war. Along with other Australian casualties whose remains could be recovered, he was buried in a canvas bag in what is now the United Nations Memorial Cemetery at Pusan. This was standard practice; few bodies were returned to Australia from overseas in those times. There was

---

xxii Squadron Leader Leonard Thomas McGlinchey, a weapons officer on attachment from 91 Wing.

no established unit to deal with burials, and Ross Glassop and Bill Collings were tasked with escorting the body to Pusan and overseeing the burial—and did so on their way home to Australia.[45]

Many reasons are given for the final ending of the war, but in simple terms the time was finally right. For the key participants, the costs of continuing could now no longer be justified if peace could be arranged instead. For China, their disastrous cost/benefit equation was emphasised by the latest Communist offensive, which had cost them 72 000 lives for very small territorial gain and was soon stalled. Even for someone as indifferent to casualties as Mao, this was an obvious waste of life and effort.

As July proceeded, an armistice became more and more likely. Air power had again played a major role in containing the offensive, but in a bizarre twist was now more in demand than ever. Armistice conditions were expected to limit the introduction of new forces into North Korea post-war, giving the Communists a powerful incentive to have the best possible air force *in situ* when the armistice took effect. UN leaders, wishing otherwise, kept their aircraft very active up until the last minute, attacking North Korean airfields and aircraft on the ground.

As a result, some UN aircraft flew right up until the armistice took effect at 10 a.m., Korean time, on 27 July 1953. No. 77 Squadron's activities dropped off in the last weeks as many targets were well to the north and so outside the Meteor's radius of action. They continued to attack targets within range, however, and flew their last operational combat flight of sixteen aircraft on 20 July over North Korea. Appropriately, four aircraft were flown by RAF pilots, who had become an integral part of the squadron in its last year in Kimpo.

The final mission was a familiarisation flight of four over the border on the 27th, bringing the squadron's grand total of sorties in the Korean War to 18 872. Their time in Korea was not yet over, however. There was no certainty that the armistice would hold, and they would need to stay on until things stabilised, continuing to fly out of Kimpo and later Pusan before finally leaving Korea in October 1954.

7

Aftermath

The fighting had stopped, but no one was confident it would not erupt again, and 77 Squadron flew to keep their skills alive. Left to their own devices, they drew up a training program concentrating on ground attack and trials of new tactics based on recent combat experience. They also joined in exercises with the USAF and practised rapid reactions to alerts. This kept them reasonably busy, but the hectic pace of combat operations was no longer needed and a lower rate of effort was used until the squadron left Korea in October 1954.

In September, a North Korean pilot arrived unannounced in a MiG-15 and landed in order to defect, causing great excitement and reminding them that things were still tense. Bill Monaghan moved quickly to have a look, but the cordon of MPs the USAF threw around the aircraft formed even quicker and ordered him away. The aircraft was soon test-flown by USAF test pilots, including Chuck Yeager,[i] who came back to Kimpo and briefed the pilots on the MiG's performance.

Flying in Korea continued to present challenges. In

---

i A World War II veteran and the first man to break the sound barrier.

December, a Meteor caught in wake turbulence crashed without injuring the pilot and was written off. In May 1954, two Meteors, now operating out of Kunsan, collided in mid-air, destroying both aircraft and killing Pilot Officer H. Andrews, the last 77 Squadron pilot to die in Korea.

In August and September 1953, the seven POW pilots were released at Panmunjom, the site of the armistice talks and now a Joint Security Area. As the squadron's executive officer, Neville McNamara 'was sent up to Panmunjom to meet fellows like "Butch" Hannan and Gordon Harvey who were being returned from captivity by the communists'.[1] The POWs had known for some time they would be released, but the process took time.[ii] In the interim the UN built special facilities to accommodate them on release.

The actual release was through a structure like a cattle chute. As the prisoners passed through it, anti-bacterial sprays were directed inside their clothes and de-licing sprays into their hair, after which they took off their prison clothes, showered thoroughly, dressed in clean clothes and walked out free men. Following that, they all went to the purpose-built facilities where they were served drinks and later an informal dinner, accompanied by a band. In all, it was, Neville McNamara recalls, 'very well organised' and a very pleasant way to welcome back the POWs.

All were hungry for news, especially about things like family and friends. This could not always be provided, but the occasion was otherwise an ideal chance for them to relax and enjoy the moment. With time, they spoke of their ordeals. Some of their stories were horrific. Gordon Harvey was the first released after 32 months in captivity. His first five months in captivity were the worst, being spent in a North Korean prison they called 'Pok's Palace' after the ruthless major in charge. They were up

---

ii   The POWs were not all released at the same time and Don Pinkstone was the last squadron POW released.

at 5.30 each morning, went to bed when night fell and were given two meagre meals a day of rice or sorghum and some weak vegetable soup.

In late April 1951 Gordon and two Americans escaped, but were captured after six days and treated so badly one of the Americans died. Gordon was placed in a 2-metre-deep hole in the ground for 45 days until the prisoners were moved to a Chinese camp near the Yalu River. There they were treated a little better physically, but had to listen attentively (or at least appear attentive) to political lectures for eight hours a day. As the peace talks got going, things improved enough that they had some free time and were eventually allowed to write three letters a month.

Ron Guthrie also spent three months with the North Koreans, who paraded him through the local villages and cross-examined him. Taken to Pyongyang, he escaped with an American and an Englishman, only to be captured and marched to the Manchurian border with 35 other POWs. The March took fourteen days and a third of the POWs died along the way from malnutrition and dysentery. Camps were organised according to rank and Ron was placed in the officer's camp at Pinchon-ni, where he met Gordon Harvey and later Vance Drummond and Bruce Thompson.

Food and clothing at Pinchon-ni were in short supply and were not supplemented by Red Cross parcels as the Chinese did not let them in. There was no mail throughout 1952. Later on, when a mail exchange was arranged, it depended on the whim of the Chinese guards and many letters were not delivered. The other Australians were in a different camp, but were treated in much the same way. The death rate in all the camps was high and the survival of all seven of the 77 Squadron POWs owes a good deal to luck and their strong personal resolve.[2]

The survival of their POWs brought home to the squadron how much luck there was in life and how the Koreans didn't seem to have any of it. South Korea had been freed, but much of it was now in ruins and the Korean people were separated into two countries. Millions had died and the bitterness ran deep; South Korea refused to sign the armistice and North and South Korea are still technically at war today. It had been, as Dick Cresswell had prophesised in 1950, 'a dirty war'.

But on the positive side, it had seen the United Nations stand up to aggression and had checked the spread of the particularly ruthless strain of Communism Mao was practising in China. It was a limited war, as all wars since have been, with geographical and political boundaries setting the military agenda. This frustrated some military commanders and aided the enemy by providing sanctuaries and limiting UN air power, but the political aims were achieved. The war did not spread, aggression was met head-on and the required (limited) victory was won.

And from the first days of the war, 77 Squadron had been part of that victory, helping demonstrate that Australia was prepared to play its part in opposing aggressive Communist expansion. To do so, in three years the squadron had flown almost 19 000 sorties from six different airfields; made a significant operational contribution, especially at the Pusan Perimeter; and destroyed 3700 enemy buildings, 1408 vehicles, 98 railway trains and carriages, sixteen bridges and at least five MiG-15s.

This was a proud record, but, as Alan Stephens tells us, perhaps their

greatest contribution to Australian security came during a meeting in the White House only three months after the war started. Since the end of World War II both the Chifley and Menzies governments had worked assiduously to convince the United States to conclude a 'Pacific pact' with Australia, convinced that the proposed treaty was critical to national security. The American response had, however, been cautious …

No. 77 Squadron's early success in Korea proved to be the key to overcoming American diffidence. Australian Minister for External Affairs Sir Percy Spender visited Washington in September 1950 where he was received by President Harry Truman. Only days before Spender's visit, United States Assistant Secretary of State Dean Rusk had expressed his 'warmest thanks and admiration' to Australian officials for 'the work of the RAAF in Korea' ...

President Truman reflected that goodwill. Spender was supposed to make only a brief formal call, but at the president's encouragement he took the opportunity to raise the subject of the proposed Pacific pact. Robert O'Neill has concluded that 'there can be no doubt' that the Truman/Spender meeting was a critical event leading to the Anzus Treaty ... In particular, O'Neill credited 'the high proficiency shown by No. 77 Squadron' as the main reason for the excellent reputation Australia enjoyed in Washington.[3]

That a single squadron achieved so much for its country, albeit indirectly, is remarkable and something of a bargain for Australia. For the RAAF, however, Korea was no bargain, with 35 dead and 58 aircraft lost, 44 of them Meteors. It was a high cost for a small air force, but in the long term Korea would be seen as a turning point for the RAAF.

When the war began the RAAF was stumbling along, with very poor government direction and too little knowledge of the adjustments needed to fully enter the jet age. Now, the lessons learned in Korea would transform operational training, and add practical combat experience to the CVs of many men who would shape the RAAF in future years.

Dick Cresswell was one of the most important early shapers. While head of Fighter Operations, he had visited the squadron in Japan and Korea during April–May 1953. While there he flew as wingman for Don Smith, one of the RAF pilots, and with some of the younger RAAF pilots and found some important gaps in RAAF training. The most notable of these were weak air-combat instruction and patchy instrument flying standards.

Operational Training Units (OTUs) had been set up in Australia in 1951, but there was clearly still work to do. In late 1953, Dick Cresswell was put in charge of the fighter OTU and left a lasting legacy. At Dick's funeral in December 2006, the then air commander, Air Vice Marshal John Quaife, a previous CO of 77 Squadron and long-time friend of Dick's, said that he

> was an instrumental player in the recovery of air to air training and of capturing the doctrine for squadron employment. As part of this effort, No. 2 OTU introduced formal training for Fighter Combat Instructors. The Fighter Combat Instructor's course remains a vital part of our force preparation to this day ...[4]

In doing so he drew on the knowledge of other Korean veterans. The example they set soon permeated the rest of the RAAF and has shaped its operational training and standards ever since.

Korea also reinforced the value of being able to examine all the facts. There is no doubt that the Meteor was a first-generation jet in a world transitioning to the next generation of fighters with their higher top speeds and better high-altitude performance. This fact is often used to support the common view that 'the Meteor couldn't match it with the MiG-15'. The complete facts, however, tell us this was not always so.

We now know that in its early days of war, the Meteor was opposed by elite Russian pilots operating in greater numbers and controlled by master tacticians sitting above the battle. In these early engagements five Meteors were lost and one MiG downed (although this was not known at the time). Later on, the Meteors fought on more level terms against the normal MiG force and shot down at least four more MiGs with no Meteors lost during combat. The Korean War Meteor versus MiG-15 scorecard was, in fact, a draw—five kills on each side and many damaged.

Ground attack cannot be scored this way, but two facts are

clear: the squadron performed very well in this role and ground attack became increasingly dangerous as the war progressed and target defences steadily built up. Eight more pilots were lost in the second half of the war than in the first 18 months, mostly to ground fire. Attacking with rockets, rather than dropping bombs, may have been a factor here. One who thinks so is Keith Williamson,[iii] a RAF pilot who flew with the squadron in the last few months of the war when ground fire was at its most lethal. In a contribution to an article on the Meteor,[5] he wrote that to fire the rockets

> the Meteor had to be flown steadily for a few seconds at the very time that it was most vulnerable to ground fire, and by mid-1952 the North Koreans and the Chinese were becoming very proficient at directing their ground fire against attacking aircraft. This, I believe, was the single most important reason for the high casualty rate suffered by 77 … in the ground attack role.

He then contrasts the Meteor rocket attacks with USAF dive bombers that

> turned in for their attacks from about 20 000 feet and released their bombs at a height that enabled then to avoid the worst of the anti-aircraft fire. Their casualty rate was low indeed, while the amount of high explosive delivered to their targets was much higher than that achieved by the Meteors … Notwithstanding all these difficulties, the pilots of the RAAF flew their aircraft aggressively, and, in doing so, they managed to establish a first class reputation for themselves while in Korea.

Wally Rivers, with the experience of 319 missions in Korea to draw on, agrees, pointing out that 'rocket attacks were low

---

iii   See later paragraph for personal details.

level against selected targets that were heavily fortified ... Fighter bombers had more potential.'[6] The RAAF too seems to come to such thinking by the third year of the war. During the last months, the then Squadron Leader Jim Rowland[iv] in Iwakuni was working on a bomb rack that was not used operationally because the armistice was imminent.[v] However, several trial drops proved that the prototype rack worked well, and had the war continued the squadron would have had the option to use bombs as well as rockets.

Whatever the facts, the good and bad of Meteor air-to-air and ground-attack performance were debated for years in the RAAF (and are still not entirely agreed by veterans). This ongoing debate stimulated thought and improved knowledge in both areas. Lessons learned in Korea flowed through into fighter and bomber lore, with many Mustang and Meteor veterans going on to senior ranks or simply sharing their combat experience in post-war squadrons.

Neville McNamara, 77 Squadron's executive officer in 1953, went on to be chief of the Air Staff and then chief of the Defence Staff and Sir Neville. Jake Newham too later became the RAAF's chief. Keith Williamson also commanded his service and is now Sir Keith and a marshal of the Royal Air Force. John Price (RAF), Bay Adams, Bill Collings, Bill Simmonds, Fred Barnes, Ray Trebilco and Jim Flemming became air vice marshals and quite a few made air commodore and group captain.

These men took the Korean experience with them through to executive levels. Others served in RAAF squadrons in the 1950s and 1960s, working as COs, flight commanders, instructors and mentors to younger men and passing on what was to be the RAAF's only fighter combat experience for the next 50 years. At an international level, many friendships made with USAF and RAF personnel endured, giving the RAAF

---

iv   Later Air Marshal Sir James Rowland, Chief of the Air Staff and then Governor of NSW.

v   Information provided by Jake Newham.

invaluable connections with two of the world's premier air forces and opening many doors to technology, training and knowledge until well into the 1980s.

Without question, by reshaping RAAF operational training and influencing so many important careers, Korea left a lasting and positive legacy for the RAAF. This is also true in reverse, and the legacy the RAAF left for South Korea has not been forgotten. In 2001, Dick Cresswell and other veterans went to Korea to help commemorate the 50th Anniversary of Commonwealth Forces participation in the Korean War. The centrepiece of the commemorative schedule was a service at the UN Memorial Cemetery in Pusan where most of the Australians who died in Korea, including 77 Squadron pilots like Lou Spence, are buried.

The Korean Government hosted the visitors, taking them to points of interest and into the schools. There, they were introduced to the students as men who had come from faraway countries 50 years ago to fight for our freedom, and to whom we owe the fact that we live in freedom and prosperity instead of in oppression and poverty like the North. This type of language has gone out of style in Australia, but it is still most apt in Korea. The students knew it and showed their gratitude however they could.

It was a moving time for everyone and Dick later told me that 'we spent a week with tears in our eyes' and a feeling of great pride for what they had done there. South Korea has not forgotten and nor should we. 77 Squadron fought above its weight, helped keep a grateful country free and did its own country proud as it did so. We will all be the poorer if they once more become the Forgotten Few and quietly fade into the mists of history.

Notes

1 To War

1. Milt Cottee, 'A Tour of Operations, No. 77 Fighter Squadron', unpublished writings, 2006.
2. Stephen Lund, 'Divided Nation' in 'Unfinished Business', *Weekend Australian*, July 26–27, 2003.
3. Steve Neal, *Harry & Ike*, Scribner, New York, 2001, p. 178.
4. Ibid.
5. George Odgers, *Remembering Korea*, Landsdowne Publishing, Sydney, 2000, p. 10.
6. Interview with Dick Cresswell, 8 December 2006.
7. Figures vary greatly with sources. These are drawn from Robert F. Futrell, *The United States Air Force in Korea, 1950–53*, Duell, Sloan and Pearce, New York, 1961, and Robert O'Neill, *Australia in the Korean War*, Australian War Memorial and AGPS, Canberra, 1985.
8. George Odgers, *Remembering Korea*, p. 10.
9. James Morris, *History of the US Navy*, Bison Books, London, 1984, p. 173.
10. Ibid.

11. George Odgers, *Across the Parallel*, William Heinemann Ltd, Melbourne, 1942, p. 7.
12. Milt Cottee, op cit.
13. Ibid, p. 7.
14. Incident account provided by Jim Flemming, 1 Dec 2006.
15. Milt Cottee, op cit.
16. George Odgers, *Across the Parallel*, p. 11.
17. Ibid, p. 18.
18. Figures vary with references. Those quoted reconcile veteran's memories of one front-line aircraft per pilot, plus a spare, with figures from Robert O'Neill, *Australia in the Korean War*.
19. Les Reading, 'Mustang', undated RAAF Museum Aerogram, provided by author.
20. George Odgers, *Across the Parallel*.
21. Australia, Belgium, Canada, Colombia, Ethiopia, France, Greece, Luxembourg, the Netherlands, New Zealand, the Philippines, Thailand, Turkey, Union of South Africa, the United Kingdom and the United States sent combat forces, and Denmark, Italy, India, Norway and Sweden sent medical units.

2 Iwakuni Ops

1. George Odgers, *Across the Parallel*.
2. Ibid, p. 34.
3. David Wilson, *Lion over Korea*, Banner Books, Belconnen, 1994, p. 13.
4. Notes provided by Dave Hitchins, 14 March 2007.
5. Milt Cottee, op cit.
6. Interview with Dick Cresswell, December 2006.
7. Description of the Suwon Incident based on information from George Odgers, *Across the Parallel*, David Wilson, *Lion over Korea,* and Alan Stephens, *Going Solo*.
8. Milt Cottee, op cit.
9. Interview with Jim Flemming, 24 January 2007.

10. Les Reading, op cit.
11. Lyall Klaffer, unpublished memoirs, provided to the author in January 2007.
12. Ibid.
13. George Odgers, *Remembering Korea*, p. 29.
14. George Odgers, *Across the Parallel,* p. 72.
15. Ibid, p. 73.
16. Milt Cottee, op cit.
17. Ibid.
18. Ben Evans, *Out in the Cold, Australia's Involvement in the Korean War 1950–1953*, Australian War Memorial and Department of Veterans' Affairs, 2000.
19. George Odgers, *Across the Parallel*, p. 70.
20. George Odgers, *Remembering Korea*, p. 32.
21. Ibid, p. 79.
22. Interview with Jim Flemming, 24 January 2007.
23. Ibid.
24. Ibid.
25. Norman Bartlett, *With the Australians in Korea*, Australian War Memorial, Canberra, 1954, p. 14.
26. George Odgers, *Across the Parallel*, p.78.
27. Lyall Klaffer's memoirs, op cit.
28. Bill Harrop's body was later recovered and buried in the UN cemetery at Pusan. Accounts of what happened to him in the orchard vary—this one is based mainly on Lyall Klaffer's unpublished writing.

3 Mustangs in Korea

1. Transcript of Australian War Memorial interview with Buster Brown in 1989, from a series printed in undated 77 Squadron Association newsletters.
2. Interview with Dick Cresswell, December 2006.
3. Lyall Klaffer, unpublished memoirs, provided to the author January 2007.
4. Interview with Jim Flemming, 24 January 2007.

5. George Odgers, *Across the Parallel*, p. 89.
6. George Odgers, *Remembering Korea*, p. 38.
7. Lyall Klaffer, op cit.
8. George Odgers, *Across the Parallel*, p. 33.
9. Notes from Les Reading, August 2007.
10. Transcript of AWM interview with Dinny O'Brien.
11. Ibid.
12. Transcript of AWM interview with Dick Cresswell.
13. Milt Cottee, op cit.
14. George Odgers, *Remembering Korea*, p. 44.
15. Milt Cottee, op cit.
16. Robert F. Futrell, op cit, p. 263.
17. Jung Chang and John Halliday, *Mao: The Unknown Story*, Jonathan Cape, 2005, p. 383.
18. Ibid.
19. George Odgers, *Remembering Korea*, p. 51.
20. Interview with Dick Cresswell, December 2006.
21. Ibid.
22. Lyall Klaffer, op cit.
23. Transcript of AWM interview, Extract 2, with Dinny O'Brien.
24. Based on descriptions in George Odgers, *Across the Parallel*, op cit, pp. 105–6.
25. Based on Lyall Klaffer's memoirs, op cit.
26. Les Reading, op cit.
27. David Wilson, op cit, p. 46.
28. Transcript of AWM interview with Dinny O'Brien, op cit.
29. George Odgers, *Remembering Korea*, p. 58.
30. Quote and account of the attack from George Odgers, *Across the Parallel*, op cit, pp. 137-9.

4 Mustangs to Meteors

1. Based on data from Robert F. Futrell, op cit.
2. Alan Stephens, *Going Solo: The Royal Australian Air Force 1946–1971*, AGPS, 1995, p. 229.
3. Transcript of AWM interview, Extract 4, with Dick Cresswell.

4. Robert F. Futrell, op cit, p. 261.
5. Ibid.
6. Barnes and Olorenshaw missions accounts based on descriptions in Brian Cull and Denis Newton, *With The Yanks in Korea*, Grub Street, London, pp. 86, 90.
7. Lyall Klaffer, op cit.
8. Ibid.
9. Based on information supplied by Keith Meggs, May 2007.
10. Steve Neal, op cit, p. 212.
11. Ibid.
12. From a copy of an unidentified Australian newspaper article of the times, supplied by Keith Meggs.
13. Account of Cec Sly's rescue based on notes provided by him in June 2007 and material from Keith Meggs in May 2007.
14. Notes by Keith Meggs, May 2007.
15. George Odgers, *Across the Parallel*, p. 160.
16. Lyall Klaffer, op cit.
17. Alan Stephens, *Going Solo*, op cit, p. 232.
18. Transcript of AWM interview, Extract 5, with Dick Cresswell.
19. Interview with Dick Cresswell, 8 December 2006.
20. Telecom interview with Les Reading, 13 March 2007.
21. Notes from Keith Meggs, May 2007.
22. Colin King, *Luck Is No Accident*, Australian Military History Publications, Loftus, p. 52.
23. Based on account in David Wilson, *Lion over Korea*, op cit, pp. 75-6.
24. George Odgers, *Across the Parallel*, p. 198.

5 Air to Air

1. Robert F. Futrell, op cit.
2. Alan Stephens (ed.), *The War in the Air*, RAAF Aero Space Centre, 1994, p. 112.
3. Colin King, op cit, p. 55.
4. AWM transcript, No. 5 of Interview with RCC.

5. Brian Cull and Dennis Newton, op cit, p. 180.
6. Interview with Les Reading, 13 March 2007.
7. Ibid.
8. Alan Stephens, *Going Solo*, p. 234.
9. Ibid, p. 234.
10. Comments provided by Wally Rivers following his review of the draft chapter, March 2007.
11. Based on notes provided by Les Reading, 15 June 2007.
12. George Odgers, *Across the Parallel,* p. 204.
13. Interview with Les Reading, 13 March 2007.
14. Ibid.
15. Brian Cull and Dennis Newtown, op cit, p. 251.
16. A.D. Garrison, *Australian Fighter Aces: 1914–1953*, Air Power Studies Centre, Canberra, 1999, p. 167.
17. Alan Stephens, *The War in the Air*, p. 120.
18. Presentation on the Korean War by AVM Simmonds AO MiD at the RAAF History Conference 1996.
19. George Odgers, *Across the Parallel*, pp. 206-7.
20. Alan Stephens, *Going Solo*, p. 235.
21. Ibid, p. 234.
22. Details of the mission and Dick Wilson's travails from Brian Cull and Dennis Newtown, *With the Yanks in Korea*, op cit, pp. 195–6 and discussions with him.
23. Details of the two fights in late October 1951 drawn from Alan Stephens, *Going Solo*, op cit; George Odgers, *Across the Parallel*, op cit; and Brian Cull and Dennis Newtown, *With the Yanks in Korea*, op cit.
24. Telecom discussion with Les Reading, 16 March 2007.
25. Notes provided by Ross Glassop, 20 May 2007.
26. Brian Cull and Dennis Newtown, op cit, p. 241.
27. David Wilson, op cit, p. 101.

6 Ground Attack Meteors

1. Notes provided by Bill Murphy, who was later commissioned and retired as a Squadron Leader.

2. Brian Cull and Dennis Newtown, op cit, p. 256.
3. Robert F. Futrell, op cit, p. 413.
4. George Odgers, *Across the Parallel*, op cit, p. 224.
5. Colin King, op cit, p. 66.
6. George Odgers, *Across the Parallel*, op cit, p. 222.
7. 'History's Faithless Scribe', *Weekend Australian*, 23–24 December 2006, p. 20.
8. Colin King, op cit, p. 72.
9. Notes provided by Owen Zupp, 27 June 2007.
10. Colin King, op cit, p. 76.
11. George Odgers, *Across the Parallel*, op cit, p. 225.
12. Talk by AVM W. H. Simmonds, RAAF History Conference, 1996, 'Korean War – Air Operations Meteor Phase'.
13. Doug Hurst, *The Part-timers: A History of the RAAF Reserves 1948–1998*, Defence Force Journal Publication, p. 35.
14. Colin King, op cit, p. 85.
15. Ibid, based on account on p. 92–3.
16. Telephone interview with Group Captain Doug Hurst, DFC, (Ret'd), 2 April 2007.
17. Description of both missions based on Colin King, *Luck is No Accident*, op cit, p. 104.
18. Ibid, p. 106.
19. John Price's comments from a transcript of a talk he gave on Korea, published in the Royal Air Force Historical Society Journal 21, 2000.
20. Jim Turner, *The RAAF at War*, Kangaroo Press, Sydney 1999.
21. Ibid.
22. Notes provided by Ross Glassop, 20 May 2007.
23. Based on account in Robert O'Neill, *Australia in the Korean War*, op cit, p. 394.
24. Based on Jung Chang and Jon Halliday, *Mao: The Unknown Story*, op cit, pp. 392–4 and Robert F. Futrell, *The United States Air Force in Korea*, op cit, p. 606.
25. Notes provided by Jake Newham, April 2007.

26. Details and quotes from David Wilson, *Lion over Korea*, op cit, p. 123 and Norman Bartlett, *With the Australians in Korea*, op cit, p. 118.
27. Notes provided by Ross Glassop, 20 May 2007.
28. Based on an account provided by Bill Collings, who was his No. 2 at the time.
29. Account of George Hale's aerial battle reviewed and confirmed by him, as was the incident in the mess that evening.
30. Based on notes provided by Jake Newham, April 2007.
31. Notes provided by Don Smith, 13 May 2007.
32. Based on notes provided by Jake Newham, April 2007.
33. From Don Smith's email of 23 May 2007.
34. Notes provided by Don Smith, op cit.
35. Notes provided by Bill Murphy, April 2007.
36. Notes from Jake Newham April 2007.
37. Notes provided by Bill Murphy, April 2007.
38. Robert O'Neill, op cit, p. 398.
39. Email notes from Bill Monaghan, May 2007.
40. Notes provided by Don Smith, 13 May 2007.
41. Notes provided by Bill Monaghan, May 2007.
42. The CO, John Hubble, told Bill Collings some years later of the protracted battle he fought to end the use of re-tread tyres—which were obviously cheaper than new ones, and just as obviously inferior.
43. Copy of Crash Report, dated 16/7/53.
44. Based on notes from Bill Collings and Don Smith, provided during May 2007.
45. Based on notes from Bill Collings provided during May 2007.

7 Aftermath

1. From Neville McNamara, *The Quiet Man*, the auto–biography of Air Chief Marshal Sir Neville McNamara, RAAF Air Power Development Centre, 2005, p. 97.
2. Details of POWs from Norman Bartlett, *With the Australians*

in Korea, op cit, an interview with Sir Neville McNamara in April 2007 and other material from his autobiography, *The Quiet Man*, op cit..

3. Alan Stephens, Going Solo, op cit, p. 243–4.
4. Copy of John Quaife's speech provided on the day to the author.
5. David Oliver, *British Combat Aircraft in Action Since 1945*, publisher unknown.
6. Comments from Wally Rivers following his review of relevant drafts of the book.

Bibliography

Books

Bartlett, Norman, *With the Australians in Korea*, Australian War Memorial, Canberra, 1954.

Chang, Jung and Halliday, Jon, *Mao: The Unknown Story*, Jonathan Cape, London, 2005.

Cull, Brian and Newton, Dennis, *With the Yanks in Korea*, Volume 1, Grub Street, London, 2000.

Evans, Ben, *Out in the Cold: Australia's Involvement in the Korean War 1950–1953*, Australian War Memorial and Department of Veterans' Affairs, Canberra, 2000.

Futrell, Robert F., *The United States Air Force in Korea 1950–53*, Duell, Sloan & Pearce, New York, 1961.

Gibney, Frank, *The Pacific Century*, Macmillan Publishing Company, New York, 1992.

Ilbery, Peter, *Hatching an Air Force*, Banner Books, Maryborough, Australia, 2002.

King, Colin, *Luck Is No Accident*, Australian Military History Publications, Loftus, 2001.

McNamara, Neville, *The Quiet Man*, RAAF Air Power Development Centre, Canberra, 2005.

Morris, James M., *History Of The US Navy*, Bison Books, London, 1984.

Neal, Steve, *Harry & Ike*, Scribner, New York, 2001

Odgers, George, *Across the Parallel*, William Heinemann Ltd, Melbourne, 1952.

Odgers, George, *The Royal Australian Air Force*, Child & Henry, Brookvale, 1984.

Odgers, George, *Remembering Korea*, Lansdowne Publishing, Sydney, 2000.

Oliver, David, *British Combat Aircraft in Action Since 1945*, publisher unknown.

O'Neill, Robert, *Australia in the Korean War 1950–53*, Volumes 1 and 2, Australian War Memorial and AGPS, Canberra, 1985.

Stephens, Alan (ed.), *The War in the Air 1914–1994*, RAAF Aerospace Centre, Canberra, 1994.

Stephens, Alan, *Going Solo: The Australian Air Force 1946–1971*, AGPS, Canberra, 1995.

Turner, Jim, *The RAAF at War*, Kangaroo Press, Sydney, 1999.

Wilson, David, *Lion Over Korea*, Banner Books, Belconnen, 1994.

Articles, Written Notes and Emails

Collings, Bill, Notes and comments on drafts.

Cottee, Milt, Extracts of Milt's draft autobiography, supplied by the author.

Flemming, Jim, Various written (email) comments on drafts supplied by the author. Roll of pilots in Korea in July 1950.

Hitchens, David, Notes from 2002 talk to the Australian Defence College on RAAF transport support in Korea.

Hurst, Doug, The Air Force Career of Group Captain Douglas Charles Hurst, DFC 1942–1970—private publication supplied by the author.

Klaffer, Lyall, Extracts of Lyall's draft autobiography, supplied by the author, and email comments on drafts.

Murphy, Bill, Notes about his time in Iwakuni and Kimpo and email comments on drafts.

National Geographic, 'The Forgotten War: Three Long Years in Korea' maps, pictures and text, July 2003.

Newham, Jake, Notes on flying Meteors in Korea and various email comments on drafts.

Reading, Les, Two articles from the RAAF Museum *Aerogram* both titled 'Mustang' and dealing with Korean operations. Comments on drafts and feature item on MiG versus Meteor operations.

Rivers, Walter, Notes provided to author, 23 April 2007, and comments on drafts.

Royal Air Force Historical Society, *Journal 21*, Fotodirect Ltd, East Sussex, 2000.

Simmonds Bill, Notes from a talk given at RAAF History Conference, 1996.

Stubbs, Denis, Notes on air power theory and comments on drafts.

Treadwell, Jim, 77 Squadron Association details of key personnel and statistics from Korea. Transcripts of Australian War Memorial interviews with Dick Cresswell, Buster Brown and Dinny O'Brien. Notes on the RAF and the Korean War. Various email comments on drafts.

Weekend Australian, 'Unfinished Business, The Korean War 50 Years On', various contributors, July 26–27, 2003.

Weekend Australian, 'History's Faithless Scribe', 23–24 December 2006, p. 20.

Williamson, Sir Keith, Contribution to an article on the Meteor in Oliver, David, *British Combat Aircraft*, publisher unknown.

Other Sources

Transcripts of Australian War Memorial interviews with Buster Brown, Dinny O'Brien and Dick Cresswell. Various email comments on drafts.

Index